R for Microsoft® Excel Users: Making the Transition for Statistical Analysis

Conrad Carlberg

800 East 96th Street,
Indianapolis, Indiana 46240 USA

D0898668

R for Microsoft® Excel Users

ISBN-13: 978-0-7897-5785-2
ISBN-10: 0-7897-5785-0

Library of Congress Control Number: 2016955450

1   16

Trademarks

All terms mentioned in this book that are known to be trademarks or service marks have been appropriately capitalized. Que Publishing cannot attest to the accuracy of this information. Use of a term in this book should not be regarded as affecting the validity of any trademark or service mark.

Warning and Disclaimer

Every effort has been made to make this book as complete and as accurate as possible, but no warranty or fitness is implied. The information provided is on an "as is" basis. The author and the publisher shall have neither liability nor responsibility to any person or entity with respect to any loss or damages arising from the information contained in this book or from the use of the programs accompanying it.

Special Sales

For information about buying this title in bulk quantities, or for special sales opportunities (which may include electronic versions; custom cover designs; and content particular to your business, training goals, marketing focus, or branding interests), please contact our corporate sales department at corpsales@pearsoned.com or (800) 382-3419.

For government sales inquiries, please contact governmentsales@pearsoned.com.

For questions about sales outside the U.S., please contact intlcs@pearson.com.

Editor-in-Chief
Greg Wiegand

Senior Acquisitions Editor
Trina MacDonald

Development Editor
Wordsmithery, Inc.

Managing Editor
Sandra Schroeder

Project Editor
Mandie Frank

Indexer
Erika Millen

Proofreader
Sasirekha

Technical Editor
Michael Turner

Editorial Assistant
Olivia Basegio

Cover Designer
Chuti Prasertsith

Compositor
codeMantra

Contents

About the Author

Conrad Carlberg (www.conradcarlberg.com) is a nationally recognized expert on quantitative analysis and on data analysis and management applications such as Microsoft Excel, SAS, and Oracle. He holds a Ph.D. in statistics from the University of Colorado and is a many-time recipient of Microsoft's Excel MVP designation.

Carlberg is a Southern California native. After college he moved to Colorado, where he worked for a succession of startups and attended graduate school. He spent two years in the Middle East, teaching computer science and dodging surly camels. After finishing graduate school, Carlberg worked at US West (a Baby Bell) in product management and at Motorola.

In 1995 he started a small consulting business which provides design and analysis services to companies that want to guide their business decisions by means of quantitative analysis—approaches that today we group under the term "analytics." He enjoys writing about those techniques and, in particular, how to carry them out using the world's most popular numeric analysis application, Microsoft Excel.

Acknowledgments

My thanks go to Charlotte Kughen and Michael Turner. Charlotte has guided the development of my books in the past, and Michael has provided technical suggestions that both simplify and clarify. I was delighted to learn that both of them would be working on this book—one that promised to be a little tricky because its intent is to cover two applications, not just one. And my thanks as well to Trina MacDonald, for pulling it all together.

We Want to Hear from You!

As the reader of this book, *you* are our most important critic and commentator. We value your opinion and want to know what we're doing right, what we could do better, what areas you'd like to see us publish in, and any other words of wisdom you're willing to pass our way.

We welcome your comments. You can email or write to let us know what you did or didn't like about this book—as well as what we can do to make our books better.

Please note that we cannot help you with technical problems related to the topic of this book.

When you write, please be sure to include this book's title and author as well as your name and email address. We will carefully review your comments and share them with the author and editors who worked on the book.

Email: feedback@quepublishing.com
Mail: Que Publishing
        ATTN: Reader Feedback
        800 East 96th Street
        Indianapolis, IN 46240 USA

Reader Services

Register your copy of *R for Microsoft® Excel Users: Making the Transition for Statistical Analysis* at informit.com for convenient access to downloads, updates, and corrections as they become available. To start the registration process, go to informit.com/register and log in or create an account*. Enter the product ISBN, 9780789757852, and click Submit. Once the process is complete, you will find any available bonus content under Registered Products.

*Be sure to check the box that you would like to hear from us in order to receive exclusive discounts on future editions of this product.

My father once told me that in academia, the knives are so sharp because the stakes are so small. He was speaking of the squabbling that goes on among faculty in colleges and universities. I've heard that old observation many times since then, in different versions. I was reminded of it when I was researching what different people have to say about the application called R and about the application called Microsoft Excel. The feelings seem to run surprisingly high.

If I'm biased about R and Excel, you might expect that bias to favor Excel. I've been using Excel to run quantitative analyses since the late 1980s. I've been very happy with Excel when it comes to financial analysis, and fairly happy with its capabilities in the area of statistical inference. I make my living primarily as a consultant, and it's worth a lot to me that my clients have Excel on their systems and are generally familiar with its use.

It's also helpful that Excel can display the details of many statistical analyses—that is, what goes on inside the black box. My clients don't necessarily *want* to follow the trail of bread crumbs from the raw data to the final probability statement. But they like knowing that the trail is there, if and when it's needed.

Furthermore, Excel can be a powerful learning tool. You can construct a binomial logistic regression analysis using nothing more than Excel's worksheet functions and the Solver. There's no better way to understand what a statistical analysis is all about than assembling it from scratch.

From a more technical perspective, it's clear that Excel is not an ideal statistical application. (And it's fair to remember that Excel was never intended as one.) You still find annoyances and outright errors in Excel's statistical features that, 30 years after their first release, you just don't find in SAS, SPSS, Stata, Minitab, and so on. Over time, Microsoft has addressed and corrected many problems with its statistical capabilities. But it took far too long to fix the problems with a constant of zero in the LINEST() function, and to shift from traditional matrix algebra inversions to QR decomposition. Judging from new analyses in Excel 2016, that *sort* of problem is still around.

But Excel is definitely usable for statistical analysis, and more so if you want to pair its native worksheet functions with added capabilities you can arrange using VBA. On the other hand, there are limits to Excel's statistical reach. For an Excel user who is accustomed to analyzing P&L statements and balance sheets, it's a gentle learning curve to get from there to beginning-to-intermediate statistical analyses such as multiple regression, and that's about as far as most want to go. It's also about as far as Excel *can* go.

R is different. You'd be hard put to name any statistical analysis that R won't run for you. And it's free, so the price is right. Figuring out how to use it is another matter entirely. The principal method of interaction between the user and R is a command-line interface, supplemented by a very spare menu structure. (Several front-end GUIs are available for R, none of them satisfactory in my view.) Here are some of R's characteristics that can get in the way:

- *The R language is case sensitive*, and it's your responsibility to make sure that you've used upper- and lowercase letters appropriately. For example, there's an *Anova* function and an *anova* function. Although both functions return an analysis of variance table (hence the acronyms), only one of the two is capable of properly handling factorial designs with different numbers of observations per cell.

  Or, there's a function named *XLGetRange*, handy for importing data directly from an open Excel worksheet into R, ready to analyze. But you'd better not type *xlgetrange* because R will tell you that the object *xlgetrange* cannot be found.

- *There are no straightforward rules regarding the management of number formats*. With some functions you're expected to specify, in the function's arguments, the number of decimals to display in the function's results. With other functions, you're expected to supply that information in a separate *options* statement, or in a separate *print* statement. In some cases, you can specify the character to use as a thousands separator in integers, but you must do it again for numbers that include fractional values.

- *Backslashes don't behave as you'd expect in file addressing*. You might be used to specifying the path to, say, a csv file by entering this:

  C:\Users\Fred\Desktop\jr.csv

  But if you use R's *read.csv* function to open that file, you'll get an error message. R does not interpret a backslash as a means of separating folders from their subfolders.

R interprets a backslash as an escape character. If you want to specify a path to that file, you must either double the backslashes:

C:\\Users\\Fred\\Desktop\\jr.csv

or use forward slashes instead:

C:/Users/Fred/Desktop/jr.csv

Now, these behaviors are better termed "annoyances" than "errors" or "bugs." They're analogous to Excel's problem with the order that it returns regression coefficients in LINEST() and the fact that CORREL() and PEARSON() are exactly equivalent functions. Nevertheless, they represent hurdles to successfully learning how to carry out statistical analysis in R.

And the problems I've cited are just examples. So, how do you take advantage of the benefits of a free application, one with extensive functionality, without getting bogged down in its idiosyncrasies? The only way I know of is practice, practice, practice.

But if you've been using Excel for your statistical analyses, I know the sort of analysis you've been running. You've been getting descriptive statistics such as averages, standard deviations, medians, and inferential statistics such as confidence intervals, so that you can understand your data's distributional characteristics better. To get those analyses you've probably applied a mix of worksheet functions such as AVERAGE() and tools such as the Data Analysis add-in.

You've been running bivariate analyses such as simple correlations and breakdowns of numeric variables by factor levels. In Excel that usually means worksheet functions such as CORREL(), scatter charts with trendlines, and pivot tables.

If you have access to samples of records with several variables each, you might have analyzed them using multiple regression analysis. Excel functions such as TREND() and LINEST(), and the Regression tool in the Data Analysis add-in, are useful ways to carry out that sort of statistical inference.

You might want to go beyond the simple descriptive breakdown of a numeric variable by factor levels and make inferences about the population that the data came from. In that case, you could use the analysis of variance, or ANOVA. You can put together an ANOVA using standard worksheet functions, but the tools in the Data Analysis add-in can also help you out here.

Or you might have gone a step further and looked at the probability of a binary outcome, such as Buys/Doesn't Buy) as a function of factors such as *Product Line* and covariates such as *Time on Page*. Then you would likely have deployed logistic regression as I suggested earlier in this introduction, using LN() and EXP() along with Solver to formulate an equation to predict that binary outcome.

It's even possible that you have pushed the boundaries of statistical analysis in Excel and picked up some VBA code that extracts principal components from a correlation matrix. This is a standard method to reduce a data set with too many observed variables to deal with sensibly, and reduce it to just a handful of latent variables that get expressed in the variables that you already have access to in your Excel workbook.

There may be a few additional statistical analyses that you routinely run in Excel, but the ones I just outlined account for the great majority of those that users apply in Excel. That fact makes them ideal starting points for exploring R.

Suppose that you begin by focusing on the functions in R that perform the same tasks that you now handle with Excel. Then you can focus on the five or ten procedures in R that are most similar to what you're accustomed to doing in Excel. You can compare the results from the two applications. You can become familiar with the idiosyncrasies of five or ten R functions just as you once became familiar with the idiosyncrasies of similar capabilities in Excel.

Just knowing how to do that eases the learning curve considerably. And then you're in a position to start pushing the boundaries. Perhaps your data set involves two or more factors and an unequal number of observations per cell, or it has both a factor and a covariate that you'd like to analyze via the analysis of covariance. You can handle these situations in Excel, and there are good reasons to do so, even though it can be an exacting process.

But if you've already experimented with R's ANOVA functions as applied to a balanced factorial design, you have only to check which option to set so that your unbalanced design will be analyzed as you want. And then it's just another small step to knowing how to test the factor by covariate interaction in an analysis of covariance. Although Excel is a great application for seeing what's actually happening inside the analysis, it can be tedious to set things up in a way that clarifies the details. That's when R, with all its mutually contradictory settings, starts to look really attractive.

So that's the approach that I've taken in this book. If you've used Excel for statistical analysis, you're already familiar with at least some of the general analyses I discussed earlier: univariate descriptive statistics, bivariate analysis, simple and multiple regression, the analysis of variance and covariance, logistic regression and principal components analysis.

I show you, for introductory or review purposes, how those analyses are carried out in Excel. I also demonstrate how to reach the same correct outcome using R, including which packages to install and how to access them. Then you're in a position to decide which application to use in a particular situation: perhaps, Excel for a colleague who would appreciate a step-by-step explanation of the analysis, or R for a skeptic who has run across and bought into a screed by someone who doesn't understand Excel very well.

Chapter 1 starts things off with a discussion of what you might find new and different if you've never used R before.

Making the Transition

1

Many experienced Excel users at some point decide to give R a try, and there's a variety of reasons for that. Perhaps you routinely use Excel to arrange for statistical analyses that compare product lines, that forecast numbers of website hits or hospital patients, that break down voter surveys by sex and political affiliation. For that sort of statistical analysis, Excel nearly always performs very well.

Furthermore, Excel is often a convenient way to perform numeric analysis and to get the results out. In most business, education, and government environments, you'd be hard pressed to find a computer that *doesn't* have access to Excel, or a person who doesn't know how to use it.

Still, you run into situations in which Excel just doesn't do the statistical job. It *is* a general analysis package and can't be expected to include all the tools that a specifically statistical application should have.

For example, multivariate analyses often require you to extract principal components from a correlation matrix. Excel can do that, but not without external help from, say, VBA subroutines. Or, following an analysis of variance (ANOVA), you might want to run a multiple comparisons procedure that requires access to the q distribution instead of the more common t or F distributions. In most situations, Excel can't help you there. And if you want to work with more so-called "robust" statistics such as ranges, medians, and quantiles, Excel isn't fully up to the task: You can calculate and show a mean value in a pivot table easily enough, but the first quartile is a different matter altogether.

It complicates matters even further that many offices have just a whiff of application snobbery: The hint that anyone who can't perform statistical analysis in R might not be quite smart enough to work here.

Adjusting Your Expectations

I might as well get it off my chest right here: It's not easy to add R to your Excel toolbox. R differs from Excel in a variety of ways, such as these:

■ We're all so accustomed to menu-driven applications (such as every application in the Office suite) that R's user interface can seem like a radical departure from the norm. R expects you to type what you want to do in a command line. You find that command line in the *R console*. Figure 1.1 shows what that console looks like immediately after you open R.

Figure 1.1

The greater than sign is the command prompt. You type your command immediately to the right of the prompt.

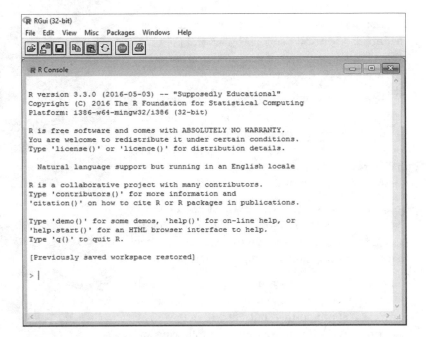

■ Excel saves formulas in cells and displays their results in the worksheet, making automatic recalculation possible when the precedents change. R shows you static results, which means that you have to recalculate dependents if those precedents change.

■ Function names and arguments in Excel are not case sensitive. You can type "=average(A1:A10)" or "=AVERAGE(A1:A10)" or "=AvErAgE(A1:A10)" and get the same result. But R recognizes "DescTools" and doesn't recognize "desctools."

So if you're going to migrate from Excel, or any menu-driven application, to R, you have to prepare yourself for some radical adjustments to long-held habits. I'll mention some of them here to give you a sense of their extent, and revisit them from time to time as necessary.

Analyzing Data: The Packages

R comes with several pre-installed packages that have names such as *base* and *stats*. These packages offer a variety of functions (*mean*, for example) and you could probably get along for a while with just that amount of statistical functionality. But R also gives you access to a large range of *contributed packages*, which extend the functionality in the base application. R lists thousands of contributed packages as I write this. There will probably be more as you read it.

For example, one of the more basic packages is *DescTools*, which Chapter 2 discusses in some detail. Using the function *Desc* in the DescTools package, you can quickly get distributional information about individual variables, whether measured on a nominal or on a numeric scale. You can also get bivariate analyses such as these:

- Correlations between numeric variables (and optionally provide scatter charts)
- Breakdowns of numeric variables by nominal variables (which R often terms *factors*)
- Contingency tables, often termed *crosstabs*, of one factor by another.

You might expect R to supply this sort of information from the base application (and it does) but the DescTools package goes into some depth, reporting not only Pearson correlations but Spearman's *r* and Kendall's tau; the Kruskal-Wallis one-way breakdown by rankings; and the likelihood ratio for contingency tables in addition to Pearson's chi-square.

Storing and Arranging Data: Data Frames

R relies heavily on what it terms *data frames*. If you're familiar with one of the popular database management systems such as Oracle, DB2, or SQL Server, you'll recognize a data frame as very similar to a table in a database. A data frame is rectangular, so that each row has the same number of columns and each column has the same number of rows. This aspect limits the sort of structure that can be placed in a data frame—so, you can't necessarily store a statistical report in a data frame. You usually store raw data in data frames.

Data frames carry more information than just the data values themselves. They know the names of the variables, which you might supply or which R might supply by default if you choose not to do so. They automatically recognize the type of data values included in each variable: normally text, numeric, and logical (that is, the Boolean values TRUE and FALSE).

Data frames are typically the sources of data used by R's statistical procedures, whether those are in R's base system or in its contributed packages. Various ways exist to create data frames. You can do that from R's console, although that's usually the most time-consuming and tedious method. You can also pull the data into R from CSV (comma-separated values) files created by other applications such as Access or Excel. And you can use R functions such as XLGetRange to grab data directly from an open Excel worksheet.

NOTE Various functions, including many that I refer to in this book, belong to specific contributed packages. Therefore, R won't recognize the name of such a function unless you have installed the contributed package and loaded it into your current instance of R. For example, you have to use *library(DescTools)* to use XLGetRange because the function XLGetRange is defined in the package DescTools and not elsewhere in R.

Both the R base system and its contributed packages contain data frames that you can use to compare the results you get from a given analysis with the results that documentation leads you to expect.

The User Interface

Most of your interaction with R takes place in the console (refer to Figure 1.1). The more adept you are at navigating the console the more efficiently you'll spend your time. The R console does include a menu structure (File, Edit, View, and so on) but it's quite sparse. Most of the instructions you send to R get there via commands you type into the console.

It's easy enough to mistype R commands—for one thing, they're case-sensitive and you can find yourself typing *Mean* instead of *mean*. So you'll often want to go back one (or sometimes more) commands to the point where you made your error. You might then want to copy the erroneous command, return to the command prompt, paste it, and then correct the error.

Sometimes that works reasonably well, particularly if the command in question hasn't yet scrolled off the console. But a better way is to press the up arrow key until the erroneous command shows up again next to the command prompt. Use the left arrow key, or click, to get to the point where you need to make a correction. Do so, and then press Enter—even if your cursor is still in the middle of the command. The Enter key doesn't stick a carriage return in the middle of the command: It just tells R to run the command as it stands.

During an R session you generally create objects that are kept in memory: data frames, lists, and vectors, even the results of statistical analyses if you've arranged to save them in a variable. Collectively, those objects are saved in what R terms a *workspace*.

When you quit an R session, before R actually closes it asks whether you want to save the workspace. If you answer Yes, an image of that workspace is saved in the working directory. That workspace is opened, and its objects made available, when you next start R.

R has a number of functions that help you deal with the workspace from the console. Here are a few of the most valuable. Although some are available from the console's menu, you can call each of them from the command prompt (from www.statmethods.net/interface/workspace.html):

- Return the path of the working directory: getwd().
- Change the working directory: File, Change Dir, or setwd("file path and name").
- Return a list of the workspace contents: Misc, List Objects, or ls().

- Show a list of the current session's commands in a separate window: history().
- Save the current session's commands in the working directory, in a file named .Rhistory: File, Save History, or savehistory().
- Load the commands in the .Rhistory file into the console: File, Load History, or loadhistory().
- Save a copy (an *image*) of the workspace in the working directory. The workspace is saved in a file named *.Rdata*: File, Save Workspace, or save.image().
- Load the previously saved workspace: File, Load Workspace, or load("myfile.Rdata").

Special Characters

R makes liberal use of the tilde (~) and a combination of the less-than character (<) and the dash (–). The tilde is probably more easily explained than the combination, which works out to <–.

Using the Tilde

An English translation of the tilde as used in R is "is a function of." A few examples follow:

If you use the DescTools package (discussed at some length in Chapter 2), you often find yourself analyzing two variables at once. You might want to get the Pearson, Spearman, and Kendall correlations between the length of time it takes to deliver pizzas and the temperature of those pizzas when they are delivered. (The DescTools package includes a data frame named *d.pizza* with operational data on hundreds of pizza deliveries.)

To run those analyses using the DescTools package, you could use this command, which employs the package's Desc function:

Desc(temperature ~ delivery_min, d.pizza)

You would get the results that appear in Figure 1.2.

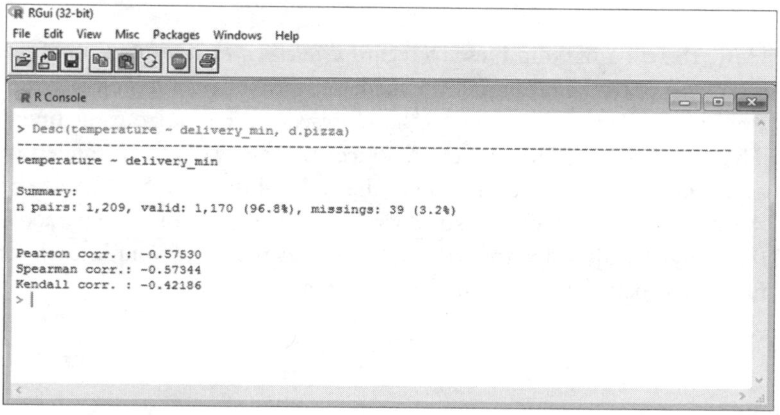

Figure 1.2
An additional argument to Desc (plotit) would provide you with a scatter chart of the two variables.

Here, you supply the Desc function with the names of two variables in the data frame named *d.pizza*. The tilde informs Desc that it should regard temperature as a function of minutes to delivery. Because both variables are numeric, Desc responds with the three correlation coefficients shown in Figure 1.2.

Suppose instead that you were interested in whether it takes much longer to deliver a pizza to one area rather than to another. Then you could use this command:

Desc(delivery_min ~ area, d.pizza)

The results are shown as in Figure 1.3.

Figure 1.3
Kruskal-Wallis tests for differences in medians rather than differences in means.

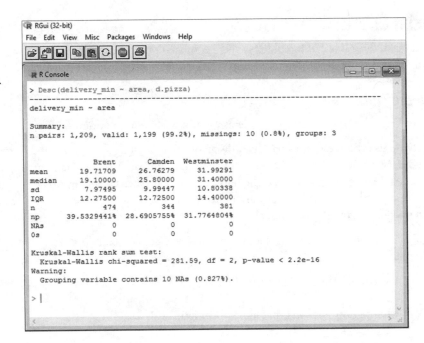

Here, the tilde has told Desc to regard *delivery_min* as a function of *area*, and the results show you both the mean and the median values of time to delivery for each of the three areas in the *d.pizza* data frame. The analysis is different from the one shown in Figure 1.2. That's because the Desc function notices that the variable to the left of the tilde is numeric, as in Figure 1.2, but the variable to the right of the tilde has character values—in terms shared by R with much statistical writing, *area* is a factor. It's characteristic of data frames that they already know the sort of data values that are found in each variable, and therefore functions such as Desc can make use of that information.

Lastly, what about two character variables? Two such are in the *d.pizza* data frame, named *area* (as in the prior example) and *quality* (which can be low, medium, or high). This command:

Desc(quality ~ area, d.pizza)

provides a crosstabulation of the two variables, as shown in Figure 1.4.

Figure 1.4
Tests of the strength of association between the variables accompany the contingency table.

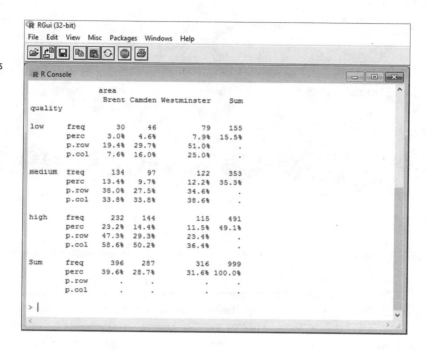

In this case, Desc regards *quality* as a function of area, as indicated by the order of the variables and the presence of the tilde.

Now, it's clear that just sticking a tilde between the names of two variables doesn't render one of them causal. And the order that you use to name two numeric variables doesn't mean the second variable causes the first. But early on in your investigation of R; it's helpful to think of the tilde as calling for an analysis of two variables *as though* one were truly a function of the other. In that case, R returns the bivariate analysis that's appropriate for the scales of measurement of the two variables you name.

Using the Assignment Operator <—

R has five—*five!*—assignment operators. Other languages make do with one. Excel's assignment operator is the equals sign. So when you enter this formula into cell C3:

=A2/2

you're using the equals sign to assign the formula A2/2 to cell C3.

Here are R's five assignment operators:

- <-
- ->
- <<-
- ->>
- =

In formal documentation, and in other writing about R, you most frequently tend to see the <- operator. It's a way of telling R to put what's to the right of the operator into what's on the left of the operator. Figure 1.5 shows an example.

Figure 1.5
The result of the formula is assigned to VarA.

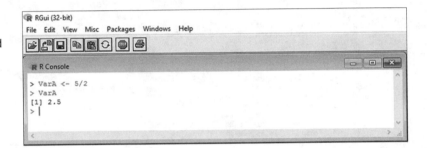

The first statement uses the <- operator to assign the result of the formula 5/2 to the variable VarA. The variable is declared simply by using it in that statement. Depending on what you put into it, VarA could be a scalar (that is, a single value), a vector or list of values, or a matrix. In the R console, one way to find out what's in a variable or other object is just by typing its name in the command line and pressing Enter. In this case, VarA contains one value only, identified by the [1] entry.

> **NOTE** In R, all the values in a *vector* must share the same scale of measurement: typically, character, numeric, or logical values. A *list* can mix values measured on different scales.

In R, the equals sign handles assignment in the same way as the <- operator: whatever is to the right of the equals sign is assigned to whatever is on its left. As a practical matter, you generally see this usage in an argument list: For example, to set the optional *scores* argument to TRUE, you would use *scores = TRUE*.

> **NOTE** In general, you can save a little time by abbreviating TRUE and FALSE in function arguments to T and F.

Should you wish, you can turn things around with the –> assignment operator, as I've done in Figure 1.6.

Figure 1.6
The outcome is the same as in Figure 1.5.

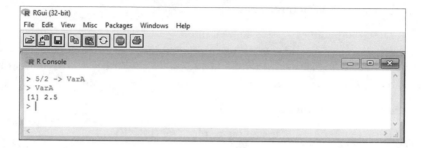

```
> 5/2 -> VarA
> VarA
[1] 2.5
>
```

I admit that the only places where I've seen the –> operator used is in R documentation. The strong tendency seems to be to use <– in preference to –>. I suspect that's due to the influence of programming languages such as FORTRAN and BASIC, in which the orientation of the assignment always puts what's to the right of the operator into what's on the left; for example:

StDev = Var^(0.5)

That's speculation, of course, and a Wikipedia editor would doubtless delete it as OR. Nevertheless, you frequently see advice on R to the effect that you can use the <– assignment anywhere but that other operators are restricted to certain contexts.

I'm afraid that's oversimplifying things. Consider Figure 1.7.

Figure 1.7
The Desc function responds differently depending on the assignment operator.

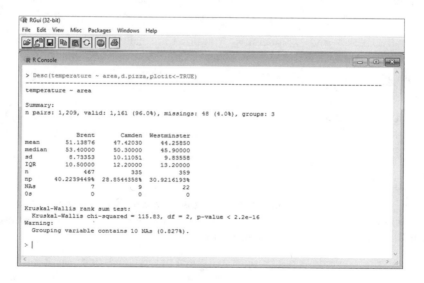

```
> Desc(temperature ~ area,d.pizza,plotit<-TRUE)
------------------------------------------------------------------------------
temperature ~ area

Summary:
n pairs: 1,209, valid: 1,161 (96.0%), missings: 48 (4.0%), groups: 3


                Brent       Camden   Westminster
mean         51.13876     47.42030     44.25850
median       53.40000     50.30000     45.90000
sd            8.73353     10.11051      9.83558
IQR          10.50000     12.20000     13.20000
n               467          335          359
np        40.2239449%  28.8544358%  30.9216193%
NAs              7            9           22
0s               0            0            0

Kruskal-Wallis rank sum test:
  Kruskal-Wallis chi-squared = 115.83, df = 2, p-value < 2.2e-16
Warning:
  Grouping variable contains 10 NAs (0.827%).

>
```

As you'll see in Chapter 2, when you use the Desc function (from the contributed package DescTools) to analyze two numeric variables, you can include the *plotit* argument to call for a scatter chart of the two variables (including a LOESS smoother). Suppose that you call for that analysis using this command:

Desc(temperature ~ area, d.pizza, plotit = TRUE)

You will get the results shown in Figure 1.7 *and* a scatter chart. The syntax of that command conforms to what the function's documentation recommends.

But if you use the syntax:

Desc(temperature ~ area, d.pizza, plotit <- TRUE)

substituting the <- operator for the equals sign operator, you do not get the scatter chart: You get only what's shown in Figure 1.7. Substituting the operator does not result in an error message, but neither does it bring about the same result as does the equals sign.

That's what I mean by "oversimplifying things." It may well be that you can use the <- assignment operator anywhere you would use any of the assignment operators, but you won't necessarily get the same result.

This book is intended for people who use and have used Excel for statistical analysis, and want to extend their reach by using R where it's appropriate to do so. I urge those readers to pay close attention to the documentation and usage examples for a given package and function. Use the syntax suggested there, especially including operators and the distinctions between upper- and lowercase.

If you do so, you're much less likely to go wrong than if you believe and act on statements such as "You can use <- anywhere you'd use any assignment operator."

Finally, the <<- and ->> operators: You don't normally find them used in the R console—that is, in commands that you enter next to the command prompt. They tend to show up only in functions: the code that R developers write that defines functions such as *Desc* and *mean*.

As a practical matter, get used to seeing and using the <- and the equals sign. Those two are likely to be the only ones you ever need to actually run statistical analysis in R.

Obtaining R

There's nothing mysterious or arcane about installing R on your own system. It's free to download, install, and use. You need about 70MB of disk space to download the installation file and about 200MB to contain the expanded files.

If you use a Windows operating system then before you begin you might want to check to see if your computer is running a 64-bit system. The reason is that there are some files that R can use if you're running a 64-bit system. Those files enable to address *much* more memory than if you're running a 32-bit system. Therefore, R documentation recommends that you download the 64-bit files for a 64-bit system and not otherwise.

To be sure which system you're running in Windows 10, take these steps:

1. Click the Start Menu.
2. Click Settings in the lower-left corner of the menu.
3. Click System in the Settings window.
4. Click About in the navbar.

You'll see a summary of your system's attributes, including whether it's a 64- or a 32-bit system.

> **NOTE** In Windows 8 you need to start with the Charms bar to get to the Control Panel, but after that the sequence is similar.

After you've found out whether you're using a 32- or a 64-bit system, you're ready to download the R installer file. To begin, open this site in a browser (the abbreviation *cran* stands for Comprehensive R Archive Network):

https://cran.r-project.org/

Toward the top of the page are three download links: one for Linux systems, one for Mac systems, and one for Windows systems. The three links take you to three different pages, each tailored to issues of interest to users of each type of operating system. I'll assume that you're a Windows user. When you click the Download R for Windows link, you'll get a new page with an Install R for the First Time link. Click that link to reach another page with a Download R 3.3.0 for Windows link. At the time I'm writing this, the most current version for Windows is 3.3.0, but by the time this book reaches you a more recent release is probably current.

Here are the steps to take to download and install R:

1. Quit applications other than your browser.
2. Click the Download R 3.3.0 for Windows link to initiate the download.
3. You're prompted to save the file. When you click Save File you can navigate to a location where you'd like to save it. All you're downloading and saving at this point is the installation file, which you can delete after the installation procedure is complete.
4. Click Save. The download starts.
5. When the download is complete (and it takes place very quickly) navigate to the location where you saved it and double-click the file's icon. This initiates a wizard that guides you through the installation process.

The wizard offers you choices such as whether to place a shortcut to R on your desktop. Most, perhaps all, the choices involve defaults that you can live with, certainly as a new user. The one exception is the 64-bit versus 32-bit issue. You should choose 64-bit files or 32-bit files, and you can choose both if you want.

When the installation is complete, double-click the R shortcut on your desktop (assuming you accepted that option in the installation wizard) to start R. Or you can start R from the Start Menu if you prefer. Either way, you'll get a window that looks much like the one shown earlier in Figure 1.1.

Contributed Packages

Getting a contributed package into R is much like the procedures you have to complete to get an add-in into Excel. If you want to use Excel's Data Analysis add-in, you have to make it available to your computer by installing it either locally or on a shared server. (Back in the day, you chose an option to install the add-in from the CDs that you got when you bought Excel. Now, it's more likely that you rely on a technical services department or on the Microsoft website's installation routine to install the full application.)

Once the add-in is installed and accessible to Excel, you have to alert Excel to its existence, so that (for example) the Data Analysis command or the Solver command appears in the Ribbon's Data tab. That Excel add-in installation process is version-dependent so I'll skip it here, except to mention that in recent releases you initiate the process by clicking Excel's File tab and selecting Options.

Similarly, to get a contributed package for R installed on your computer, you need to download it from one of the available mirror sites. Suppose you wanted to use DescTools and have not already installed it. You might take these steps:

1. Choose Install Packages from R's Packages menu.
2. R asks you to select a mirror site. You can choose an https site or one of the http sites. (Some R documentation recommends that you use an https mirror for security.) R recommends that you select a site that is geographically closest to your location, to ease the load on the network.
3. After you have chosen a mirror site, you'll get a list box with the names of thousands of contributed packages. Scroll down to find the one you want and click it. This can be an onerous task because the thousands of packages are not categorized, and their names do not always clearly represent their purpose, but at least they're alphabetized. Fortunately, you need do this once only for a given package.
4. When you have clicked the name of the package you're after, click OK. The CRAN site takes over, downloads, and unzips compressed files on your own installation, tests checksums, and finally returns control to you in the R console.

> **NOTE** I recently purchased a new laptop and nearly drove myself crazy trying to download and install some of R's contributed packages. They would not install in the intended locations and there was no hint as to the reason. The new laptop came with a virus protection package that was instrumental in helping me fail to install the packages I wanted. I finally realized that I needed to turn of the package's "Real Time Scanning" off. That by itself did not do the trick. I also had to choose Run as Administrator when I started R from the Start menu (click R's jump list in the Start menu, choose More, and then choose Run as Administrator). Only with those two conditions met was I able to install the packages I wanted in the locations that R prefers. In fairness, this was not truly R's fault, but that of the trolls in the distribution channels who think they know what we want better than we do.

After R has finished downloading and installing the package, you still have to tell R it's there. This step is analogous to the series of steps you use to direct Excel's attention to a recently installed add-in:

1. Click Excel's File tab.
2. Click Options in the navbar.
3. Click Add-Ins in the navbar.
4. Click to manage Excel add-ins at the bottom of the window.
5. Fill the checkbox of all the add-ins that Excel could find to have them show up in the Ribbon.

In R, all you have to do is enter this command, assuming that DescTools is the package you're interested in:

```
library(DescTools)
```

In subsequent R sessions you skip the download and install steps, and simply use the *library* command to load the package. To unload a contributed package, just enter this command:

```
remove.packages("cp")
```

where *cp* is the name of a contributed package. Notice that to load a package into the current session of R, you use something such as this:

```
library(DescTools)
```

which does not employ double quotes. However, to remove the package from the workspace, you would use this:

```
remove.packages("DescTools")
```

which *does* use the double quotes. R's language is a quirky one and this is one of the quirks that you just have to get used to.

> **TIP**
>
> To get a listing of the packages that have been installed, use this command:
>
>   library( )
>
> To get a listing of the packages that have been loaded into the current session, use this command:
>
>   search( )

Running Scripts

I often find that I want to run some commands in R every time I use the application. When those commands are long and involved and have nested levels of parentheses, I'm liable to get something wrong. This is just the sort of situation that makes scripts so convenient.

For example, when I want to use the Desc function in the DescTools package (discussed at some length in Chapter 2), I want to change some of the number formats that it uses. I want it to use scientific (that is, exponential) notation only as a last resort. I'm usually happy with two decimal places and my bias is that three decimals clutters things up. I'm from the U.S. and I'm used to seeing a comma, rather than an apostrophe or a period, as the thousands separator in large numbers. And by the way, I don't want to forget to load DescTools with the *library* command.

For this particular situation I have a small text file, created with Notepad, that contains the R commands needed to carry out those tasks. It looks like what's shown in Figure 1.8.

Figure 1.8
These commands are executed one by one, just as though you had entered them into the R console.

```
MyScript.R - Notepad                                    —    □    ×
File  Edit  Format  View  Help
library(DescTools)
options(scipen=10)
options(fmt.abs=structure(list(digits=0, big.mark=","), class="fmt"))
options(fmt.num=structure(list(digits=5, big.mark=","), class="fmt"))
```

It doesn't really make much difference what's in my script file, or for that matter yours. What matters is that the commands are ones that you normally want executed, and that the more involved they are the less you want to retype them. (However, the *library* command loads DescTools; the command with the keyword *scipen* controls the use of scientific notation; the two format commands control the thousands separator and the number of decimals in integers and floating point numbers.)

When I've typed the commands into a text editor like Notepad, I save the file to some convenient location such as this one:

    C:\Users\ellen\Documents\R

and I give it a filename such as *myscript.txt*. (The filename could also be George.txt or Jean.R. You might also have several different script files, tailored to the requirements of different contributed packages. In that case you might have one named DescTools.txt and another named stats.txt.)

Now I'm all set. I start R and enter this command into the console:

    source("C:/Users/ellen/Documents/R/myscript.txt")

The commands to load the DescTools package and set certain formatting options are executed automatically.

You can also browse to and run a script file by choosing *Source R code* from R's File menu.

You may want to include a *print* command in the script to see results in the console.

Notice these two points about the *source* command:

- The path and filename are enclosed in quote marks.
- The slashes that separate the folder names are forward slashes, not backslashes. Even when interpreting a text constant, as here, R interprets a single backslash as an escape character. One way to get around that is to use forward slashes instead, as here. You can also use two consecutive backslashes, such as \\, instead of one to separate the folder names.

Importing Data into R from Excel

It often happens that, for any of a variety of reasons, you want to copy data that's in an Excel worksheet to a data frame in R. Suppose you have a table or a simple list in a worksheet like the one in Figure 1.9.

Figure 1.9
A single range consisting of two contiguous columns and eleven contiguous rows.

	A	B	C	D
1	Variable A	Variable B		
2	73	55		
3	12	50		
4	3	13		
5	47	80		
6	57	56		
7	44	73		
8	0	24		
9	74	96		
10	11	87		
11	83	19		
12				
13				

There's an easy way to import that data directly into R, and I'll show that to you shortly. First, though, I want to show you another way, for two reasons: There might come a time when you need it, and it will help you appreciate how easy the other method is.

You can think of the hard way as the *csv method*. With the worksheet shown in Figure 1.9 active, save the file as a CSV file:

1. Click the File tab and then click Save As in the navbar.

2. Click the Browse link and navigate to the location where you want to save the file, at least temporarily. Suppose that location is C:\.

3. Locate the Save As Type dropdown in the Save As window. Use it to select *CSV (Comma delimited) (*.csv)*.

4. You'll see a warning that some features might not be retained in a CSV file. Go ahead and save it. I'll assume that the file is named *mydata.csv*.

5. Make a note of the fully qualified file path and filename. Better yet, locate the saved CSV file using something like File Explorer, right-click it and choose Properties from the shortcut menu.

6. Drag through the file's Location in the Properties window: In this example, that's just C:\. Use Ctrl + C to copy the selected text.

7. Switch to the R console and at the command prompt type this text:

    mydf<–read.csv(file="

8. Use Ctrl + V to paste the path you just copied.

9. Either add a backslash to every existing backslash in the path, or change each existing backslash to a forward slash. (R interprets a single backslash as an escape character.)

10. At the end of the pasted path, type

    \mydata.csv",header=TRUE)

    You should now see this command following R's command prompt:

    mydf<–read.csv(file="C:\\mydata.csv", header = TRUE)

    or, if you prefer a forward slash:

    mydf<–read.csv(file="C:/mydata.csv", header = TRUE)

    Including the argument *header = TRUE* causes R to interpret data in the first row of the CSV file as variable names rather than variable values.

11. Press Enter.

    You'll get another command prompt. R has now read the contents of the CSV file and put it into a data frame named *mydf*. (R terms this process "coercing": R coerces the data into a data frame.)

    At the command prompt, type:

    mydf

R responds by listing the contents of the CSV file, which have now been copied into the mydf data frame. See Figure 1.10.

Figure 1.10
Both the header and the data are placed in the data frame.

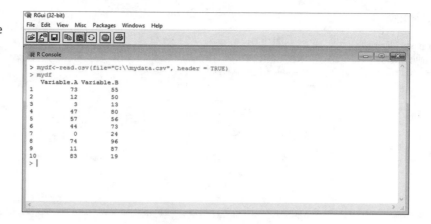

So far, you might have noticed a couple of difficulties in the process, both pertaining to how you preset the file's path and name to R.

- It's easy to forget that you need to change every instance of \ in the path to either \\ or to /.

- Paths are so long in Windows that you're almost forced to copy and paste the file path and name from the Properties window. As in this example, you might save a CSV file as, say, C:\mydata.csv, but such easily specified locations are often off limits in Windows security arrangements.

There's another potential problem. Suppose that you have a random value in your CSV file, such as the one in cell F13 of Figure 1.11.

Figure 1.11
The value in F13 is usually no problem for whatever you're doing in Excel.

F13			f_x	32		
	A	B	C	D	E	F	G
1	Variable A	Variable B					
2	73	55					
3	12	50					
4	3	13					
5	47	80					
6	57	56					
7	44	73					
8	0	24					
9	74	96					
10	11	87					
11	83	19					
12							
13						32	
14							

The difficulty arises when you use *read.csv* to import this CSV file. Figure 1.12 shows what happens in R.

Figure 1.12
The value in F13 comes over, along with NA values that you probably don't want.

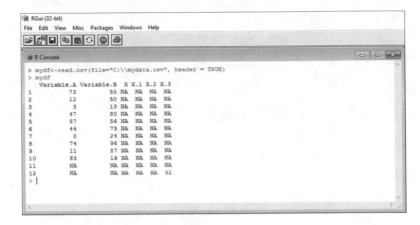

R replaces all those blank cells in columns C through F with NA values. Your best bet now is probably to switch back to Excel, get rid of the (probably) unwanted value in F13, resave the CSV file, switch back to R, and import the file once again.

Those are among the reasons that I no longer use *read.csv* to pull data into R from Excel (or from any application that writes CSV files). Pulling from Excel, I use the DescTools package, that calls a package named RDCOMClient. Using this method, I don't need to specify a file path—or a filename, for that matter.

The DescTools package calls RDCOMClient using its XLGetRange function. To get ready for the import, you'll need to take these steps:

1. Use R's Packages menu to install the DescTools package and the RDCOMClient packages. (You need to do this one time only.)

2. Make the DescTools package available to R using the *library* command. DescTools will automatically make RDCOMClient available.

3. Switch to Excel and select the range of data that you want to import. Leave that range's worksheet active and leave the Excel workbook open. It should look like the worksheet in Figure 1.13, complete with the (unselected) value in cell E14.

Figure 1.13
The value in E14 won't be imported.

	A	B	C	D	E
1	Variable A	Variable B			
2	73	55			
3	12	50			
4	3	13			
5	47	80			
6	57	56			
7	44	73			
8	0	24			
9	74	96			
10	11	87			
11	83	19			
12					
13					
14					74

4. Switch to R and enter this command:

mydf<–XLGetRange(header=TRUE)

R imports the selected range of data. In Figure 1.14, notice that only the cells selected in Excel are imported into R. Also, notice that using the direct import method as in Figure 1.14 does not alter the headers. The csv method, shown in Figure 1.12, inserts periods in place of the spaces in the headers (cells A1 and B1 of Figure 1.11).

Figure 1.14
If you started by selecting a single range of cells, you get a single data frame.

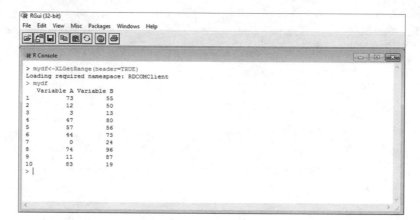

The results of using the XLGetRange function differ from what you see in Figure 1.14 if you start out with a multiple selection in Excel. I'm not recommending that you do so. I assume that you're comfortable with Excel and can rearrange the data on the worksheet before the fact rather than deal with problems after the fact. This is just an example of how it's possible to create problems unnecessarily. See Figure 1.15.

Figure 1.15
Here the user starts with a multiple selection.

	A	B	C	D	E
1	Variable A	Variable B	Variable C	Variable D	
2	73	55	28	53	
3	12	50	12	82	
4	3	13	21	65	
5	47	80	41	26	
6	57	56	97	91	
7	44	73	46	69	
8	0	24	66	70	
9	74	96	69	92	
10	11	87	55	64	
11	83	19	39	40	
12					
13					

D1   ✕ ✓ *fx*   Variable D

In this case, the user has selected A1:B21 by dragging through it with the mouse pointer, then held down the Ctrl key and dragging through D1:D21. This is a multiple selection.

Suppose the user now switches to R and (with the DescTools package loaded by means of the *library* command) uses the XLGetRange function as here:

multsel<–XLGetRange(header=TRUE)

where "multsel" represents "multiple selection".

The result is that the multiple selection in the active Excel worksheet is "coerced" into a data frame named *multsel*. To see what's in the data frame, just enter its name, multsel, at the command prompt. Figure 1.16 shows the result.

Figure 1.16
This data frame has two components, named for the Excel columns.

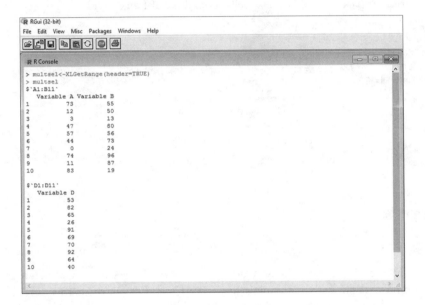

So the multiple selection in the Excel worksheet results in two components in R's data frame, one named 'A1:B11' and one named 'D1:D11'. To see, for example, the contents returned from Excel column D, you could enter this in the R console:

multsel$'D1:D11'

The results are in Figure 1.17.

Figure 1.17
The second of the data frame's two components.

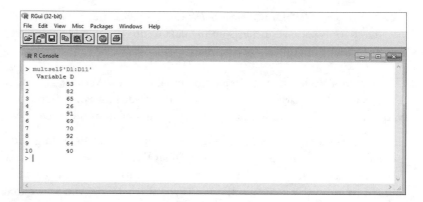

Notice that R uses the dollar sign to separate the name of the data frame, multsel, from the name of the component, 'D1:D11'. You can use that component in a statistical analysis, but a little more work is needed first.

For example, R's base system includes the function *mean*. If you tried to use the mean function with 'D1:D11' you would get the NA value—a missing value. When the mean function runs into a text value, it can't proceed.

> **NOTE**
> The base system's *mean* function accepts an *na.rm* argument, such as *na.rm=TRUE*. This instructs R to strip off NA values—again, missing data—before calculating the mean. But this does not work in the current instance, in which we're stuck with two component headers, 'D1:D11' and 'Variable D'.

So we need to qualify matters a little more fully. Use another $ operator to separate the 'Variable D' component from the 'D1:D11' component:

    mean(multsel$'D1:D11'$'Variable D')

That command returns 65.2, the mean of the values in cells D2:D11 shown in Figure 1.15.

Similarly, if you wanted to use the Desc function in the contributed package DescTools, you would follow this sequence of events. The following assumes that you have already installed DescTools and that the data frame *multsel* has been created in the present session or that you have loaded it into R by means of the *load* command:

    load("C:/Users/ellen/Desktop/multsel.rda")

With the data frame loaded there are just two steps:

1. *library(DescTools)* loads the contributed package DescTools into R. Because you have already downloaded and installed the package where R can find it, you don't need to specify anything other than the package's name. But remember that those names are case sensitive.

2. *Desc(multsel$'D1:D11'$'Variable D')* calls the Desc function, which belongs to the DescTools package. It picks up the data in the Variable D component of the multsel data frame and returns several statistics.

The statistics are based on the ten numeric values in the Variable D component, including the mean, the standard error of the mean, the median, maximum, range, coefficient of variation—you'll see much more of what you can obtain from the Desc function in Chapter 2.

In sum, R presents some added difficulties when it comes to dealing with data frames that are based directly on multiple selections in an Excel worksheet. If it's at all feasible, you should try to rearrange the data in the worksheet so that you can capture everything you want R to import as a single selection. If you do that, you won't have to deal with component names based on worksheet addresses—and there's little benefit in having those addresses as part of an R data frame anyway.

Nevertheless, if you're forced into importing a multiple selection into R, you have a method of dealing with them by stringing out a series of components demarked by the $ operators.

Exporting Data from R to Excel

Just as there's a way to use CSV files to import data from Excel into R (see the prior section for the reasons why that's not usually the best option), there's a way to go from R to Excel using the same technique.

I can think of a few occasions when I've needed to move raw data from an R data frame to an Excel workbook, but as a practical matter the need comes up infrequently. The installed base of instances of both the Excel application and its workbooks means that people store much more data in Excel workbooks than they do in data frames. So the need and opportunity to move raw Excel data into R occur much more frequently than to move raw R data into Excel.

But it does happen on occasion that a colleague may want to replicate, in the Excel context, an analysis that you've run in R. In that case you might want to export the raw data from a data frame into an Excel worksheet. Here's the long way, after which I'll demo the shortcut.

The DescTools package, which I mentioned earlier in this chapter, contains a data frame named *d.pizza*. It's a useful test bed because it contains an appreciable number of records (roughly 1,200), some 15 variables including numeric, nominal and logical, and enough missing values to test how and how well an analysis package handles them. I'll use d.pizza here to show how to export data from R via a CSV file, and then how to export it directly into Excel. (You'll see quite a bit more of d.pizza in Chapter 2.)

Figure 1.18 shows an abbreviated subset of the records and variables in d.pizza.

Figure 1.18

Use the head command to examine details on the first few records in a data frame.

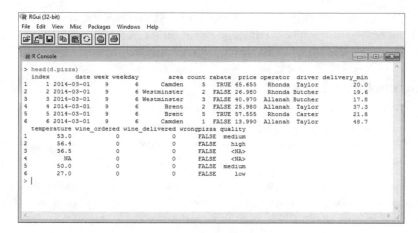

Exporting via a CSV File

To save the entire data frame to a CSV file, you can use the *write.csv* command:

write.csv(d.pizza,file="C:/Users/ellen/desktop/pizza.csv",na="")

The data frame will be saved in a CSV file named *pizza.csv* on the desktop that belongs to the user named *ellen*. Missing values, represented conventionally by *NA* in R, will be exported to the CSV file as empty cells.

> **NOTE** If you omit the *na* argument from the *write.csv* command, you'll get empty cells in the Excel file. If you specify *na* in this way:
>
>   write.csv(d.pizza,file="C:/Users/ellen/desktop/pizza.csv",na="#N/A")
>
> you'll get the standard #N/A error value in the Excel worksheet.

You can either double-click the resulting CSV file or open it from the Excel user interface. More recent versions of Excel open CSV files and place the data in columns defined by comma delimiters (back in the day it was necessary to use Excel's text-to-columns utility in order to break the data out of column A and distribute it across as many columns as necessary). Figure 1.19 provides a look at the results for the first few cases.

Figure 1.19

Notice that empty cells represent the missing data.

	A	B	C	D	E	F	G	H	I	J	K	L	M	N	O	P	Q
1		index	date	week	weekday	area	count	rabate	price	operator	driver	delivery_mi	temperatur	wine_order	wine_delive	wrongpizza	quality
2	1		1	3/1/2014	9	6	Camden	5	TRUE	65.655	Rhonda	Taylor	20	53	0	0	FALSE	medium
3	2		2	3/1/2014	9	6	Westminsti	2	FALSE	26.98	Rhonda	Butcher	19.6	56.4	0	0	FALSE	high
4	3		3	3/1/2014	9	6	Westminsti	3	FALSE	40.97	Allanah	Butcher	17.8	36.5	0	0	FALSE	
5	4		4	3/1/2014	9	6	Brent	2	FALSE	25.98	Allanah	Taylor	37.3		0	0	FALSE	
6	5		5	3/1/2014	9	6	Brent	5	TRUE	57.555	Rhonda	Carter	21.8	50	0	0	FALSE	medium
7	6		6	3/1/2014	9	6	Camden	1	FALSE	13.99	Allanah	Taylor	48.7	27	0	0	FALSE	low
8	7		7	3/1/2014	9	6	Camden	4	TRUE	89.442	Rhonda	Taylor	49.3	33.9	1	1	FALSE	low
9	8		8	3/1/2014	9	6	Brent				Allanah	Taylor	25.6	54.8			FALSE	high
10	9		9	3/1/2014	9	6	Westminsti	3	FALSE	40.97	Allanah	Taylor	26.4	48	0	0	FALSE	high

This approach to exporting by means of a CSV file is not as cumbersome as the process of importing via a similar method, discussed earlier in this chapter. I'll leave it to you to decide whether it's as useful as the direct method, discussed next.

Using the Direct Export

The DescTools package, in addition to the XLGetRange function discussed earlier, has an XLView function that exports data frames "directly" to Excel. I put "directly" in quotes because the process is not perfectly direct: It involves the creation of a CSV file, but you never need to see it or do anything with it.

You need to have DescTools package loaded via the *library* command. You also need to have the RDCOMClient package downloaded and installed, but you need not load it: DescTools takes care of that for you. With those tasks taken care of, you can export the d.pizza (or any other) data frame to Excel with this command:

XLView(d.pizza)

The data frame is exported into a new Excel workbook, in CSV format. Figure 1.20 shows the results.

Figure 1.20
Notice that the actual records begin in row 2.

	A
1	index;"date";"week";"weekday";"area";"count";"rabate";"price";"operator";"driver";"delivery_min";"t
2	1;2014-03-01;9;6;"Camden";5;TRUE;65.655;"Rhonda";"Taylor";20;53;0;0;FALSE;"medium"
3	2;2014-03-01;9;6;"Westminster";2;FALSE;26.98;"Rhonda";"Butcher";19.6;56.4;0;0;FALSE;"high"
4	3;2014-03-01;9;6;"Westminster";3;FALSE;40.97;"Allanah";"Butcher";17.8;36.5;0;0;FALSE;
5	4;2014-03-01;9;6;"Brent";2;FALSE;25.98;"Allanah";"Taylor";37.3;;0;0;FALSE;
6	5;2014-03-01;9;6;"Brent";5;TRUE;57.555;"Rhonda";"Carter";21.8;50;0;0;FALSE;"medium"
7	6;2014-03-01;9;6;"Camden";1;FALSE;13.99;"Allanah";"Taylor";48.7;27;0;0;FALSE;"low"
8	7;2014-03-01;9;6;"Camden";4;TRUE;89.442;"Rhonda";"Taylor";49.3;33.9;1;1;FALSE;"low"
9	8;2014-03-01;9;6;"Brent";;;;;"Allanah";"Taylor";25.6;54.8;;;FALSE;"high"
10	9;2014-03-01;9;6;"Westminster";3;FALSE;40.97;"Allanah";"Taylor";26.4;48;0;0;FALSE;"high"
11	10;2014-03-01;9;6;"Brent";6;TRUE;84.735;"Rhonda";"Carter";24.3;54.4;1;1;FALSE;"medium"

There are several points to note about the worksheet in Figure 1.20:

- The data values are all found in column A, beginning in row 2, separated by semicolons.
- The variable names are all found in cell A1, also separated by semicolons.
- The first number in each row, beginning with row 2, is a record number. The original data frame *d.pizza*, contains record numbers in a variable named *Index*, which contains the record number that's written at the beginning of each record.

If your data frame does not contain a variable such as *Index* in *d.pizza*, you can arrange for a record ID to be written to the Excel worksheet. The *XLView* function has a *col.names* argument and a *row.names* argument. They control whether XLView writes variable names for the columns and record IDs for the rows.

The effects of these arguments aren't entirely what you'd expect. Here are the possible combinations and the results:

- XLView(d.pizza, col.names = TRUE, row.names = TRUE): Record numbers inserted to the left of the first variable in the data frame. Variable names are inserted as the first row in the Excel worksheet. Variable names occupy cell B1; values occupy column A below row 1.

- XLView(d.pizza, col.names = FALSE, row.names = FALSE): No record numbers or variable names are inserted. The first record occupies cell A1.

- XLView(d.pizza, col.names = TRUE, row.names = FALSE): No record numbers are inserted. Variable names are inserted in cell A1. TRUE and FALSE are the default values for *col.names* and *row.names*, and they produced the layout shown in Figure 1.20.

- XLView(d.pizza, col.names = FALSE, row.names = TRUE): Record numbers are inserted to the left of the first variable. No variable names are inserted. The first record's values are in cell in B1.

So, if you assign TRUE to the *row.names* argument, the data in the first row of the resulting Excel worksheet is found in cell B1, rather than cell A1, where you might expect to find it.

I always want the variable names. But if my data frame already has record IDs, as is the case with the d.pizza data frame, I don't want to bother with them. So I tend to use this form of the XLView function with d.pizza:

```
XLView(d.pizza,col.names=TRUE,row.names=FALSE)
```

or, equivalently:

```
XLView(d.pizza,row.names=FALSE)
```

or simply:

```
XLView(d.pizza)
```

The downside to using this direct export method instead of the two-step, CSV file route is that you get all the data mashed up in column A, and all the variable names run together in cell A1 or B1. Excel's text-to-columns capability can take care of that for you, but you still have to call for it. Using the layout shown in Figure 1.20, here's how to go about it:

1. Select cell A1.
2. Select the remaining records in column A by holding down the Ctrl and Shift keys while you press the down arrow key.
3. Click the Text-to-Columns link on the Data tab. A three-step wizard starts.
4. Make sure that the Delimited option button is selected. Click Next.
5. Clear all Delimiter checkboxes except the Semicolon option box. Click Finish or click Next if you want to use the wizard's third step to apply special formats.

The result is shown in Figure 1.21.

Figure 1.21
Empty cells replace
NA values.

	A	B	C	D	E	F	G	H	I	J	K	L	M	N	O	P
1	index	date	week	weekday	area	count	rabate	price	operator	driver	delivery_t	temperatu	wine_ord	wine_deli	wrongpizz	quality
2	1	3/1/2014	9		6	Camden	5	TRUE	65.655	Rhonda	Taylor	20	53	0	0	FALSE	medium
3	2	3/1/2014	9		6	Westmins	2	FALSE	26.98	Rhonda	Butcher	19.6	56.4	0	0	FALSE	high
4	3	3/1/2014	9		6	Westmins	3	FALSE	40.97	Allanah	Butcher	17.8	36.5	0	0	FALSE	
5	4	3/1/2014	9		6	Brent	2	FALSE	25.98	Allanah	Taylor	37.3	#N/A	0	0	FALSE	
6	5	3/1/2014	9		6	Brent	5	TRUE	57.555	Rhonda	Carter	21.8	50	0	0	FALSE	medium
7	6	3/1/2014	9		6	Camden	1	FALSE	13.99	Allanah	Taylor	48.7	27	0	0	FALSE	low
8	7	3/1/2014	9		6	Camden	4	TRUE	89.442	Rhonda	Taylor	49.3	33.9	1	1	FALSE	low
9	8	3/1/2014	9		6	Brent				Allanah	Taylor	25.6	54.8			FALSE	high
10	9	3/1/2014	9		6	Westmins	3	FALSE	40.97	Allanah	Taylor	26.4	48	0	0	FALSE	high
11	10	3/1/2014	9		6	Brent	6	TRUE	84.735	Rhonda	Carter	24.3	54.4	1	1	FALSE	medium

WARNING

Using XLView, if you suppress the column names (that is, the variable names) but not the row names, using a command such as this one:

XLView(d.pizza,col.names=FALSE, row.names=TRUE)

the first row of actual data replaces the cell with variable names, normally B1 when you call for the column names and the row names. The remaining data records start out in column A, as described above. You'll need to account for this when you run the Text-to-Columns utility.

Descriptive Statistics

2

Regardless of the sort of analysis you have in mind for a particular data set, you want to understand the distribution of the variables in that set. The reasons vary from the mundane (someone entered an impossible value for a variable) to the technical (different sample sizes accompanying different variances).

Any of those events could happen, whether the source of the data is a sales ledger, a beautifully designed medical experiment or a study of political preferences. No matter what the cause, if your data set contains any unexpected values you want to know about it. Then you can take steps to correct data entered in error, or to adjust your decision rules if necessary, or even to replicate the experiment if it looks like something might have gone wrong with the methodology.

The point is that sophisticated multivariate analyses such as factor analysis with Varimax rotation or Cox Proportional Hazards Regression do not alert you when someone entered a patient's body temperature on Wednesday morning as 986 degrees instead of 98.6 degrees. In that case, the results of your sophisticated procedure might turn out cockeyed, but you would have no special reason to suspect a missing decimal point as the cause of your findings.

You can save yourself a lot of subsequent grief if you just look over some preliminary descriptive statistics based on your data set. If a mean value, the range of the observed values, or their standard deviation looks unusual, you probably should verify and validate the way the data is collected, entered and stored before too much time passes.

Descriptive Statistics in Excel

If you're using Excel to analyze the data, either as a preliminary check or as your principal numeric application, one way to carry out this sort of work is to point Excel's various worksheet functions at the data set. MIN() gets you the minimum in a set of values, MAX() gets you the maximum, and MAX() – MIN() gets you the range. COUNT() counts the numeric values, AVERAGE() returns the mean, and either STDEV.S() or STDEV.P() gets you the standard deviation.

Excel comes equipped with a Descriptive Statistics tool in the Data Analysis add-in (which was at one time termed the Analysis ToolPak or ATP). The Descriptive Statistics tool is good news and bad news.

The good news is that using the tool on an existing data set gets you up to 16 different descriptive statistics, and you don't have to enter a single function on the worksheet. See Figure 2.1.

Figure 2.1
You can analyze multiple variables in one pass.

	A	B	C	D	E	F	G	H
1	MPG	IPS				MPG		IPS
2	28	0.41						
3	17	0.61			Mean	26	Mean	0.52
4	24	0.18			Standard Error	2.63	Standard Error	0.07
5	32	0.24			Median	28	Median	0.43
6	22	1			Mode	28	Mode	0.42
7	33	0.78			Standard Deviation	8.72	Standard Deviation	0.24
8	28	0.73			Sample Variance	76	Sample Variance	0.06
9	11	0.43			Kurtosis	-0.67	Kurtosis	0.09
10	17	0.42			Skewness	-0.20	Skewness	0.62
11	40	0.42			Range	29	Range	0.82
12	34	0.51			Minimum	11	Minimum	0.18
13					Maximum	40	Maximum	1
14					Sum	286	Sum	5.73
15					Count	11	Count	11
16					Largest(3)	33	Largest(3)	0.73
17					Smallest(3)	17	Smallest(3)	0.41
18					Confidence Level(95.0%)	5.86	Confidence Level(95.0%)	0.16

Figure 2.1 shows 11 values of two different variables in the range A1:B12. A univariate analysis of the variable named *MPG* appears in the range E3:F18, and a similar analysis of *IPS* appears in G3:H18. Notice that each statistic reported pertains to one variable only: None of the statistics correlates, for example, MPG with IPS, or reports the means of IPS according to specific values of MPG. The reported statistics are exclusively univariate.

You get them without having to know that Excel has a STDEV.S() function that reports the standard deviation of a sample of records, or that the standard errors reported in the fourth row are the standard error of the mean of each variable. The reported statistics are largely useful when you're getting acquainted with a data set. You'll normally want to know a lot more than that, of course, but it's a good place to start.

The bad news is that the reported statistics represent static values. For example, in Figure 2.1, cell F3 contains the value 26 rather than this formula:

=AVERAGE(A2:A12)

Therefore, if you want to change the input values in A1:A12 by adding or deleting a record, or editing an existing value, none of the statistics would change in response. A worksheet formula recalculates when the values it points to change, but the results calculated by the Descriptive Statistics tool do not: They don't point to anything because they're just numbers.

Using the Descriptive Statistics Tool

Using the tool is easy enough. You'll want your active worksheet to have one or more lists or tables, such as the two shown in columns A and B of Figure 2.1. Go to the Ribbon's Data tab and locate the Data Analysis link in the Analyze group. When you click it, you see the list box shown in Figure 2.2.

Figure 2.2
Descriptive Statistics is the list box entry you want for these analyses.

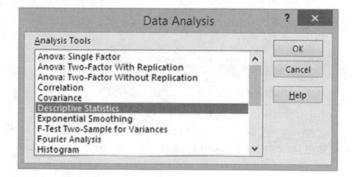

Click Descriptive Statistics and click OK. You'll get the dialog box shown in Figure 2.3.

Figure 2.3
It's usually best to keep the output on the active worksheet.

Then take these steps:

1. Click in the Input Range box and drag through the range your data occupies. In Figure 2.1, that's A1:B12. If you have one variable, the range might be A1:A25, or if you have three variables, the range might be B1:D85. Don't worry if your variables have different numbers of records, but leave unoccupied cells empty and don't substitute #N/A for an empty cell.

2. Accept the default of Grouped By Columns.

3. If the first row in the input range has labels such as variable names, fill the Labels in First Row checkbox. This instructs Excel not to treat a label as a legitimate data value, which would usually result in an error message that the input range contains non-numeric data.

4. Click the Output Range option button, unless you want the results to be written to a new workbook or a new worksheet. (*Worksheet Ply* is just an old term for *worksheet*.) Careful! If you click the Output Range option button, the Input Range box is re-activated and gets filled with any cell or range that you click next. First, click the Output Range edit box and only then indicate where you want the output to begin.

5. Fill the Summary Statistics checkbox if you want the statistics shown in row 3 through row 15 in Figure 2.1.

6. Fill the Confidence Level for Mean checkbox if you want to put a confidence interval around the mean. Enter the confidence level you want in the edit box (often that will be 90, 95, or 99, taken as a percent).

7. Fill the Kth Largest and the Kth smallest checkboxes if you want that information. Also supply a value for K. That is, if you want the 5th largest value, fill the checkbox and enter **5** in the edit box. (I can't recall the last time I needed either of these two statistics.)

8. Click OK. Within a few seconds you should see results such as those shown in columns E through H of Figure 2.1.

Understanding the Results

Here's a closer look at some of the statistics shown in Figure 2.1. Most of them are precisely what you would expect (mean, median, mode, range, minimum, maximum, sum, count, kth largest, and smallest values). The following may require a little additional information.

Standard Error of the Mean

Suppose that the 11 values in A2:A12 of Figure 2.1 are a sample from a population. Now suppose that you took hundreds or even thousands of similar 11-record samples from the same population. Each of those samples would have its own mean value, such as the one shown in cell F3 of Figure 2.1. If you calculated the standard deviation of all those mean values, you would have a statistic called the *standard error of the mean*. The value in cell

F4 of Figure 2.1 estimates that value, so that you don't have to actually take hundreds or thousands of additional samples. You can calculate that estimate using this formula:

$$S_{\bar{X}} = S/\sqrt{n}$$

where:

- $S_{\bar{X}}$ is the standard error of the mean.
- S is the sample standard deviation.
- n is the number of records in the sample (the *count*).

The standard error of the mean is often useful when you want to test the difference between an obtained sample mean and a hypothesized value. It is also an integral part of a confidence interval placed around a sample mean.

Standard Deviation

Excel (and the general field of statistics) offers two types of standard deviation:

- Your data constitutes a population. For example, you might have 100 items made in a special production run, after which the mold was broken.
- Your data constitutes a sample. You might have 100 items sampled randomly from an ongoing process that yields millions of products per year.

In the first case, where you have an entire population of values, the formula for the standard deviation uses the actual count of values, n, in its denominator. In the second case you are estimating the population's standard deviation on the basis of your sample, and you use $n-1$ instead of n in the denominator.

In Excel, you use the worksheet function STDEV.P() when your data is the population. You use STDEV.S() when you have a sample. Possession of a sample occurs much more frequently than possession of a population, so the Descriptive Statistics tool returns the value that you would get if you were using the STDEV.S() function.

Sample Variance

The variance is the square of the standard deviation, and it's subject to the same conditions as the standard deviation: That is, the variance has a population form (n) and a sample form ($n-1$). The Descriptive Statistics tool returns the sample form of the variance.

Skewness

Skewness measures the symmetry in a distribution of values. An asymmetric distribution is said to be *skewed*. One popular way of calculating skewness is the average of the cubed standard scores (also termed *z-scores*):

$$\sum_{i=1}^{n} z^3 / n$$

The formula that Excel uses approaches the value of the average cubed z-score as n increases:

$$n\sum_{i=1}^{n}z^3/((n-1)(n-2))$$

A symmetric distribution is expected to have a skewness of 0.

Kurtosis

Kurtosis measures the degree to which a distribution of scores is taller or flatter with respect to its width. Here's one textbook definition of kurtosis:

$$(\sum_{i=1}^{n}z^4/n)-3$$

It's very similar to one definition of skewness, except here the z-scores are raised to the fourth instead of the third power. A distribution such as the normal curve would have an average z-score, raised to the fourth power, of 3. Therefore, 3 is subtracted in the formula so that a normal curve would have kurtosis of 0.

Again, Excel's formula for kurtosis is slightly different and attempts to remove bias from the calculation of kurtosis based on a sample:

$$\text{Kurtosis}=\frac{n(n+1)}{(n-1)(n-2)(n-3)}\sum_{1}^{n}z^4-\frac{3(n-1)^2}{(n-2)(n-3)}$$

I'm inflicting these formulas on you so that if you need to contrast the reason that R returns different values for skewness and kurtosis than Excel, you'll be better placed to understand the differences.

Confidence Level

The Descriptive Statistics tool's results refer to the confidence interval value as the *Confidence Level* (see cell E18 in Figure 2.1). That's a misnomer. The confidence *level* is the percentage of sample confidence intervals that you expect to capture the population mean: typically, 90%, 95%, or 99%.

In contrast, the Descriptive Statistics tool reports the quantity that you add to and subtract from the calculated mean so as to arrive at the confidence interval. That quantity is calculated, using Excel function syntax, as

=T.INV.2T(0.05,10)*F4

where cell F4 contains the standard error of the mean. Excel's T.INV.2T() worksheet function returns the positive t value that cuts off some percentage of the area under the t-distribution, such that the remaining percentage is divided evenly between the two tails. So, this use of the function

=T.INV.2T(.05,10)

returns 2.23. That means

- Take a t-distribution, which is very similar to a normal curve but is a little flatter in its center and a little thicker in its tails. Its shape depends partly on the number of observations in the samples used to build the distribution. In this example, the number of observations is 11 and therefore the degrees of freedom is 10.

- The mean of that t-distribution is 0. If you cut the distribution at two points, −2.23 and +2.23, you'll find that 95% of the area under the curve is between those two cuts.

- And of course, 5% is outside the cuts, with 2.5% in the distribution's right tail and 2.5% in its left tail.

But we're not working in a scale of t values, which has a standard deviation that's slightly larger than 1.

> **NOTE** The standard deviation of the t-distribution is given by this formula:
>
> $$\sqrt{v/(v - 2)}$$
>
> where v is the degrees of freedom. So in a t-distribution built on samples of size 5, the degrees of freedom is 4 and the standard deviation is the square root of (4/2), or 1.414. As the sample size increases the standard deviation decreases, so a t-distribution built on samples of size 11 has a standard deviation of 1.12.

Instead, we're working with a scale that in Figure 2.1 describes whatever MPG is, with a standard error of 2.63. So, to cut off 2.5% of the distribution at each tail, we multiply ±2.23 by 2.63 or ±5.86. Adding ±5.86 to the mean of 26 shown in cell F4 of Figure 2.1 gives a 95% confidence interval of from 20.14 to 31.86. Another way of saying this is that we want to go up from the mean by 2.23 standard deviations. In this scale, a standard deviation is 2.63 units, so we go up from the mean by 2.23×2.63 units. We go down from the mean by the same amount. The resulting range of values is the 95% confidence interval for this data.

You interpret the confidence interval as follows: If you were to take 100 random samples, each from the same population, and put a 95% confidence interval around each of 100 sample means, 95 of those confidence intervals would capture the mean of the population. It is more rational to suppose that the one confidence interval that you *did* construct is one of the 95 that captures the population mean than one of the 5 that do not. That's what's meant by saying that a confidence interval makes you 95% confident that it captures the true population mean.

Using the Excel Descriptive Statistics Tool on R's Pizza File

Let's take a look at what Excel's Descriptive Statistics tool has to say about the numeric variables in R's pizza delivery database. The first step is to export that database so it's available to Excel. To arrange that, take these steps:

1. Start R.

2. Load the DescTools package using this R command:

    library(DescTools)

3. Export the data frame named *d.pizza* by entering this command:

    write.csv(d.pizza, file="C:/Users/Jean/Desktop/pizza.csv")

You can use any legitimate destination name and location for the file. It will be formatted as a comma-separated values file, or csv file, so you might as well use *csv* as the filename extension. Also notice the use of forward slash (/) rather than backslashes (\) in the file path: R interprets a backslash as an escape character. You can instead use the forward slash (/) or two consecutive backslashes (\\).

When control returns to the R interface—it only takes a second or two—quit R and start Excel. Open the csv file from the location where you stored it. It looks something like the worksheet shown in Figure 2.4.

Figure 2.4

A csv file that's opened in Excel has none of the frills such as currency formats that we're used to seeing in Excel workbooks.

	index	date	week	weekday	area	count	rabate	price	operator	driver	delivery min	temperature	wine ordered	wine delivered	wrongpizza	quality
1																
2	1	3/1/2014	9	6	Camden	5	TRUE	65.655	Rhonda	Taylor	20	53	0	0	FALSE	medium
3	2	3/1/2014	9	6	Westminster	2	FALSE	26.98	Rhonda	Butcher	19.6	56.4	0	0	FALSE	high
4	3	3/1/2014	9	6	Westminster	3	FALSE	40.97	Allanah	Butcher	17.8	36.5	0	0	FALSE	NA
5	4	3/1/2014	9	6	Brent	2	FALSE	25.98	Allanah	Taylor	37.3	NA	0	0	FALSE	NA
6	5	3/1/2014	9	6	Brent	5	TRUE	57.555	Rhonda	Carter	21.8	50	0	0	FALSE	medium
7	6	3/1/2014	9	6	Camden	1	FALSE	13.99	Allanah	Taylor	48.7	27	0	0	FALSE	low
8	7	3/1/2014	9	6	Camden	4	TRUE	89.442	Rhonda	Taylor	49.3	33.9	1	1	FALSE	low
9	8	3/1/2014	9	6	Brent	NA	NA	14.22	Allanah	Taylor	25.6	54.8	NA	NA	FALSE	high
10	9	3/1/2014	9	6	Westminster	3	FALSE	40.97	Allanah	Taylor	26.4	48	0	0	FALSE	high
11	10	3/1/2014	9	6	Brent	6	TRUE	84.735	Rhonda	Carter	24.3	54.4	1	1	FALSE	medium
12	11	3/1/2014	9	6	Westminster	3	FALSE	66.41	Allanah	Miller	11.7	28.8	1	1	FALSE	low
13	12	3/1/2014	9	6	Brent	5	TRUE	62.955	Rhonda	Carter	19.5	51.3	0	0	FALSE	medium
14	13	3/1/2014	9	6	Camden	4	TRUE	46.764	Allanah	Taylor	32.7	24.05	0	0	FALSE	low
15	14	3/1/2014	9	6	Camden	1	FALSE	49.95	Rhonda	Carter	38.8	35.7	1	1	FALSE	low
16	15	3/1/2014	9	6	Brent	6	TRUE	73.746	Rhonda	Carter	23	53.6	0	0	FALSE	medium
17	16	3/1/2014	9	6	Westminster	5	TRUE	57.555	Rhonda	Miller	30.8	51.3	0	0	FALSE	NA
18	17	NA	NA	NA	Brent	2	FALSE	26.98	Allanah	Carter	27.7	51	0	0	FALSE	high
19	18	3/1/2014	9	6	Brent	2	FALSE	27.98	Rhonda	Butcher	29.7	47.7	0	0	FALSE	medium
20	19	3/1/2014	9	6	Brent	3	FALSE	41.97	Rhonda	Carter	9.1	52.8	0	0	FALSE	medium
21	20	3/1/2014	9	6	Westminster	1	FALSE	11.99	Rhonda	Miller	37.3	20	0	0	FALSE	low

In Figure 2.4, notice the *NA* values sprinkled among the legitimate values. The *NA* values mean *not available* and, because they're text, the Descriptive Statistics tool has difficulty dealing with them when they're supposed to be numbers.

If you want to use Excel's worksheet functions, you're in the clear. When a function such as SUM() or AVERAGE() or STDEV.S() encounters a text value such as *NA*, it simply ignores it. See Figure 2.5 for some examples.

Figure 2.5
Excel ignores records
on a pairwise basis for
correlation functions such
as CORREL().

A13	▾	:	✕	✓	*fx*	=AVERAGE(A2:A11)			

	A	B	C	D	E	F	G	H
1	temperature			delivery_min	temperature		delivery_min	temperature
2	53			20	53		20	53
3	56.4			19.6	56.4		19.6	56.4
4	36.5			17.8	36.5		17.8	36.5
5	NA			37.3	NA		21.8	50
6	50			21.8	50		48.7	27
7	27			48.7	27		49.3	33.9
8	33.9			49.3	33.9		25.6	54.8
9	54.8			25.6	54.8		26.4	48
10	48			26.4	48		24.3	54.4
11	54.4			24.3	54.4			
12								
13	46.00000000			-0.74494935				-0.74494935
14	=AVERAGE(A2:A11)			=CORREL(D2:D11,E2:E11)			=CORREL(G2:G10,H2:H10)	
15								
16	46.00000000							
17	=AVERAGE(A2,A3,A4,A6,A7,A8,A9,A10,A11)							

The first ten records in the Pizza database from DescTools appear in cells A2:A11 of Figure 2.5, where the delivery temperature is recorded. This formula is entered in cell A13:

=AVERAGE(A2:A11)

Notice that the formula's argument includes the text value NA in cell A5. The formula returns the result 46.00.

This formula is entered in cell A16:

=AVERAGE(A2,A3,A4,A6,A7,A8,A9,A10,A11)

The second AVERAGE formula includes every cell in A2:A11 except A5. Both AVERAGE() formulas return the same result, 46.00, and you can depend on Excel worksheet functions such as AVERAGE() and SUM() to ignore text values such as NA when they expect numeric values.

Still in Figure 2.5, the range D2:E11 contains the same records as A2:A11, but both the temperature and the minutes to delivery appear. If you want to calculate the correlation between those two variables on the basis of those records, Excel manages the missing data by ignoring the entire fourth record because it has a missing value for one of the variables. Notice the correlation between the values in D2:D11 and E2:E11, and −0.7449. That value is returned by this formula:

=CORREL(D2:D11,E2:E11)

In the range G2:H10 I have omitted the record with one missing value. The formula that calculates the correlation for that range of data is

=CORREL(G2:G10,H2:H10)

Both formulas return the same result, so the CORREL() function ignores the full record when either of the values is text.

Therefore, you're in good shape if you decide to get the summary statistics from a data set such as the Pizza database using worksheet functions. Things aren't as straightforward if you decide you want to use the Descriptive Statistics tool in Excel's Data Analysis add-in.

If you point the Descriptive Statistics tool at a worksheet range that contains text data, it returns an error message to the effect that the range contains text data. See Figure 2.6.

Figure 2.6
Although all the worksheet functions operate smoothly with text values, the Descriptive Statistics tool doesn't.

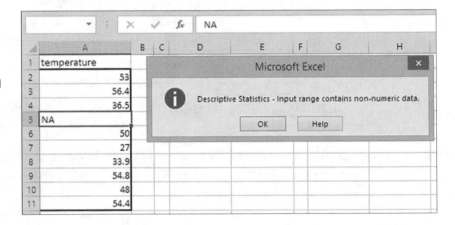

To get the Descriptive Statistics tool to process the data, you have to replace the text data with something else. Obviously, you can't just make up numbers and enter them in place of the *NA* values. As it turns out, though, the Descriptive Statistics tool can manage if you replace the text values with empty cells.

> **TIP**
> Worksheet functions ignore empty cells just as they ignore text values, so you can use either to indicate a missing value. You can use the #N/A error value or the NA() function instead of an empty cell or text value, but if you do so any worksheet function that has the cell in its arguments will return the #N/A error value.

So, one possibility is to do a global replace of the NA values with nothing—that is, in the Find and Replace dialog box, enter NA in the Find What box and enter nothing in the Replace With edit box. Excel treats a truly empty cell as missing data, and functions such as AVERAGE() and SUM() return the correct summary values for those cells that contain numeric values.

Unfortunately, with a data set as full of NA values as R's Pizza data set, those replacement empty cells cause another problem. With as many as 1209 records in the worksheet, you're apt to want to select a variable for analysis by clicking its label (for example, cell M1 in Figure 2.4), then holding down the Ctrl key and pressing the down arrow. This sequence selects all the cells from the active one to the final contiguous non-empty cell below the one that's active.

But that probably just takes you partway through the data set—perhaps even just 10 records. As soon as you replace an *NA* value, making (say) M5 an empty cell, your search for the actual final value in the column ends at M4.

An acceptable workaround is to select the entire column by clicking its column header to enter, for example, M:M in the Input Range box (see Figure 2.3). This slows processing down just a bit, but it's better than hitting the down arrow once for every blank cell in the data's column.

Another possibility is to use a worksheet function that is designed to handle text values in an otherwise numeric field. AVERAGEA() treats text values as legitimate zero values, however, and in averages there's a difference between a missing value and a zero value. That is, this formula:

    =AVERAGEA(1,2,"NA,"4,5)

returns 2.4. Treating NA as a zero value means that the sum is 12 and the count is 5, so the result is 2.4. It's likely that the result you're after completely ignores the NA value, so the sum would still be 12 but the count would be 4, and the result would be 3.

There's no entirely satisfactory solution to these problems in Excel. You could define names based on the top row of the selection, and use a defined name instead of a worksheet address in the Input Range edit box. But Excel does not include the column headers as part of a range that's named using that method, and so Descriptive Statistics cannot show the variable's label as part of its results. If only from the standpoint of convenience, then, R is probably the better bet than Excel in this sort of situation.

Using R's DescTools Package

R has a package named DescTools. It combines a large variety of functions: basic analyses that you might well want to carry out before undertaking a more advanced, perhaps more demanding analysis.

For example, one difficulty that can crop up when you want to compare the means of two or more groups is the *Behrens-Fisher problem*. The difficulty arises if you want to test the statistical significance of the difference between the group means.

When two groups have an unequal number of observations and also unequal variances, one of two outcomes is possible:

- **The larger group has the larger variance.** The process of pooling the variances of the two groups gives the larger group a greater effect on the pooled variance. This artificially increases the denominator of the t-test, making it more conservative than the t-distribution would lead you to believe. The tables may tell you that your alpha level, the probability of rejecting a true null hypothesis, is 0.01 when—because of the relationship between the group sizes and the group variances—alpha is actually something like 0.005.

■ **The larger group has the smaller variance.** In this case, the larger group still exercises a greater effect on the pooled variance, just because it has more records. But in this case the effect is the reverse: to artificially reduce the denominator of the t-test, making the t-test more liberal than you would otherwise expect. Again, if the nominal alpha level is 0.01, the actual alpha level might be 0.05. You will reject a true null hypothesis more often than the tables say you will.

This is the sort of thing you'd like to know before you go to the trouble of running the t-test. Depending on the reason for the unequal group sizes, it may be legitimate to add or remove records so that both groups have the same number of observations. (With equal group sizes, unequal variances do not pose a problem to the statistical test.) Or you might decide to use Welch's correction, which is a not entirely satisfactory solution to the Behrens-Fisher problem.

The point is that R's DescTools package gives you the tools you need to make that sort of test, one that you would want to run early on in the analysis process. Before 2015, most of the tools in the package were available in R, but scattered across different packages. That made it a time-consuming task to get specific preliminary analyses done. Now you can get access to them by loading just the one DescTools package.

Entering Some Useful Commands

DescTools comes equipped with the Pizza data frame that I used to illustrate, earlier in this chapter, Excel's Descriptive Statistics add-in. Therefore, this section uses the Pizza data frame to illustrate R's functions. There's no need to go through the steps to import data from either another application or from the standard comma-separated values ASCII format.

DescTools includes the very useful Desc function, which you can deploy to obtain descriptive statistics on any of the following:

■ A single numeric variable

■ A nominal (or *category*) variable

■ Two numeric variables to obtain a correlation

■ A nominal and a numeric variable to get, for example, mean values of the numeric variable by individual levels of the nominal variable

■ Two nominal variables to obtain a contingency table

You can get univariate statistics for a single numeric variable by using the Desc function in this way, on the Temperature variable in the Pizza data frame:

Desc(d.pizza$temperature)

> **CAUTION**
>
> I have capitalized variable names such as Temperature in the text to make them more readable. The Pizza data frame does not capitalize them, and when you type a command into R's user interface you should be careful to follow the case given in this text's examples, such as the one immediately preceding this caution. R's syntax is case sensitive, so *Temperature* does not identify the variable *temperature*, just as *true* is not the same thing as *TRUE*.

Controlling the Type of Notation

Just as a personal matter I find it irritating to go looking for the mean weight of a group of subjects and find that R reports that its value is 1.49e+02. You know and I know that means 149, and maybe the fractional portion of the mean weight is irrelevant—but on the other hand maybe it's critically important.

The DescTools package routinely and by default reports results in scientific notation, under which the "e" is understood to mean "times 10 raised to the power of." This can be a convenient way to represent large numbers, but it also obscures what might be significant digits.

Therefore, I generally enter the following command early in an R session that will use the DescTools package:

    options(scipen = 10)

The keyword *scipen* in this case is set equal to 10. (The option does not belong exclusively to DescTools.) The option applies a penalty—hence the *pen* part of *scipen*—to the results of the function so that the use of scientific—hence the *sci* part—notation is replaced by fixed decimal notation such as 149.41. In this case, DescTools waits until fixed notation would be 10 characters longer than scientific notation before it switches from fixed to scientific.

Figures 2.7 and 2.8 show the difference in displayed results, first without the *scipen* option and then with it in use.

Figure 2.7
You can tell that the default number formats for the summary data aren't too informative.

	A	B	C	D	E	F	G
1							
2	> library(DescTools)						
3	> Desc(d.pizza$temperature)						
4	--						
5	d.pizza$temperature (numeric)						
6							
7	length	n	NAs	unique		0s	mean	meanSE
8	1.00E+03	1.00E+03	4.00E+01	4.00E+02		0	4.79E+01	2.91E-01
9							
10	0.05	0.1	0.25	median		0.75	0.9	0.95
11	2.67E+01	3.33E+01	4.22E+01	5.00E+01		5.53E+01	5.88E+01	6.05E+01
12							
13	range	sd	vcoef	mad		IQR	skew	kurt
14	4.55E+01	9.94E+00	2.07E-01	9.19E+00		1.31E+01	-8.42E-01	5.06E-02
15							
16	lowest :	1.93E+01	1.94E+01	2.00E+01	2.020e+01 (2e+00)	2.04E+01	
17	highest:	6.38E+01	6.41E+01	6.46E+01		6.47E+01	6.48E+01

Figure 2.8
By setting the *scipen* option to a relatively large value, you override the default scientific notation.

	A	B	C	D	E	F	G	H
1	> options(scipen=10)							
2	> Desc(d.pizza$temperature)							
3	--							
4	d.pizza$temperature (numeric)							
5								
6		length	n	NAs	unique	0s	mean	meanSE
7		1'209	1'170	39	375	0	47.937	0.291
8								
9		0.05	0.1	0.25	median	0.75	0.9	0.95
10		26.700	33.290	42.225	50.000	55.300	58.800	60.500
11								
12		range	sd	vcoef	mad	IQR	skew	kurt
13		45.500	9.938	0.207	9.192	13.075	-0.842	0.051
14								
15	lowest :	19.3	19.4	20	20.2 (2)	20.35		
16	highest:	63.8	64.1	64.6	64.7	64.8		

Overriding the scientific notation with fixed decimal notation certainly improves matters, but we're not there yet. Notice that the thousands separator in the results' first row is an apostrophe. In the United States it's conventional to use a comma instead. You can call for the comma *in the integer fields* of the results—that is, length, *n*, NAs, unique, and 0s—by means of this command:

    options(fmt.abs=structure(list(digits=0, big.mark=","), class="fmt"))

Because the values are all integers, you can call for the number of decimals, here termed *digits*, to equal 0. The thousands separator is termed *big.mark*, and here it's set to the comma.

A quick side trip to explain some more R terminology. In Figures 2.7 and 2.8, the first five values are each counts and are therefore integers. The meanings of the labels are as follows:

- **Length:** The number of records in the data frame d.pizza
- **N:** The number of legitimate values of the variable Temperature
- **NAs:** The number of *not applicable* values of the variable Temperature
- **Unique:** The number of unique values of Temperature
- **0s:** The number of times that the value 0 appears for Temperature

The effect of setting the big.mark option to a comma for the integer variables appears in Figure 2.9.

Figure 2.9
The thousands separator for Length through 0s is now the comma.

	A	B	C	D	E	F	G	H	I	J
1	>options(fmt.abs=structure(list(digits=0,big.mark=","),class="fmt"))									
2	>Desc(d.pizza$temperature)									
3	--									
4	d.pizza$temperature(numeric)									
5										
6		length	n	NAs	unique	0s	mean	meanSE		
7		1,209	1,170	39	375	0	47.937	0.291		
8										
9		0.05	0.1	0.25	median	0.75	0.9	0.95		
10		26.700	33.290	42.225	50.000	55.300	58.800	60.500		
11										
12		range	sd	vcoef	mad	IQR	skew	kurt		
13		45.500	9.938	0.207	9.192	13.075	-0.842	0.051		
14										
15	lowest :	19.3,	19.4,	20.0,	20.2 (2),	20.35				
16	highest:	63.8,	64.1,	64.6,	64.7,	64.8				

Although the Options statement has had its intended effect on the integer variables (no decimals; thousands separator is now the comma) it has had no effect on the statistics such as the mean through the kurtosis, nor on the values of the five smallest ("lowest") and largest ("highest") values in the data frame.

That's because the Options statement set the format for the integers only; the *fmt.abs* argument restricts its effect to integer variables only. You need a separate Options statement for what DescTools terms *numeric* variables: the mean, the meanSE, and so on. Notice that although the Options statement for integers called for zero digits, the numeric variables still display three digits following the decimal point. To control the format for numeric (which you might also think of as floating point or double-precision) variables, you need to specify *fmt.num* instead of *fmt.abs*. Suppose that you want numeric values to use the comma as the thousands separator and five digits following the decimal point. You could use this command in DescTools:

```
options(fmt.num=structure(list(digits=5, big.mark=","), class="fmt"))
```

Figure 2.10
The numeric statistics now display five digits following the decimal point.

⊿	A	B	C	D	E	F	G	H
1	>options(fmt.num=structure(list(digits=5,big.mark=","),class="fmt"))							
2	>Desc(d.pizza$temperature)							
3	--							
4	d.pizza$temperature(numeric)							
5								
6		length	n	NAs	unique	0s	mean	meanSE
7		1209	1170	39	375	0	47.93667	0.29055
8								
9		0.05	0.1	0.25	median	0.75	0.9	0.95
10		26.70000	33.29000	42.22500	50.00000	55.30000	58.80000	60.50000
11								
12		range	sd	vcoef	mad	IQR	skew	kurt
13		45.50000	9.93820	0.20732	9.19212	13.07500	-0.84187	0.05058
14								
15	lowest:	19.3,	19.4,	20.0,	20.2 (2),	20.35		
16	highest:	63.8,	64.1,	64.6,	64.7,	64.8		

The Reported Statistics

Now that we can actually see the summary statistics, let's have another look at Figure 2.10 to see what they actually represent. Recall that you can call for these statistics using DescTools' Desc function:

The Mean

The average of the numeric values in the variable, so R omits the NA values from the calculation. In the Pizza data frame, I have found that the mean of the Temperature variable, as calculated by R, differs from the mean as calculated by Excel by 0.000000000000071, thirteen zeros followed by a 7 and a 1.

The Standard Error of the Mean (meanSE)

This chapter has already discussed the meaning of this function and touched on its use. R uses the sample version of the standard deviation rather than the population version to calculate the standard error—appropriately, in my view. If you really have your hands on a population of values, there's no point in calculating an inferential statistic such as the standard error. Excel's calculation of the standard error differs from R's at the fourteenth decimal place.

The Seven Quantiles

The seven values that occupy the second row of statistics for a numeric variable analyzed by the Desc function are collectively termed *quantiles*. They represent the values found at the 5th, 10th, 25th, 50th, 75th, 90th and 95th percentile ranks of the variable's distribution.

For example, Figure 2.10 shows that the Desc function returns 26.70000 as the 5th percentile, labeled ".05." To verify that statistic, you could take these steps:

1. Note that the Temperature variable has an *n*, or count, of 1,170 legitimate numeric records.

2. Calculate that five percent of the way through those 1,170 records is 0.05 times 1,170, or 58.5.

3. Sort the records using Temperature as the sort key, in ascending order.

4. Note that both the 58th and the 59th of the sorted records have a value of 26.7.

5. Therefore, the 5th percentile of the distribution of Temperature values is 26.7.

Similarly, the 90th percentile rank of 1,170 records is the 1,053rd record (that's 0.9 times 1,170). Sorted by Temperature, the 1,053rd record in the data set has a Temperature value of 58.8, just as reported by the Desc function.

The emphasis in Desc's results on quantiles reflects the DescTools package's emphasis on "robust" statistics. In this context, the term *robust* has little to do with the robustness of inferential analyses such as the analysis of variance with respect to the violation of their assumptions. It has to do with a statistic's stasis when a value in the distribution changes.

The clearest example of this quality is the range of a distribution. You can change any value, or any values, in the distribution other than the largest or the smallest, by any amount, and the range remains fixed. The same is not necessarily true of the quantiles that Desc reports, but the effect is similar. For example, to change the value of the 5th percentile, you would have to add a new value below that percentile or move a value from a spot below that percentile to a spot above it.

Personal opinion: I'm uncomfortable referring to that sort of property as "robust." The term connotes a generally desirable quality. Certainly, there are times when you prefer to see a distribution's characteristics unaffected by a record's minor change in ranked position. But statistics such as the variance or correlation that do change automatically in response to moving a single record are often preferred for that very reason. For more on this matter, see the section later in this chapter on the median absolute deviation, or MAD.

You will often want to call the Desc function with the *plotit* argument, as follows:

```
Desc(d.pizza$temperature, plotit = TRUE)
```

When you use it as above to return univariate statistics, the plotit argument calls for the charts as shown in Figure 2.11.

Figure 2.11
The charts are a handy way to judge the nature of the variable's distribution.

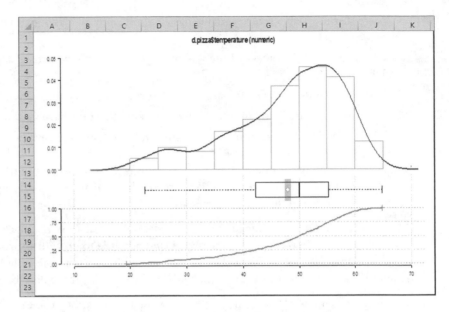

Figure 2.11 shows four charts:

- A line chart that shows the relative frequency of different observations, superimposed over a histogram
- A box-and-whiskers plot
- A cumulative frequency line chart

The line chart, and the histogram it superimposes, are based on groups of observations whose Temperature ranges are five degrees wide. They are the same charts you would get with Excel by inserting a pivot chart that groups the Temperatures into bins of five degree each, and then charting the results as a combination column-line chart.

The box-and-whiskers plot requires a little more explanation. The first and third quartiles—that is, the 25th and 75th percentiles, which John Tukey terms the *hinges*—define the endpoints of the chart's central box.

The endpoints of the whiskers are more complex. Tukey, who originated the idea of box-and-whisker plots, recommended that the whiskers extend no more than 1.5 times the size of the *interquartile range*, often referred to as the *IQR*, which is the distance from the first quartile to the third quartile. As Desc (and other functions in R and applications other than R) implement the recommendation, a whisker's endpoint is the actual observation that is

- Most distant from the median to one side or the other
- No more than 1.5 times the IQR from its side of the box

So in Figure 2.11, the endpoint of the lower whisker is 22.6, and the endpoint of the upper whisker is 64.8. Figure 2.12 shows how these endpoints are calculated.

Figure 2.12
The calculations behind the endpoints are not complicated but they are obscure.

F2 =QUARTILE(A2:A1171,1)

	A	B	C	D	E	F	G	H	I	J	K
1	temperature		Quartile	Percentile	Percentile's rank	Percentile's value	IQR	IQR * 1.5	Q1 - (IQR * 1.5)	Q3 + (IQR * 1.5)	Max value
2	19.3		Q1	25%	292.5	42.225	13.075	19.613	22.6125		
3	19.4		Q3	75%	877.5	55.300				74.913	64.8
4	20										
5	20.2										
6	20.2										
7	20.35										
8	20.4										

Here's how to calculate the endpoint of the lower and upper whiskers, given the references in Figure 2.12:

1. The lower and upper edges of the box—the hinges—are at Quartile 1 and Quartile 3, shown in cells C2 and C3. These quartiles correspond to the 25th and 75th percentile ranks, shown in cells D2 and D3.
2. Cells E2 and E3 show the ranks of the records that occupy the 25% and 75% percentiles. With the records sorted in Temperature order, those ranks are 292.5 and 877.5.
3. The records at ranks 292 and 293 have the same Temperatures, as do the records at ranks 877 and 878. Therefore, we can take their actual Temperature values as defining the first and third quartiles, or the hinges of the chart's box. Those actual values are shown in cells F2 and F3.
4. The interquartile range, IQR, is shown in cell G2. It is the difference between the Temperature values for the third and first quartiles. Multiplying the IQR by 1.5 results in 19.613, shown in cell H2.
5. Almost there. Subtract 19.613 from the Temperature value for the first quartile to get the lower whisker endpoint. Cell I2 shows that the result is 22.6125. Compare that with the location of the lower whisker's endpoint in Figure 2.11's box-and-whisker plot.
6. Finally, add 19.613 to the Temperature value for the third quartile. The result, 74.913, appears in cell J3. *However*, that value is greater than the maximum observed value for Temperature. Therefore, we take the maximum observed value as the endpoint for the upper whisker. That maximum value is 64.8, as shown in cell K3.

When observed values exist that are outside the calculated whisker endpoints, R plots them and terms them *outliers*.

NOTE

Excel's box-and-whisker plots use the same approach for calculating the whisker endpoints and for showing outliers.

The Range

The range is simply the difference between the maximum and the minimum legitimate numeric values of the variable you're analyzing. It is an extremely static—some would say robust—measure of the variability in a set of values. You can change every value in the set except the minimum and maximum without changing the range.

Historically, the range has been a useful measure of variability for statistical process control in factory settings where access to computing power was limited. Estimates of control limits could be made quickly with pencil and paper by basing them on the range. More recently, easy access to computers has eliminated that reason to employ the range. It remains a good way to look for errors in data entry. If the range of a patient's body temperature runs from 98.0 to 990.0, it's a good bet that someone dropped a decimal point.

The Standard Deviation (SD)

The standard deviation that the Desc function returns is the sample version—that is, it assumes that your data set constitutes a sample from a population, and it divides by its degrees of freedom, or $(n-1)$, to estimate the standard deviation of that population. This is consistent with the calculation of the standard error of the mean, discussed earlier in this chapter. For the Temperature variable in the Pizza data set, Excel and R return the same value for the standard deviation to the fourteenth decimal place. Beyond that they both return a sequence of zeros.

The Coefficient of Variation (vcoef)

The coefficient of variation, in the context of univariate analysis, is the ratio of a variable's standard deviation to its mean. The result has no special intuitive meaning by itself. But it can tell you whether two different variables have different degrees of variability. The idea is that the standard deviation and the mean are measured using the same unit. So, by dividing the standard deviation by the mean, you remove the effect of the scale of measurement and you're left with an indicator of the intrinsic amount of dispersion measured by a variable.

It's customary to multiply the ratio by 100, in order to work less frequently with ratios less than 1.0. The Desc function does not do this.

Suppose that you wanted to look into the variability in the salaries of computer programmers in 1990 as compared to 2010. Your research shows that the mean salary in 1990 was $40,000 and the standard deviation was $4,000, for a coefficient of variation of 10; in 2010 the mean was $60,000 and the standard deviation was $6,000, and the coefficient of variation is still 10. By that measure, the variability did not change over the 20-year period, even though the standard deviation increased from $4,000 to $6,000, as the scale—in this case, the purchasing power of a dollar—changed over the years.

The same approach is sometimes taken with units instead of variables. For example, suppose that your company manufactures pistons for internal combustion engines. You manufacture one size of piston for automobile engines and a smaller piston for two-stroke engines. The piston ring diameter for the larger engine might be 75 millimeters, with a standard deviation of 0.01 millimeters. Your two-stroke pistons might average 30 millimeters in diameter with a standard deviation of 0.007 millimeters. So the coefficient of variation would be

0.01 / 75 = 0.0001

for the auto engine piston rings, and

0.007 / 30 = 0.0002

for the two-stroke engine. Therefore, even though the auto engine ring diameters have a larger standard deviation than the two-stroke engine rings, when the effect of the unit of measurement is removed from the comparison it turns out that the diameters of the two-stroke engine rings have greater intrinsic variation.

There are various caveats for the use of the coefficient of variation, and accompanying workarounds. For example, you're usually advised to take the absolute value of the mean or of the ratio, to avoid a negative value for the coefficient of variation. And variables whose mean value is zero, or close to zero, are usually avoided so that you don't wind up with a division by zero error or a huge coefficient of variation.

The Median Absolute Deviation (mad)

The median absolute deviation, or *MAD*, is one way to estimate the variability in a set of values. The general approach is to take the absolute values of deviations of individual values from a measure of their central tendency.

Standard measures of variability such as the variance and the standard deviation are built on *sums of squares,* shorthand for *sums of squared deviations*. If you were to find the deviations of, say, ten values from their mean and total the deviations, the result would be zero. It would always be zero, regardless of the values themselves or the number of values. So the average deviation is useless as a measure of variability.

Approaches based on sums of squares get around this difficulty by squaring the deviations before summing. The square of a number is always positive, and therefore—given that there's any variation in the numbers at all—the greater the variation the greater the sum of squares.

You get to the variance by dividing the sum of squares by the number of values. This makes the variance independent of the number of observations: it's the average squared deviation. And you get to the standard deviation by taking the square root of the variance.

But squaring the deviations can lead to an over-estimate of the variance. One outlier can cause a large deviation, and squaring that large deviation can cause an estimate of the variance that does not stand up in subsequent samples. So an alternative to squaring the deviations that nevertheless returns a positive number as its result is to take their absolute values.

One approach to doing so is to take the deviation of each value in the data set from the set's mean (that is, its arithmetic average). Get each deviation's absolute value and find their average.

The approach that the Desc function takes is to use the *median* instead of the mean. (Unfortunately, the fact that both *median* and *mean* begin with the letter "m" causes the acronym to be MAD in either case.) The Desc function calculates the deviations from the median of the original data set, and then finds the median of the absolute values of the deviations.

Certain properties describe different statistics. Unbiasedness, for example, is one desirable property. An unbiased statistic does not routinely underestimate or overestimate the population parameter that it's meant to estimate. The sample mean is an unbiased statistic. It may not equal the population mean—in fact, it almost certainly doesn't—but it does not routinely underestimate or overestimate that parameter.

In contrast, the average squared deviation from a sample mean, which is the variance, *is* a biased statistic. It routinely underestimates the population variance. That's the reason the sample variance divides the sum of the squared deviations by $(n-1)$ rather than by n: to correct the bias. (The standard deviation, though, is still slightly biased. The square root of an unbiased statistic is not itself necessarily unbiased.)

Another desirable property of a statistic is *consistency*. A consistent statistic comes nearer to a population parameter as the size of the sample on which it's based gets larger. Suppose that the mean age of all residents of the state of Illinois is 55. A random sample of 10 people who live in Illinois might have an average age of 45 years, a 10-year underestimate. Because the mean is a consistent statistic, a random sample of 100 Illinois residents would tend strongly to be much closer to the population parameter—say, 52 instead of 45. That's a *consistent* statistic.

Users of the MAD often like to use it as an estimator of the population standard deviation. The median of the absolute deviations from the median is not a consistent estimator of that parameter. It turns out that if you multiply the median of the absolute deviations from the median by a constant, 1.4826, that version of the MAD is a consistent estimator of the population standard deviation.

Figure 2.13 shows the calculation of what the Desc function reports as the MAD.

Figure 2.13
I have omitted the NA values from column A's list of temperatures.

	A	B	C	D	E	F	G
		Median		Absolute values of	Median Absolute		
1	temperature	temperature	Deviations	deviations	Deviation	Constant	MAD
2	53	50	3	3	6.2	1.4826	9.19212
3	56.4		6.4	6.4			
4	36.5		-13.5	13.5			
5	50		0	0			
6	27		-23	23			
7	33.9		-16.1	16.1			
8	54.8		4.8	4.8			
9	48		-2	2			

G2 · ✕ ✓ f_x =E2*F2

The Interquartile Range (IQR)

This statistic is easily calculated as the distribution's 75th percentile (or third quartile) less its 25th percentile (or first quartile). The IQR defines the distance between the hinges of the box in the box-and-whisker plot (see Figure 2.11).

The Skewness

Skewness is a measure of a distribution's departure from symmetry. Skewed distributions tend to have values that bunch up in one tail of the distribution, often resulting in an opposite tail that's relatively long and thin. If that long, thin tail is on the left side of the distribution, the variable is said to be negatively skewed; if to the right side, positively skewed. The distribution shown in Figure 2.11 is negatively skewed.

Skewness is conventionally calculated as a distribution's average cubed z-score. That is:

1. Calculate the distribution's mean and standard deviation.
2. Subtract the mean from each value and divide the result by the standard deviation, to get each value as a z-score.
3. Cube the z-scores.
4. Find the average of the cubed z-scores to determine the skewness of the original values.

Figure 2.14 illustrates the process. The Desc function calculates the skewness in the same way. (A normal distribution, by the way, has a skewness of 0.0.)

Figure 2.14
The negative skewness indicates an asymmetric distribution.

| | F2 | ▾ | ⋮ | ✕ | ✓ | fx | =AVERAGE(E2:E1171) | |

	A	B	C	D	E	F
1	temperature	Mean temperature	Standard Deviation	Zs	Cubed z	Mean cubed z
2	53	47.93666667	9.93820393	0.50948173	0.132247	-0.841868
3	56.4			0.85159586	0.61759053	
4	36.5			-1.150778	-1.5239639	
5	50			0.20761632	0.00894921	
6	27			-2.1066852	-9.3497264	
7	33.9			-1.4123947	-2.817528	
8	54.8			0.69060098	0.32936812	
9	48			0.00637271	2.5881E-07	

The Kurtosis

Kurtosis measures how much more peaked (or how much flatter) a distribution is vis-à-vis the normal curve. It is calculated in much the same way as skewness, except:

- The z-scores are raised to the fourth instead of the third power.
- It's customary to subtract the constant 3 from the average of the raised z-scores.

The average of the z-scores raised to the fourth power in a normal curve is 3. Subtracting 3 from the average means that a normal curve has a kurtosis of zero—a convenient result because a normal curve also has a skewness of zero. A curve flatter than the normal has a negative kurtosis, and a curve taller than normal has a positive kurtosis. The Desc function follows the custom of subtracting 3 from the average of the raised z-scores.

Figure 2.15 illustrates the process of calculating the kurtosis.

Figure 2.15
The positive kurtosis indicates that the distribution is slightly more peaked than normal.

| | F2 | ▾ | ⋮ | ✕ | ✓ | fx | =AVERAGE(E2:E1171)-3 | |

	A	B	C	D	E	F
1	temperature	Mean temperature	Standard Deviation	z	z^4	Mean $z^4 - 3$
2	53	47.93666667	9.93820393	0.50948173	0.06737743	0.0505833
3	56.4			0.85159586	0.52593754	
4	36.5			-1.150778	1.75374416	
5	50			0.20761632	0.001858	
6	27			-2.1066852	19.6969299	
7	33.9			-1.4123947	3.97946171	
8	54.8			0.69060098	0.22746195	
9	48			0.00637271	1.6493E-09	

Lowest and Highest Five

Mainly to help you interpret any outliers shown in the box-and-whiskers plot, Desc shows you a list of the five highest and five lowest values in the selected variable. If a tie exists, the number of tied records for a given value appears after that value in parentheses.

Running the Desc Function on Nominal Variables

The Desc function has useful information for you concerning nominal, categorical variables as well as the statistics concerning numeric variables that the prior section discussed. It's primarily frequency and percentage breakdowns, and the amount of information is sparser than with numeric variables.

Figure 2.16 shows an example of how the nominal variable Driver appears when analyzed by the Desc function.

Figure 2.16
The analysis for a nominal variable—termed *factor* by R—is limited to simple counts and percents.

	A	B	C	D	E	F
1	d.pizza$driver	(factor)				
2						
3	length	n	NAs	unique	levels	dupes
4	1,209	1,204	5	7	7	y
5						
6		level	freq	perc	cumfreq	cumperc
7	1	Carpenter	272	22.60%	272	22.60%
8	2	Carter	234	19.40%	506	42.00%
9	3	Taylor	204	16.90%	710	59.00%
10	4	Hunter	156	13.00%	866	71.90%
11	5	Miller	125	10.40%	991	82.30%
12	6	Farmer	117	9.70%	1,108	92.00%
13	7	Butcher	96	8.00%	1,204	100.00%

The data provided for a nominal variable forms the basis for the Pareto charts, sorted histograms, shown in Figure 2.17. You get the charts by specifying *plotit = TRUE* in the Desc command.

2

Figure 2.17
The sorted charts make it easy to identify the most and least frequently occurring values.

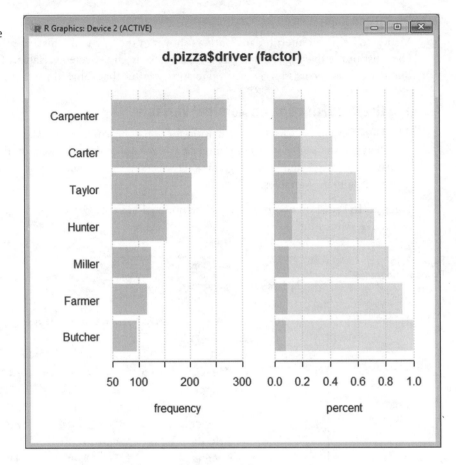

The default order is descending by frequency. But you can use an *ord* argument to change that default. For example:

Desc(d.pizza$driver,ord="asc")

returns the values in order of ascending frequency. And:

Desc(d.pizza$driver,ord="level")

returns the values in alphabetic order by the driver's name. (The Desc function uses the term "level" to refer to the different values that a factor can take.)

Running Bivariate Analyses with Desc

The Desc function can handle bivariate analyses as well as the univariate analyses discussed so far in this chapter. For example, analyzing two numeric variables gets you correlations between the two variables, and analyzing a numeric variable and a factor gets you a breakdown of the numeric variable by each level of the factor.

In Excel, and in most applications that are intended specifically for statistical analysis, you decide which analysis you want (ANOVA, multiple regression, correlation, factor analysis and, so on) and supply the names of the variables that you want the analysis to work with.

In the DescTools package, you can supply the names of two variables separated by a tilde (~) to inform the Desc function that you want to analyze the first variable by the second. For example:

> Desc(temperature ~ delivery_min, data=d.pizza, plotit=TRUE)

Here, the command instructs the Desc function to analyze Temperature by Delivery_min (minutes required to deliver the order). You also see an alternative way to identify the data frame and the variables of interest. It was easy enough to use this sort of structure:

> d.pizza$temperature

in earlier examples of univariate analysis in this chapter. That gets a little clumsy when two or more variables are involved, so the Temperature by Delivery_min analysis simply names the variables, followed by "data =" and the name of the data frame. If you're really in a hurry, you could even omit the "data =" portion, along these lines:

> Desc(temperature ~ delivery_min, d.pizza, plotit=TRUE)

Two Numeric Variables

In the previous example, the Desc function notices that the two variables specified in the arguments are both numeric variables, and therefore selects correlations as the type of analysis to carry out. This is a very different approach than an experienced Excel user is accustomed to. Excel requires that the user choose a type of analysis—for example, CORREL() for correlation or LINEST() for regression. Then the user hands the worksheet addresses of the variables of interest to the function. For example:

> =CORREL(A1:A50,B1:B50)

But using DescTools, the user chooses the sort of analysis by naming the variables to analyze. The Desc function notices the type of each variable and chooses accordingly the sort of results to return. In the prior example, Desc notices that both variables are numeric and therefore correlations are called for.

Figure 2.18 shows the statistical analysis of Temperature with Delivery_min.

Figure 2.18
The user's knowledge of the nature of the variables determines which correlation is the one to attend to.

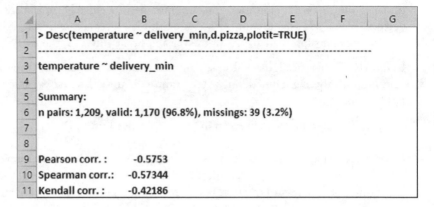

Figure 2.19
This is the approach that R uses to calculate Kendall's tau.

> The data analyzed in Figure 2.19 is taken from M.G. Kendall's *Rank Correlation Methods*, 4th Ed (Hodder Arnold, 1976), which is cited in "Kendall rank correlation and Mann-Kendall trend test" by A.I. McLeod (https://cran.r-project.org/web/packages/Kendall/Kendall.pdf).

Figure 2.19 shows how R's DescTools package (as well as R's supporting Kendall package) calculates Kendall's tau. Recommendations for how best to calculate tau have changed over the years, but they all are based on counting *agreements* and *inversions* (termed *concordant* and *discordant* pairs in some sources). Most other efforts at developing innovative measures of correlation have depended on the original Pearson product-moment approach, pairing a record's distance from the mean on one variable with its distance from the mean on the other variable. For example, Spearman's correlation coefficient for ranks is little more than Pearson's correlation calculated on ranks rather than on interval or ratio variables.

One way to conceptualize Kendall's tau is to sort the records in descending order on, say, Variable A. Then, for each instance of Variable B, count the number of times each instance is greater than the remaining instances; that's the number of agreements. Also count the number of times each instance is less than the remaining instances; that's the number of inversions. The number of agreements less the number of inversions is often termed S. *If there are no tied ranks*, divide S by $n(n-1)/2$ to get Kendall's tau.

If you look in statistics texts dating back to the 1970s you'll find some wildly idiosyncratic calculation methods. The one I got stuck with in college had you sort the records according to the rankings on one of the two variables. Then you drew a line between the two 1's, another between the two 2's, and so on. Finally, you counted the number of intersecting lines. That gave you the number of inversions. And yes, we had personal computers back then, but that method seemed to be more geared to an Etch-a-Sketch than to an HP.

Matters are more sophisticated now, although I admit that you get a better sense of the nature of the difference between Kendall's approach and Pearson's product-moment approach by thinking through the old agreement/inversion dichotomy. The approach taken by Desc, and shown in Figure 2.19, begins (as do most of the approaches to calculating Kendall's tau) by sorting the records with one of the two sets of ranks as the sort key. Then, Figure 2.19 makes use of this array-formula in cell D2:

    =SUM(SIGN(A2-A3:A$13)*SIGN(B2-B3:B$13))

In close to 30 years of using Excel, and looking over Excel worksheets prepared by others, I don't believe that I've encountered the SIGN() worksheet function more than two or three times. It takes a number as its argument and it returns a 1 if the number is positive, 0 if the number is 0 and −1 if the number is negative.

As used here, the SIGN() function subtracts each value in A3:A13 from the value in A2. Because the process started by sorting the records into ascending order by the values in column A, we expect all the values in A3:A13 to exceed or equal the value in A2. The results of the subtractions will therefore be either negative or zero, and the SIGN() function will therefore return either −1 or 0.

The array formula performs a similar operation on the differences between the values in B2 and those in B3:B13. When both instances of the SIGN() function return either +1 or −1, their product is +1, and we have an "agreement" or "concordance." Setting aside the issue of ties for the moment, both the A2 value and the B2 value are either less than or larger than a pair of values in a subsequent row. And enclosing the SIGN() functions within the SUM() function adds up the results.

In Figure 2.19, notice that the values in cells A2 and B2 are less than their counterparts in rows 4, 5, and 7 through 13, resulting in 9 instances of +1 as the product of the two SIGN()

functions. Only in row 6 does one SIGN() return a 1 and the other a −1, for a product of −1. And the result for cell D2 is 8: that is, 9 plus −1.

Dragging the array formula in cell D2 down through D12 causes the cells that are compared to those in subsequent rows to increment to D3, D4, and so on. By making mixed references to the final cells in row 13 (A$13 and B$13), the comparison ranges change from A3:A$13 to A4:A$13, then A4:A$13 to A5:A$13, and so on.

Cell D14 totals the results of the array formulas in D2:D12 and returns S, the numerator for tau. When there are no tied ranks, tau is given by this formula:

Tau = S / ($n*(n-1)/2$)

But ranks are often tied. Therefore, another series of calculations is needed, shown in the range F2:I12 of Figure 2.19. We need to know the total number of records that belong to tied ranks. In Excel, the quickest way to do that is by way of Excel's Advanced Filter. I discuss that process in detail in the next section of this chapter. Briefly, though, here's how to get the necessary calculations in Figure 2.19:

1. Make sure that you have no data in columns F and H. (The Advanced Filter overwrites existing data and you can't get it back with Undo.)

2. Click the Advanced link in the Sort & Filter group of the Ribbon's Data tab.

3. Choose Copy to Another Location.

4. Click in the List Range edit box and drag through A1:A13.

5. Click in the Copy To edit box and then click in cell F1.

6. Fill the Unique Records Only checkbox.

7. Click OK. You'll get a list of the unique ranks found in column A.

8. Repeat steps 2 through 7 for the ranks in column B, placing the unique ranks in column H.

9. Array-enter this formula in cell G2:
   =SUM(IF(F2=A$2:A$13,1,0))
   Drag it down through G3:G9.

10. Array-enter this formula in cell I2:
   =SUM(IF(H2=B$2:B$13,1,0))

11. Array-enter this formula in cell G11 to get the total ties for Variable A, termed *Kx*:
   =0.5*SUM(G2:G9*(G2:G9-1))
   (Notice that subtracting 1 in the expression (G2:G9-1)) causes any non-tied rank to return a value of 0.)

12. Array-enter this formula in cell G12 to get the total ties for Variable B, termed *Ky*:
   =0.5*SUM(I2:I9*(I2:I9-1))

13. Get the total number of possible comparisons for the twelve records on one variable, returned by $n*(n-1)/2$ where n is the number of records. Enter this formula in cell G14:

=12*11/2

14. Calculate tau with this formula in cell G16:

=D14/(SQRT(G14-G11)*SQRT(G14-G12))

To demonstrate that the fourteen steps just given return the same outcome as does Desc, see Figure 2.20. That figure carries out the calculations on Temperature and Delivery Minutes from the Pizza data set. Compare the tau shown in cell M12 of Figure 2.20 with that shown in cell B11 of Figure 2.18 and calculated by Desc.

Figure 2.20
Kendall's tau applied to the relationship between the Pizza data set's Temperature and Delivery Minutes.

	A	B	C	D	E	F	G	H	I	J	K	L	M
	M12				f_x	=M5/(SQRT(M10-M7)*SQRT(M10-M8))							
1	delivery_min	temper- ature	Rank minutes	Rank temperature	S		Unique delivery_min	Count of ties, delivery_min	Unique temperature	Count of ties, temperature			
2	8.8	60.1	2	1099	-1025		8.8	3	60.1	3		Pearson	-0.57530
3	8.8	58.8	2	1052.5	-934		8.9	1	58.8	4		Spearman	-0.57344
4	8.8	57	2	963.5	-758		9	3	57	6			
5	8.9	57.6	4	993.5	-817		9.1	5	57.6	4		S	-287584
6	9	59.9	6	1096	-1017		9.2	3	59.9	3			
7	9	58.2	6	1025	-879		9.3	2	58.2	7		Kx	2016
8	9	53.1	6	735.5	-306		9.4	6	53.1	8		Ky	2308
9	9.1	63.3	10	1162	-1142		9.5	6	63.3	1			
10	9.1	60.5	10	1112	-1044		9.6	3	60.5	7		n*(n-1)/2	683865
11	9.1	56.2	10	915	-664		9.7	3	56.2	9			
12	9.1	52.8	10	720	-278		9.8	4	52.8	7		Kendall's tau	-0.42186
13	9.1	45.7	10	391.5	377		9.9	5	45.7	6			
14	9.2	56.8	14	951	-733		10	6	56.8	7			

Figure 2.20 also shows the standard Pearson correlation coefficient, calculated on the original interval variables in columns A and B, and also Spearman's rank correlation coefficient, which is simply the Pearson correlation applied to the variables' ranks. Excel's CORREL() worksheet function is used in both cases. Compare the results to those returned by Desc in the range B9:B10 of Figure 2.18.

Figure 2.21 shows the scatter chart that you get when you set the *plotit* argument to TRUE in an instance of the Desc function that names two numeric variables.

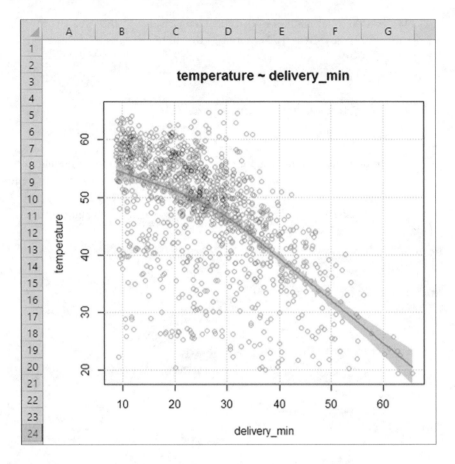

The line that resembles an Excel polynomial trendline, with shaded borders, is often termed a *smoother*. It is not a polynomial trendline but a line produced by locally weighted scatterplot smoothing, or *LOWESS* (that's the original acronym; in recent years the tendency is to put it in lower case and abbreviate it as *loess*). The technique uses local values (that is, a subset of X values near one another) on the X variable to calculate a smoothing fraction for the Y variable. The value of the fraction typically varies with the X values.

> **NOTE** Why not use running medians or means? Because the X values might not be equally spaced.

If you call for *plotit=TRUE* via the Desc function, the confidence intervals around the smoother are 95% by default. If you want to change the default values, there's just a little additional work:

```
> library(DescTools)
> plot(temperature ~ delivery_min, data=d.pizza)
> lines(loess(temperature ~ delivery_min, data=d.pizza), conf.level = 0.99,args.band
  = list(col=SetAlpha("blue," 0.4), border="black"))
```

Note in the third command, the confidence interval has been set to the 0.99 confidence level. The *plot* command enables the creation of the scatterplot itself. The *lines* command specifies the variables used in the calculation of the smoother and provides arguments that you can use to specify the size of the confidence intervals and the colors of chart components. The results appear in Figure 2.22.

Figure 2.22
Compare the size of the confidence intervals around the smoother with the 95% intervals used in Figure 2.21.

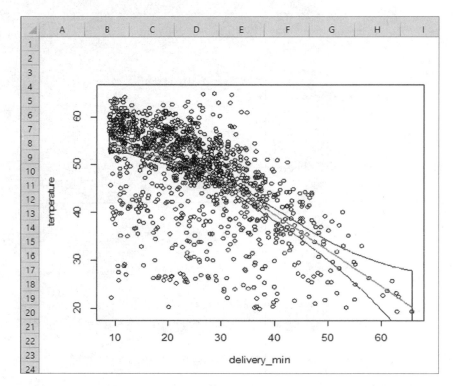

Breaking Down a Numeric Variable by a Factor

Suppose that you were interested in whether the temperature of delivered pizzas varied as a function of the area they were delivered to. You might start out by adopting an alpha level to use if you decided eventually on an inferential test such as the analysis of variance (ANOVA). You would want to do this beforehand in order that your choice of alpha could not be based on before-the-fact knowledge of how the mean temperatures turned out.

That choice made, you could get preliminary information about the mean temperatures using the Desc function:

> Desc(temperature ~ area, d.pizza)

The results appear in Figure 2.23. Again, the type of analysis that Desc returns depends on the scale of measurement used for each variable. In this case, it's a numeric variable viewed as a function of a factor.

Figure 2.23
The Kruskal-Wallis test is a nonparametric version of a one-factor ANOVA.

◢	A	B	C	D	E	F
1	> Desc(temperature ~ area, d.pizza)					
2	--					
3	temperature ~ area					
4						
5	Summary:					
6	n pairs: 1,209, valid: 1,161 (96.0%), missings: 48 (4.0%), groups: 3					
7						
8						
9		Brent	Camden	Westminster		
10	mean	51.13876	47.4203	44.2585		
11	median	53.4	50.3	45.9		
12	sd	8.73353	10.11051	9.83558		
13	IQR	10.5	12.2	13.2		
14	n	467	335	359		
15	np	40.22%	28.85%	30.92%		
16	NAs	7	9	22		
17	0s	0	0	0		
18						
19	Kruskal-Wallis rank sum test:					
20	Kruskal-Wallis chi-squared = 115.83, df = 2, p-value < 2.2e-16					
21	Warning:					
22	Grouping variable contains 10 NAs (0.827%).					

You can replicate some of the results in Figure 2.23 using an Excel pivot table. See Figure 2.24.

Figure 2.24
Excel's pivot tables provide much less information about quantiles than about means, standard deviations, and counts.

▲	A	B	C	D	E
1	temperature	(Multiple Items) 🔽			
2					
3		area	🔽		
4	Values	Brent	Camden	Westminster	Grand Total
5	Average of temperature	51.1388	47.4203	44.2585	47.9383
6	StdDev of temperature	8.7335	10.1105	9.8356	9.9157
7	Count of temperature	467	335	359	1161
8	Percent of observations	40.22%	28.85%	30.92%	100.00%
9					

If you include a request for charts in the command, you get a box-and-whiskers plot as well as a means plot for each grouping level. The command might look like this:

> Desc(temperature ~ area, data = d.pizza, plotit = TRUE)

See Figure 2.25.

Figure 2.25
The box-and-whiskers plots give you a quick idea of whether any serious skewness exists within a grouping level.

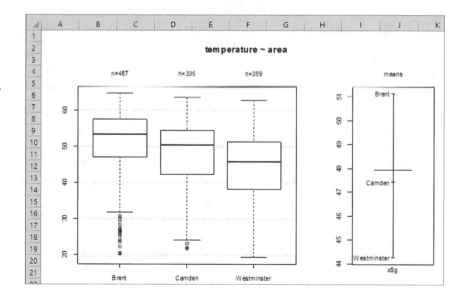

As the start of this section notes, the Desc function can break down a numeric variable such as Temperature by a factor such as Area. It provides information that's useful for assessing the reliability of differences in group means.

When you think about testing the reliability of differences in group means, you think of t tests when there are just two group means to consider, and you think of ANOVA when three or more group means are involved.

In some cases, you might also think of the Kruskal-Wallis analysis of variance by ranks. This is a nonparametric test that's designed with these considerations in mind:

- Important assumptions made by the standard ANOVA may not be met by the available data.

- The data can provide at least ordinal information. In other words, if you have three groups of cars and all you know about any given car is its make (a nominal variable), this test won't help. But if you know each car's ranking on miles per gallon, you might be in business.

- The data (in the case of the Kruskal-Wallis test, the rankings) meet various other assumptions. For example, it's assumed that the rankings can be partitioned into groups that are equally likely if the grouping factor actually has no effect on the rankings.

Now, if the data do not violate any important assumptions made by traditional ANOVA techniques to any important degree, you're better off running ANOVA than Kruskal-Wallis. Other things equal, parametric tests such as ANOVA have more statistical power than do their nonparametric counterparts.

That being so, it baffles me that the Desc function goes to the trouble of calculating and displaying a Kruskal-Wallis outcome but does not bother with an ANOVA.

Whatever the rationale, it's important to see how the Kruskal-Wallis test is implemented so that you're in a position to compare the outcome in R with the outcome in Excel. As usual, it's much easier to understand the calculations in Excel than in R. Also as usual, the steps to get to the results are more tedious using Excel than using R. But in the case of the Kruskal-Wallis test, using Excel is *much* more tedious than using R.

Figure 2.26 shows how you would start to go about a Kruskal-Wallis test in Excel.

Figure 2.26
The Kruskal-Wallis test is much less onerous if there are no tied ranks, but such ties are the norm.

	A	B	C	D	E	F	G	H	I
					Unique ranks	Count of unique ranks	Unique count of unique ranks	Instances of each number of ties	
1	area	temperature	rank						
2	Camden	53	724.0		1.0	1	1	128	
3	Westminster	56.4	920.0		2.0	1	2	63	
4	Westminster	36.5	168.0		3.0	1	3	57	
5	Brent	50	580.5		4.5	2	4	42	
6	Camden	27	65.5		6.0	1	5	28	
7	Camden	33.9	127.5		7.0	1	6	20	
8	Brent	54.8	838.0		8.0	1	7	12	
9	Westminster	48	476.5		9.0	1	8	10	
10	Brent	54.4	813.5		10.0	1	9	5	
11	Westminster	28.8	77.0		11.0	1	10	5	
12	Brent	51.3	652.5		12.0	1	11	1	
13	Camden	24.05	27.0		13.0	1	12	2	
14	Camden	35.7	153.0		14.0	1	14	1	
15	Brent	53.6	761.0		15.5	2			
16	Westminster	51.3	652.5		17.0	1		1161	
17	Brent	51	630.0		18.0	1			
18	Brent	47.7	467.0		19.0	1			
19	Brent	52.8	715.0		20.0	1			
20	Westminster	20	3.0		21.0	1			
21	Brent	52.4	696.5		22.5	2			

Cell H2: `{=SUM(IF(G2=F2:F375,1,0))}`

To prepare for the analysis in Figure 2.26, I first deleted some records from the Pizza data file. I removed all the records with the value N/A for Area (10), and also those with the value NA for Temperature (38). Of the original 1,209 records, 1,161 remained with valid values for both Area and Temperature. Those records are in the range A2:B1162 in Figure 2.26.

Column C contains the worksheet function RANK.AVG(), which returns the rank of each record. For example, this formula is in cell C2:

=RANK.AVG(B2,$B$2:$B$1162,1)

That formula returns the value 724.0. That means that the value 53, in cell B2, is the 724th lowest value in the temperatures recorded in B2:B1162: there are 723 values lower than 53.

Notice the third argument to the RANK.AVG function, the numeral 1. It tells Excel to act as though the data in B2:B1162 were sorted in ascending order. If that argument were 0 or omitted, Excel would act as though the data in B2:B1162 were in descending order. In that case, a Temperature value of 53 would be reported as the 438th highest temperature value instead of the 724th lowest.

The AVG tag to the RANK function tells Excel what value to assign in the event of identical values on the ranked variable: that is, what to do when, for example, there are two instances of a Temperature value of 27. Notice in Figure 2.26 that the value in cell B6 is a Temperature of 27 and in cell C6 a Rank of 65.5.

If the Temperature values in column B were sorted, two records with the value 27 would be adjacent. If the sort order were ascending, their ranks would be 65 and 66. The AVG tag tells Excel to assign the tied records the average of their ranks—in this case, 65.5.

If the RANK.EQ() function were used instead of RANK.AVG(), tied records would also have the same rank. But instead of averaging two ranks as just described, Excel assigns the first available rank to both. So the numbers 21, 22, 22, and 23 would be ranked as 1, 2, 2, and 4.

The next step is to get a list of the unique ranks returned by the RANK.AVG() function. Because ties exist in the list of temperatures, resulting in average ranks such as 65.5, we can't simply list each rank as an integer running from 1 to 1161. Instead, we rely on the Advanced Filter to return unique values from column C. Here's how:

1. Copy the label in cell C1 to cell E1, or make sure that E1 is empty.
2. Select C1:C1162.
3. Go to the Ribbon's Data tab and click the Advanced icon in the Sort & Filter group.
4. Choose the Copy to Another Location option button.
5. Enter E1 in the Copy To box.
6. Fill the Unique Records Only checkbox and click OK.

The result in column E is one value for each rank, tied or not. That is, suppose that in column C, rank 5 referred to exactly one record, and rank 6.5 is shared by the records that come in 6th and 7th. In column E, we want to find one instance of rank 5 and one instance of rank 6.5. The reason we need a list of unique ranks is that we're getting ready to count the number of times that each rank occurs in column C. If we had multiple instances of the same rank in column E, such as two instances of rank 6.5, we would wind up with an over-count of the records for each rank. To continue the example, we'd count the number of records in column C associated with a rank of 6.5 the first time it occurred, and then again (erroneously) the second time it occurred.

The next step is to count the number of instances of each rank, whether tied or not. Array-enter, using Ctrl + Shift + Enter, this formula in cell F2:

=SUM(IF(E2=$C$2:$C$1162,1,0))

If you prefer, you could instead use the following formula, entered normally:

=COUNTIF($C$2:$C$1162,E2)

The formulas return the same result and the choice is a matter of personal preference. (I like the array formula approach. It's a little costlier in terms of RAM but I think it gives me better control over the conditions I set.)

Either formula counts the number of instances of each rank in column C. So, for example, cell F2 shows that column C contains one instance of rank 1.0, and cell F5 shows that column C contains two instances of rank 4.5. Those two latter cases would have ranks 4 and 5, but because they share the same value for Temperature, the RANK.AVG() function assigned each record the average of 4 and 5, or 4.5.)

At this point, our task is to get a count of the number of 2-record tied ranks, the number of 3-record tied ranks, and so on. Those counts are needed to calculate the basic inferential statistic of the Kruskal-Wallis test, denoted H. The counts are also needed to calculate a correction factor, denoted C, that is necessary when, as here, tied ranks exist.

To get those counts of 2-record ties, 3-record ties and others, begin by using the Advanced filter once again, this time with the counts in column F as the basis. The result appears in column G, which shows that column F contains at least one 1-record "tie," at least one 2-record tie, on up to at least one 14-record tie.

With the types of ties identified in column G, we can get a count of each type in column H, again using an array formula that combines a conditional IF with an arithmetic SUM. In cell H2, array-enter this formula:

=SUM(IF(G2=$F2:$F375,1,0))

or this formula, entered normally:

=COUNTIF($F$2:$F$375,G2)

Copy the formula down through column H until you reach the final unique type of tie—in Figure 2.26, that's cell H14.

Cell H2 now shows the number of 1-record "ties" to be 128, the number of 2-record ties to be 63, the number of 3-record ties to be 57, and so on. I put the word "ties" in quotes because the associated ranks are single-record ranks: There are 128 ranks that involve one record only, such as the one record with a Temperature of 53 and a rank of 724. For the moment it's useful to treat them as legitimate ties because it helps to confirm the count of the numbers so far.

For example, notice the number 1161 in cell H16. It's calculated by summing the products of the values in G2:G14 and the values in cells H2:H14. The result is the number of records that are ranked in column C. By summing H2:H14 we are summing the number of records represented by each type of tie (1-record, 2-record, 3-record, and so on). If the result of that summation differed from the number of records ranked in column C, it would tell you that an error in counting had occurred somewhere along the line.

The Kruskal-Wallis analysis finishes up in Figure 2.27.

Figure 2.27
The final calculations yield results that are identical to those provided by Desc in Figure 2.23.

	A	B	C	D	E	F	G
	Number of tied ranks	Number of instances	Calculation of correction for ties		Area	Squared sum of ranks	Squared sum / n
1							
2	2	63	378		Brent	1.05808E+11	226569012.8
3	3	57	1368		Camden	36020813472	107524816.3
4	4	42	2520		Westminster	25430202492	70836218.64
5	5	28	3360				
6	6	20	4200				
7	7	12	4032				
8	8	10	5040		H	115.8274448	
9	9	5	3600		C	0.999976462	
10	10	5	4950		H'	115.8301712	
11	11	1	1320				
12	12	2	3432		$X^2_{(.05,2)}$	5.991464547	
13	14	1	2730				

F8 | f_x | =(12/(1161*(1161+1)))*SUM(G2:G4))-(3*(1161+1))

In Figure 2.27, column A is based on column G in Figure 2.26; I have omitted the 1-record "ties" in Figure 2.27 because they no longer provide useful information after the confirmation of the counts has been made. The counts of each type of tie appear in column B of Figure 2.27.

Column C begins the process of calculating a correction for the presence of ties. The formula in cell C2 is

=B2*(A2^3-A2)

In words, take the number of records involved in each 2-record tie (obviously, that's 2) and cube it. Subtract the number of records in each 2-record tie (again, 2, obviously). In cell C2, multiply the difference by the number of such ties in the original data set, found in cell B2. Repeat this process for the remaining types of ties, found in A3:A13.

Calculate the main statistic, H. For each area (shown in the range E2:E4), calculate the sum of the ranks found in that area and square the sum. The array formula to manage that for the Brent area is in cell F2:

=SUM(IF('Fig 2.26'!$A$2:$A$1162=E2,'Fig 2.26'!$C$2:$C$1162,0))^2

The formula is an array formula and must be entered using Ctrl + Shift + Enter. It tests whether a value in A2:A1162 on the worksheet named "Fig 2.26" equals the value in cell E2, which is the area named Brent. If the value in column A equals Brent, the formula adds the corresponding value in column C; otherwise, it adds zero. More briefly, the formula sums the ranks of all the records for the Brent area. At the end of the formula, that sum is squared.

The formula is copied down into F3 and F4. That's the reason for the absolute references to the values in columns A and C: so that the formula can be copied and pasted down two rows without the references to those two columns adjusting.

Now the three squared sums in F2:F4 are each divided by the number of records that they comprise. For example, the Brent area includes 467 of the 1161 records, so the formula in cell G2 is

=F2/467

Similar formulas, adjusted to correspond to the other two areas, are in G3:G4. I could have written a formula to calculate the number of records in each area, and that's probably the safer method in case any of the original records change. But at some point we all have to decide between the simplicity of a number and the additional safety of a formula. In this sort of case, where I don't expect to conduct a particular inferential test more than once, I opt for simplicity.

Finally we're in a position to calculate H. Cell F8 contains this formula:

=(12/(1161*(1161+1))*SUM(G2:G4))-(3*(1161+1))

The formula contains several values that do not change, regardless of the number of original records you have. Let N represent the number of original records, which here is 1161. Also, let S represent the sum of the squared rank totals divided by the number of records in each group—represented in the prior formula by SUM(G2:G4). Then the formula for H is

$$H = 12/(N*(N+1))*S-(3*(N+1))$$

The only two quantities that can vary in that last formula are N, the total count, and S, the sum of the squared sums of ranks divided by the record count in the groups. The 12, the 3, and the 1s are all invariant. If there were no ties in the rankings you would compare the value of H to the chi-square distribution with $G-1$ degrees of freedom, where G is the number of groups. In this case, G equals 3, so the degrees of freedom for the chi-square test is 2, and the value of H is 115.827, shown in cell F8.

Suppose you had started out this analysis by deciding to reject the null hypothesis of no difference between the group medians if the obtained value of H exceeded the 95th percentile of the chi-square distribution. You can obtain that value in Excel with this formula:

=CHISQ.INV(0.95,2)

where 2 represents the degrees of freedom for the distribution. That formula returns the value 5.99 (see cell F12 in Figure 2.27). The obtained value of H is almost 20 times that value. You would get a value of 5.99 only 5% of the time when the populations represented by the groups have the same median temperatures. A value of 115.827 is vastly less likely than that, if the medians are equal, so you can confidently reject the null hypothesis. (I'll return to the topic of the chi-square value shortly.)

But in this case tied ranks exist, and that means that the distribution of H does not follow the chi-square distribution as closely as it does when there are no tied ranks. A correction factor, usually designated as C, is needed. It's calculated in cell F9 with this formula:

=1-SUM(C2:C13)/(1162^3-1162)

The value 1162 is of course the number of original observations plus 1. The use of the values in C2:C13 is limited to calculating C, so if you have no tied ranks you can skip calculating those values. After you have C, divide H by C to obtain H', a version of H corrected for the presence of tied ranks. With so many cases—1161—the correction made by C is very small.

However, notice that the value of H' of 115.83, in cell F10 is precisely equal to the value returned by Desc as shown in Figure 2.23.

Notice also in Figure 2.23 that R states that the likelihood of observing an H of 115.83 with 2 degrees of freedom is less than 2.22e-16. This differs from the value returned by Excel's chi-square function:

=CHISQ.DIST.RT(115.83,2)

which results in 7.04426E-26. That's an extremely large difference between two extremely small numbers. I chalk it up to differences in the algorithms used by Excel and R, and I don't worry about it. Both values mean that the obtained H is overwhelmingly unlikely in the presence of equal medians for the three groups. And I remind myself that neither value is likely to be correct. It's very difficult indeed to measure the area under a curve when you're working so far from the center of a theoretical distribution.

One other point to bear in mind: The data in the Pizza data set, first, is probably fictional, and, second, would be a grab sample if it were genuine. One of the assumptions involved in this sort of test, whether you run an ANOVA or a Kruskal-Wallis one-way sum-of-ranks test, is that the groups constitute *independent* samples. I don't know where Brent is, or Camden or Westminster, but it strikes me that if they're all served by the same pizza delivery service they must be close together. As such, the samples are spacially dependent. They may well have similar traffic patterns, crime rates, ambient external temperatures, and so on, rendering the samples much more similar than would be the case with other areas that represent the same populations.

Given that sort of threat to the validity of the statistical test, worrying about the difference between two extremely small probability measures is worry misplaced. I don't mean to ding the Pizza data set here: It serves its purpose of demonstrating the results you can expect to get from the DescTools package.

Analyzing One Factor by Another: The Contingency Table

Another type of bivariate analysis comes about when you arrange to analyze one categorical variable by another. Recall that along with most sources of information about statistical analysis, R uses the word *factor* to refer to a variable that's measured on a nominal basis, in categories such as make of car or political party. When you count the number of male and female Republicans and Democrats, the table that results is termed a *contingency table*.

Let's take a look at the results of running the Desc function on two factors from the Pizza data set, Driver, and Area. See Figure 2.28.

Figure 2.28
This tabulation usually follows the inferential statistics in the Desc results.

	A	B	C	D	E	F	G	H	I	J
1			driver							
2			Butcher	Carpenter	Carter	Farmer	Hunter	Miller	Taylor	Sum
3	area									
4										
5	Brent	freq	72	29	177	19	128	6	42	473
6		perc	6.00%	2.40%	14.80%	1.60%	10.70%	0.50%	3.50%	39.60%
7		p.row	15.20%	6.10%	37.40%	4.00%	27.10%	1.30%	8.90%	.
8		p.col	75.80%	10.80%	77.30%	16.20%	82.10%	4.80%	20.60%	.
9										
10	Camden	freq	1	19	47	87	4	41	142	341
11		perc	0.10%	1.60%	3.90%	7.30%	0.30%	3.40%	11.90%	28.60%
12		p.row	0.30%	5.60%	13.80%	25.50%	1.20%	12.00%	41.60%	.
13		p.col	1.10%	7.10%	20.50%	74.40%	2.60%	33.10%	69.60%	.
14										
15	Westminster	freq	22	221	5	11	24	77	20	380
16		perc	1.80%	18.50%	0.40%	0.90%	2.00%	6.40%	1.70%	31.80%
17		p.row	5.80%	58.20%	1.30%	2.90%	6.30%	20.30%	5.30%	.
18		p.col	23.20%	82.20%	2.20%	9.40%	15.40%	62.10%	9.80%	.
19										
20	Sum	freq	95	269	229	117	156	124	204	1,194
21		perc	8.00%	22.50%	19.20%	9.80%	13.10%	10.40%	17.10%	100.00%
22		p.row	.	.	.	.	.	.	.	.
23		p.col	.	.	.	.	.	.	.	.

(It's almost eerie to note how closely the table produced by Desc in Figure 2.28 resembles the results of the old Crosstabs procedure in SPSS.)

This portion of the results is fairly straightforward. The values taken on by one factor head the table's columns and the values of the other factor label the table's rows. In each cell you get the cell's count, as well as each cell's percent of the entire table's count. You also get the cell's count as a percent of all the records for its row, as a percent of all the records for its column.

These raw counts are often intrinsically interesting. They can reveal unexpected patterns in the data or confirm a researcher's expectations. They can also mislead seriously—see the discussion of Simpson's Paradox later in this chapter for more about that problem.

It's easy enough to get the same results in Excel as are shown using Desc in Figure 2.28. Figure 2.29 shows how you might use a pivot table to get the cross tabulation. The pivot table's data source is the list shown in Figure 2.4.

Figure 2.29
This pivot table requires a moderate amount of customizing.

	A	B	C	D	E	F	G	H	I
1		Column Labels ▼							
2	Row Labels ▼	Butcher	Carpenter	Carter	Farmer	Hunter	Miller	Taylor	Grand Total
3	**Brent**								
4	Count	72	29	177	19	128	6	42	473
5	Percent of total	6.0%	2.4%	14.8%	1.6%	10.7%	0.5%	3.5%	39.6%
6	Percent of row	15.2%	6.1%	37.4%	4.0%	27.1%	1.3%	8.9%	100.0%
7	Percent of column	75.8%	10.8%	77.3%	16.2%	82.1%	4.8%	20.6%	39.6%
8	**Camden**								
9	Count	1	19	47	87	4	41	142	341
10	Percent of total	0.1%	1.6%	3.9%	7.3%	0.3%	3.4%	11.9%	28.6%
11	Percent of row	0.3%	5.6%	13.8%	25.5%	1.2%	12.0%	41.6%	100.0%
12	Percent of column	1.1%	7.1%	20.5%	74.4%	2.6%	33.1%	69.6%	28.6%
13	**Westminster**								
14	Count	22	221	5	11	24	77	20	380
15	Percent of total	1.8%	18.5%	0.4%	0.9%	2.0%	6.4%	1.7%	31.8%
16	Percent of row	5.8%	58.2%	1.3%	2.9%	6.3%	20.3%	5.3%	100.0%
17	Percent of column	23.2%	82.2%	2.2%	9.4%	15.4%	62.1%	9.8%	31.8%
18	**Total Count**	95	269	229	117	156	124	204	1194
19	**Total Percent of total**	8.0%	22.5%	19.2%	9.8%	13.1%	10.4%	17.1%	100.0%
20	**Total Percent of row**	8.0%	22.5%	19.2%	9.8%	13.1%	10.4%	17.1%	100.0%
21	**Total Percent of column**	100.0%	100.0%	100.0%	100.0%	100.0%	100.0%	100.0%	100.0%

To create the pivot table shown in Figure 2.29, you could take these general steps:

1. Insert a pivot table on an otherwise blank worksheet using the link in the Insert tab's Tables group.

2. Supply the address of the underlying data—in this case, the list shown in Figure 2.4.

3. On the PivotTable Fields window, drag the *area* field down into the Rows area. Use the Row Labels drop-down menu to suppress the NA values in the pivot table's rows.

4. Still in the PivotTable Fields window, drag the *driver* field down into the Columns area. Use the Column Labels drop-down menu to suppress NA values in the pivot table's columns.

5. Drag the *driver* field down into the Σ Values area. You will now have a raw count of the number of records for each driver in each area.

6. Drag the *driver* field down into the Σ Values area again. Click the drop-down menu next to the second instance of the *driver* field in the Σ Values area and choose Value Field Settings. Change the field's custom name to Percent of Total. Click the Show Values As tab and select Percent of Grand Total. Click OK.

7. Notice that you now have a Σ Values entry in the Columns area. Click the drop-down menu immediately to its right and choose Move To Row Labels. (You could instead drag the Σ Values entry from the Column Labels area to the Row Labels area.)

Repeat steps 4 through 7 twice, once to insert a Percent of Row (see step 6) and a Percent of Column (also see step 6) summary into the pivot table.

If you want to suppress the grand totals at the bottom of the pivot table, to more closely emulate the layout of R's table in Figure 2.28, you can right-click any cell in the pivot table and choose PivotTable Options from the shortcut menu. Click the Totals & Filters tab in the PivotTable Options dialog box and clear either the Show Grand Totals for Rows or the Show Grand Totals for Columns checkbox, or both. You can't choose to show the grand totals for a subset of the value fields, so you can't follow R's approach and show only the count and the percent of table totals, suppressing the totals for percent of row and percent of column.

The Desc function reports several additional statistics to accompany the contingency table. They appear in Figure 2.30.

Figure 2.30
Desc reports three statistics that help you evaluate the reliability of the finding and three that quantify the strength of the relationship between the table's dimensions.

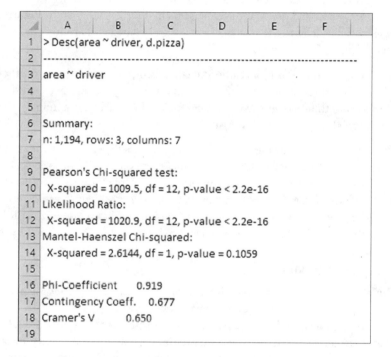

	A	B	C	D	E	F
1	> Desc(area ~ driver, d.pizza)					
2	---					
3	area ~ driver					
4						
5						
6	Summary:					
7	n: 1,194, rows: 3, columns: 7					
8						
9	Pearson's Chi-squared test:					
10	X-squared = 1009.5, df = 12, p-value < 2.2e-16					
11	Likelihood Ratio:					
12	X-squared = 1020.9, df = 12, p-value < 2.2e-16					
13	Mantel-Haenszel Chi-squared:					
14	X-squared = 2.6144, df = 1, p-value = 0.1059					
15						
16	Phi-Coefficient 0.919					
17	Contingency Coeff. 0.677					
18	Cramer's V 0.650					
19						

Suppose that instead of the names of drivers and delivery areas, you had a table that showed a breakdown of a sample of 100 adults by sex and by preference of political party. If those two variables, sex and political preference, were independent of one another, you would expect the number of observations in each cell to reflect the frequencies in the table's margins. That is, if 50 of the sampled subjects were female and 30 of the sampled subjects preferred the Republican party, and if sex and political preference were independent of one another, you would expect to find 50 times 30 divided by 100, or 15 subjects, in the cell that represents Republican women.

But if there were something about the Republican party that drew women disproportionately, you might find 30 instead of 15 Republican women in your sample (equally, you might find 5 instead of 15 if women were disproportionately drawn to the Democratic party). In either case, your observation would have departed from the expected frequency by a considerable amount. That might constitute good evidence that the two variables, sex and political preference, are not independent of one another, and that something about the parties draws or distances women disproportionately. You would have counted many more (or many fewer) people than you would expect purely on the basis that half the population is female and 30% of the population prefer the Republican party.

The three inferential statistics that R's Desc function reports help you decide whether a departure from expected frequencies in a contingency table is likely a random event that might well not show up in a subsequent sample, or is large enough that you might well expect it to repeat in that subsequent sample. These statistics are Pearson's chi-square, the likelihood ratio, and the Mantel-Haenszel chi-square, as shown in Figure 2.30. I'll discuss these statistics later in the chapter in the Excel context, where it's easier to see how the calculations come together.

The Desc function also reports the Phi coefficient, the Contingency coefficient and Cramer's V. These are three measures of the strength of the relationship between the table's variables, analogous to the Pearson correlation coefficient but used with nominal variables instead of with interval or ratio variables. Again, I'll show the details of their calculations shortly.

These three inferential statistics and relationship coefficients are somewhat more complex than those routinely used with variables measured on interval or ratio scales. Each statistic returns a chi-square value, which you can test using one of Excel's chi-square worksheet functions. Excel does not routinely provide the statistics themselves, whether via worksheet functions, the Data Analysis add-in or any command that resides on the Ribbon. It's necessary to assemble a particular set of worksheet functions as described in the next few sections.

The Pearson Chi-square

This statistic tests whether the dimensions of a contingency table such as the one shown in Figures 2.28 and 2.29 are independent of one another, or whether the dimensions have a joint effect. The question is addressed by determining the *expected* frequency for each cell. That expected frequency is found by multiplying the total frequency for a cell's row by the total frequency for the cell's column, and dividing by the total frequency for the table.

I'll show that procedure shortly, but first Figure 2.31 uses an arithmetically equivalent but quicker way to reach the same result.

Figure 2.31
A quicker way to find the chi-square value but not as helpful conceptually.

	A	B	C	D	E	F	G	H	I
	C14		f_x =I7*(SUM(B10:H12)-1)						
1				Observed counts					
2	Count	Column Labels							
3	Row Labels	Butcher	Carpenter	Carter	Farmer	Hunter	Miller	Taylor	Grand Total
4	Brent	72	29	177	19	128	6	42	473
5	Camden	1	19	47	87	4	41	142	341
6	Westminster	22	221	5	11	24	77	20	380
7	Grand Total	95	269	229	117	156	124	204	1194
8									
9									
10		0.11537	0.00661	0.28923	0.00652	0.22204	0.00061	0.01828	
11		0.00003	0.00394	0.02829	0.18971	0.00030	0.03975	0.28986	
12		0.01341	0.47780	0.00029	0.00272	0.00972	0.12583	0.00516	
13									
14	Pearson Chi Square	chisq	1009.50319						
15		df	12						
16		p	1.697E-208						

Figure 2.31 shows how to reach the chi-square value for the Pizza data set's Area and Driver variables in just a couple of steps. You can start with the contingency table itself, with the value fields restricted to the raw counts only—no percentages.

To get the matrix of values in the range B10:H12, enter this formula in cell B10:

=B4^2/(B$7*$I4)

That is, square the count in cell B4. Then divide the result by the product of the total frequency for row 4, in cell I4, and the total frequency for column B, in cell B7.

Notice the use of dollar signs in the addresses of the marginal cells B7 and I4. They make mixed references of the two addresses, so that you can drag cell B7 to the right without disturbing references to column I, and drag it down without disturbing references to row 7.

Now, copy and paste, or drag using the fill handle, from cell B10 into H10. Select B10:H10 and drag down into B12:H12. You now have the matrix in B10:H12.

Enter this formula in cell C14:

=I7*(SUM(B10:H12)-1)

That returns the value 1009.50319. Compare it to the Pearson chi-square value returned by Desc in Figure 2.30, row 10.

The analysis shown in Figure 2.32 returns the same result with an extra step, but it shows the comparison of the original to the expected values more clearly.

Figure 2.32
The range B16:H18 shows how the observed counts are compared to the expected counts.

B16		▾	:	×	✓	f_x	=(B4-B10)^2/B10		

⊿	A	B	C	D	E	F	G	H	I
1					Observed counts				
2	Count	Column							
3	Row Labels	Butcher	Carpenter	Carter	Farmer	Hunter	Miller	Taylor	Grand Total
4	Brent	72	29	177	19	128	6	42	473
5	Camden	1	19	47	87	4	41	142	341
6	Westminster	22	221	5	11	24	77	20	380
7	Grand Total	95	269	229	117	156	124	204	1194
8									
9					Expected counts				
10		37.634	106.563652	90.71776	46.34925	61.79899	49.12228	80.81407	473
11		27.13149	76.8249581	65.40117	33.41457	44.55276	35.41374	58.26131	341
12		30.23451	85.6113903	72.88107	37.23618	49.64824	39.46399	64.92462	380
13		95	269	229	117	156	124	204	1,194
14									
15					(Observed - Expected)^2/Expected				
16		31.38177	56.4556484	82.0636	16.13794	70.91658	37.85514	18.64195	
17		25.16835	43.5239519	5.177325	85.93251	36.91189	0.881193	120.3572	
18		2.242705	214.107908	63.2241	18.48571	13.24986	35.70223	31.08561	
19									
20									
21	Pearson Chi Square	chisq	1009.50319						
22		df	12						
23		p	1.697E-208						

The expected counts are calculated explicitly in the range B10:H12. Each expected count is calculated by taking the product of the marginals and dividing by the table's grand total. For example, the formula in cell B10 is

=$I4*B$7/$I$7

The dollar signs in the formula serve the same function as in Figure 2.31: They enable you to copy it and paste it through column H and down into row 12. Notice that the resulting marginals for the expected counts, in the ranges B13:H13 and I10:I12 are identical to the marginals shown for the observed counts.

Then the observed and expected counts are compared using this formula in cell B16:

=(B4-B10)^2/B10

No dollar signs are used because we don't need to constrain any addressing to the marginal cells. The formula simply squares the difference between the observed and the expected values, and divides by the expected value.

Clearly, the greater the discrepancies between the observed and the expected values, the greater the values calculated by the formula—and, therefore, the greater the sum of the values calculated in B16:H18. And the greater that total, the greater the resulting value of chi-square, which is calculated in cell C21 with this formula:

=SUM(B16:H18)

Notice that the resulting chi-square value is identical to the one reported in Figure 2.31. You can test the reliability of that value by using Excel's CHISQ.DIST.RT() function. It's used in Figure 2.31, cell C16, and Figure 2.32, cell C23. The two results are identical because the values of chi-square are identical. The formula as used in Figure 2.32 is

=CHISQ.DIST.RT(C21,C22)

The second argument, C22, is the degrees of freedom for the test. When used in this fashion, to test the independence of classifications in a contingency table, the degrees of freedom equals the number of categories in one variable, minus 1, times the number of categories in the other variable, minus 1. With seven categories for Driver and three for Area, the degrees of freedom is (7–1)*(3–1), or 12.

You'll note that the probability of getting so large a chi-square if the two variables are actually independent of one another is reported by Excel as approximately 1 in 2 times 10 to the 208th power. It's reported by Desc as approximately 1 in 2 times 10 to the 16th power.

I cannot explain the discrepancy. I can say that such discrepancies tend not to turn up with smaller, and thus much more likely, values for chi-square. Comparing such ridiculously small probabilities is akin to asking whether the volume of 208 atoms is meaningfully greater than the volume of 16 atoms.

The Likelihood Ratio

When you use it in the same sort of setup—assessing a contingency table—as you use Pearson's chi-square, the likelihood ratio provides you the same sort of inference as I discussed in the prior section. The likelihood ratio is probably used more frequently in the context of logistic regression, where it helps assess the reliability of an equation developed using maximum likelihood techniques.

Figure 2.33 shows how the likelihood ratio is calculated when used with contingency tables. The basic difference between the likelihood ratio and Pearson's chi-square is that the likelihood ratio evaluates the ratio of the observed frequencies to the expected frequencies, whereas Pearson's chi-square evaluates the result of subtracting one from the other.

Figure 2.33
Both Pearson's chi-square and the likelihood ratio depend on contrasting the observed to the expected frequencies.

	A	B	C	D	E	F	G	H	I
	B21	▼ :	× ✓	f_x	=2*SUM(B16:H18)				
1				Observed counts					
2	Count	Column .⊤							
3	Row Labels .⊤	Butcher	Carpenter	Carter	Farmer	Hunter	Miller	Taylor	Grand Total
4	Brent	72	29	177	19	128	6	42	473
5	Camden	1	19	47	87	4	41	142	341
6	Westminster	22	221	5	11	24	77	20	380
7	Grand Total	95	269	229	117	156	124	204	1194
8									
9				Expected counts					
10		37.634	106.564	90.718	46.349	61.799	49.122	80.814	473
11		27.131	76.825	65.401	33.415	44.553	35.414	58.261	341
12		30.235	85.611	72.881	37.236	49.648	39.464	64.925	380
13		95	269	229	117	156	124	204	1,194
14									
15				Observed * LN(Observed / Estimated)					
16		46.711	-37.742	118.306	-16.944	93.202	-12.615	-27.488	
17		-3.301	-26.545	-15.528	83.252	-9.642	6.005	126.506	
18		-6.995	209.584	-13.397	-13.413	-17.446	51.468	-23.550	
19									
20									
21		1020.859	Likelihood ratio						

Notice that the likelihood ratio of 1020.859 in Figure 2.33 is very close to the chi-square value of 1009.503 in Figure 2.32. In fact both statistics follow the theoretical chi-square distribution when the contingency table's variables are mutually independent. (And therefore, if you get a highly unusual chi-square or likelihood ratio, as here, you have to consider that the variables are *not* independent.) The distribution of the two statistics comes closer and closer to the theoretical chi-square distribution as the sample size increases: Both statistics are consistent estimators.

However, Pearson's chi-square converges to the theoretical distribution more quickly (that is, sooner as the sample size increases) than does the likelihood ratio. Furthermore, when the average number of observations per cell is less than 5, the likelihood ratio is usually a less accurate estimate of chi-square than Pearson's formulation.

Although you can doubtless find counterexamples, a good general approach is to regard Pearson's chi-square as your primary criterion and the likelihood ratio as a confirming measure. Because the Desc function supplies both statistics by default, you might as well use both, and it's pretty easy to calculate both using Excel worksheet formulas as shown in Figures 2.32 and 2.33.

The Mantel-Haenszel Chi-square

The third test statistic provided by the Desc function when you specify two factors such as Area and Driver is the Mantel-Haenszel chi-square. It differs in several important ways from the Pearson chi-square and the likelihood ratio. Of the differences, the two most important are these:

- The variables that define the table are assumed to be based on an *ordinal* scale. This often means that the variables take on values such as "First," "Second," and "Third." Then, Desc regards the variable as a factor (and it takes two factors for Desc to return the Mantel-Haenszel chi-square). The Desc function cannot distinguish between an ordinal "First" and a nominal "Camden," so it's up to you to decide whether the nature of the variables' scales complies with the test's assumptions.

- The Mantel-Haenszel chi-square is normally used when a third variable is in play, in addition to the two that define a two-dimensional, row-by-column contingency table. The levels of this third variable are often termed *strata*.

It's when strata exist—and when you can account for them—that analysis using the Mantel-Haenszel approach becomes most valuable. The classic study dates to the 1970s, when the University of California at Berkeley came under fire for apparent sex discrimination in admission to its graduate programs. A review of admission statistics at Berkeley for 1973 showed that 44% of male applicants were admitted, but only 35% of female applicants. The chi-square value for the 2-by-2 (admission status by sex) contingency table was significant at the 0.001 level. That appears to be prima facie evidence of sex discrimination.

On closer examination, however, it turned out that the individual departments' admissions decisions tended to *favor* female applicants. (In a breakdown of admission by sex on a department by department basis, the 2-by-2 tables for each department are the strata in Mantel-Haenszel analysis.) That's an apparent contradiction, one that occurs widely enough in different studies that it has its own name: *Simpson's Paradox*.

It's not really a paradox, though. What happened is that some departments admitted a smaller percentage of applicants, regardless of their sex. But females applied for admission to those departments more often than they did to the departments that admitted a higher percentage of applicants.

Viewed from that perspective, the apparent sex bias disappears. Consider a (hypothetical) program in thermonuclear physics. It might be that 50 men and 100 women applied for admission and 20% of each sex were admitted. In a different program on biostatistics, 50 men and 50 women applied and 50% of each sex were admitted. Combining the records for the two courses of study, 35 of 100 men were admitted, or 35%, whereas 45 of 150 women were admitted, or 30%. But viewed at the department level, 20% and 50% of each sex were admitted.

The Mantel-Haenszel chi-square test takes account of differences in the strata (which some writers have referred to as "lurkers"). As R's Desc function implements it, when only two dimensions such as Area and Driver are supplied, the test uses only that single table. Figure 2.34 shows how the statistic is calculated in that case.

Figure 2.34
It's necessary first to convert the variables' categories to ordinal, numeric values.

	K5		:	×	✓	fx	=1193*K2		

	A	B	C	D	E	F	G	H	I	J	K
1	area	driver		Area	Code		Coded area	Coded driver			
2	Brent	Butcher		Brent	1		1	1		R², Area with Driver	0.002191
3	Brent	Butcher		Camden	2		1	1			
4	Brent	Butcher		Westminster	3		1	1		Mantel-Haenszel	
5	Brent	Butcher					1	1		Chi-Square	2.614352
6	Brent	Butcher					1	1			
7	Brent	Butcher		Driver	Code		1	1		df	1
8	Brent	Butcher		Butcher	1		1	1			
9	Brent	Butcher		Carpenter	2		1	1		p	0.105901
10	Brent	Butcher		Carter	3		1	1			
11	Brent	Butcher		Farmer	4		1	1			
12	Brent	Butcher		Hunter	5		1	1			
13	Brent	Butcher		Miller	6		1	1			
14	Brent	Butcher		Taylor	7		1	1			
15	Brent	Butcher					1	1			
16	Brent	Butcher					1	1			
17	Brent	Butcher					1	1			
18	Brent	Butcher					1	1			

The values for the variables Area and Driver in the Pizza data set are given in the range A2:B1195 in Figure 2.34. Just for illustration, assume for the moment that those values are members of an ordinal scale. The first task is to convert the text values to numerics: 1 through 3 for Area and 1 through 7 for Driver. The corresponding pairs of values for the two variables are shown in D1:E4 and D7:E14.

Now Figure 2.34 uses Excel's VLOOKUP() function to convert the text values in A2:B1195 to numerics. For example, the formula in cell G2 is

=VLOOKUP(A2,$D$2:$E$4,2)

and in cell H2 the formula is

=VLOOKUP(B2,$D$8:$E$14,2)

Cells G2:H2 are copied and pasted down through row 1195.

The formula for the Mantel-Haenszel chi-square test is:

$$(n-1) * R^2$$

where n is the number of paired observations in the contingency table (here, that's 1194) and R^2 is the R squared for the paired values. Excel has a worksheet function, RSQ(), that returns the R squared value for exactly two variables, so the Mantel-Haenszel chi-square value is given in cell K5. The degrees of freedom for the test is 1, so the probability of the value in cell K5 is returned in cell K9 by

=CHISQ.DIST.RT(K5,1)

Compare the values in cells K5 and K9 with those returned by Desc in Figure 2.30.

Estimating the Strength of the Relationships

The versions of chi-square that Desc reports—Pearson's chi-square, the likelihood ratio, and the Mantel-Haenszel chi-square—are meant primarily to enable a comparison of the tabled values with a distribution, chi-square, whose characteristics are as thoroughly studied and well known as those of the normal curve. But the value of chi-square is heavily influenced by the degrees of freedom and the sample size involved, which makes it very difficult to use chi-square to assess the strength of the relationship between the variables.

That's what statistics such as the phi coefficient, the contingency coefficient and Cramer's V are for, and they're the final three statistics reported routinely by Desc when you request the bivariate analysis of two factors.

Figure 2.35 shows how all three are calculated.

Figure 2.35
Compare the values of the three coefficients calculated in this figure with those shown in Figure 2.30.

	A	B	C	D	E	F	G	H	I
E19			f_x	=SQRT(C15/(I6*2))					
1				Observed counts					
2		Butcher	Carpenter	Carter	Farmer	Hunter	Miller	Taylor	Row totals
3	Brent	72	29	177	19	128	6	42	473
4	Camden	1	19	47	87	4	41	142	341
5	Westminster	22	221	5	11	24	77	20	380
6	Column totals	95	269	229	117	156	124	204	1,194
7									
8			(Cell Count)^2/(Column Marginal * Row Marginal)						
9		0.11537	0.00661	0.28923	0.00652	0.22204	0.00061	0.01828	
10		0.00003	0.00394	0.02829	0.18971	0.00030	0.03975	0.28986	
11		0.01341	0.47780	0.00029	0.00272	0.00972	0.12583	0.00516	
12									0.84548
13									
14									
15	Pearson chisq	chisq	1009.50319		0.91950	Phi Coefficient			
16		df	12						
17		p	1.097E-208		0.67686	Contingency Coefficient			
18									
19					0.66018	Cramer's V			
20						2 is the smaller of #rows and #cols, -1			

The phi coefficient is generally used in situations that involve two dichotomous variables, therefore a 2-by-2 contingency table. The Desc function calculates and returns the phi coefficient regardless of the size of the table's dimensions, though, so it's up to you choose the proper coefficient based on your knowledge of the variables that define the table. If they're both dichotomies, the phi coefficient will quantify the strength of their relationship for you.

As usual with these statistics, the phi coefficient relies on the comparison between the observed cell frequencies and the cell frequencies that are expected, given the marginal frequencies.

Figure 2.35 shows how the phi coefficient is calculated. The Pearson chi-square is calculated in cell C15, just as is done in cell C14 of Figure 2.31. In cell E15, that chi-square value is divided by the total number of observations in the table, and the square root of the ratio is taken to return the phi coefficient.

Bear in mind that the phi coefficient is an appropriate measure of the strength of the relationship between the variables that define the table represents the cross tabulation of two dichotomies. It's interesting to note that if the table's entries were represented as an Excel list or an R data frame with each observation representing a different record with a 0 or a 1 on each variable, the ordinary Pearson correlation between the two variables would equal the phi coefficient. But the dichotomous nature of both variables imposes additional constraints on the phi coefficient, so it would be misleading to think of the phi coefficient as an exact analog of the Pearson correlation coefficient.

When you have more than two values for either or both variables, as in Figures 2.30 and 2.35, you usually prefer the *contingency coefficient* to the phi coefficient. The contingency coefficient is calculated very easily once you have the chi-square value for the table. In Figure 2.35, cell E17 returns the contingency coefficient with this formula:

=SQRT(C15/(C15+I6))

That is, the square root of the ratio of the chi-square value to the sum of chi-square and the number of observations.

Cramer's V, shown in cell E19 of Figure 2.35, again measures the strength of the association between two variables measured on nominal scales. Many analysts prefer it to the phi or the contingency coefficient because its upper limit, like Pearson's correlations, is 1.0 without any special constraints set on how the values are distributed. The formula for Cramer's V as used in cell E19 is

=SQRT(C15/(I6*2))

where cell C15 contains the value for chi-square, cell I6 contains the number of observations in the contingency table, and 2 is the smaller of

- The number of rows in the table, minus 1
- The number of columns in the table, minus 1

Regression Analysis in Excel and R

3

One of the obstacles to moving smoothly between Excel and R is the array of differences in how the two applications combine the results of a regression analysis. For example, Excel's principal regression function is LINEST(), which returns the elements of the regression equation as well as eight other statistics that enable the user to assess the equation's accuracy and its reliability. One of R's principal regression functions is *lm*, an abbreviation of *linear model*. As it's normally used, *lm* returns some useful information that LINEST() doesn't, but *lm* for some reason routinely omits the regression and residual sums of squares, which are indispensable for many associated analyses such as models comparison. If you want to find the regression and residual sums of squares, you have to look somewhere else.

If you're used to how Excel packages its results, not knowing where to find them in R's functions can be frustrating enough to send you back to the worksheet, where you can not only locate them but use them as you see fit. In this chapter I catalog regression functions, tools and results available in Excel and show you how to get at them from inside R.

Worksheet Functions

Excel offers you several worksheet functions that pertain either directly or indirectly to regression analysis. Most of Excel's regression functions work with one predictor only, and two more powerful functions work with more than one, so it's useful to have a way to distinguish a regression analysis with just one predictor variable from an analysis with more than one predictor. The standard term in the literature for single-predictor regression is *simple regression*, and regression analysis with more than one predictor is termed *multiple regression*.

The CORREL( ) Function

Excel's CORREL() function is not strictly a regression function, but it returns the Pearson correlation coefficient, and correlation coefficients are at the heart of both simple and multiple regression analysis. So it's appropriate to discuss CORREL() here.

> **NOTE** Excel also provides the PEARSON( ) function, which works exactly as does CORREL( ) and returns the same results. There's no special advantage to preferring one over the other.

Figure 3.1 shows how to use the CORREL() function. Cell E2 shows that the correlation between the Height and Weight values on the worksheet is 0.514.

Figure 3.1
It makes no difference which of the two variables you specify first in CORREL( )'s arguments.

	A	B	C	D	E
	E2		f_x	=CORREL(B2:B21,C2:C21)	
1		Height	Weight		Correlation
2		61	95		0.514
3		62	122		
4		63	142		
5		64	109		
6		65	128		
7		65	190		
8		66	119		
9		66	182		
10		67	164		
11		67	125		
12		68	103		
13		68	154		
14		69	144		
15		70	156		
16		71	203		
17		72	124		
18		72	138		
19		73	165		
20		73	191		
21		74	186		
22					
23	Mean	67.8	147		
24	Standard deviation	3.776	31.138		

The CORREL() function returns the familiar Pearson product moment correlation coefficient, usually symbolized as r. Its possible values range from −1.0 to 1.0. A correlation of 0.0 indicates no relationship between the two variables. The closer the correlation to either −1.0 or 1.0, the stronger the relationship between the two variables.

A correlation coefficient by itself does not imply causation, although of course it might exist. In the example shown in Figure 3.1, we know that as height increases, the length of bones increases, and longer bones are heavier bones. It might well be good reasoning, then, to infer that differences in height cause differences in weight, but there's nothing about the correlation itself that demonstrates causation.

The COVARIANCE.P( ) Function

Figure 3.2 repeats the correlation and also shows the covariance of the Height and Weight values that are found in B2:C21. Although you can calculate the correlation without also calculating the covariance, understanding how the two statistics are related makes the meaning of the correlation clearer.

Figure 3.2
You can bypass all these calculations by means of the COVARIANCE.P( ) function.

	A	B	C	D	E	F	G	H	I
				Height	Weight				
1		Height	Weight	Deviation	Deviation	Product		Covariance	
2		61	95	-6.8	-52	353.6		60.45	=COVARIANCE.P(B2:B21,C2:C21)
3		62	122	-5.8	-25	145		60.45	=AVERAGE(F2:F21)
4		63	142	-4.8	-5	24			
5		64	109	-3.8	-38	144.4			
6		65	128	-2.8	-19	53.2		Correlation	
7		65	190	-2.8	43	-120.4		0.514	=CORREL(B2:B21,C2:C21)
8		66	119	-1.8	-28	50.4		0.514	=H2/(B24*C24)
9		66	182	-1.8	35	-63			
10		67	164	-0.8	17	-13.6			
11		67	125	-0.8	-22	17.6			
12		68	103	0.2	-44	-8.8			
13		68	154	0.2	7	1.4			
14		69	144	1.2	-3	-3.6			
15		70	156	2.2	9	19.8			
16		71	203	3.2	56	179.2			
17		72	124	4.2	-23	-96.6			
18		72	138	4.2	-9	-37.8			
19		73	165	5.2	18	93.6			
20		73	191	5.2	44	228.8			
21		74	186	6.2	39	241.8			
22									
23	Mean	67.8	147						
24	Standard deviation	3.776	31.138						

Cell bar: C24 ▾ ✕ ✓ fx =STDEV.P(C2:C21)

Cell H2 shows the result of pointing the COVARIANCE.P( ) function at the Height and Weight values. Cell H3 shows the covariance calculated from scratch. The steps—which you never need to actually take because COVARIANCE.P( ) does that for you—are as follows:

1. Calculate the mean of each variable. In Figure 3.2, I've done that in B23:C23.
2. Subtract each individual Height and Weight value in B2:C21 from its respective mean. The differences—or *deviations*—appear in D2:E21.
3. Form the product of each pair of deviations. Those products are in F2:F21.
4. Calculate the covariance. Find the average of the products in F2:F21, as is done in cell H3.

Notice that the covariance as calculated by the COVARIANCE.P( ) function in H2 is identical to that calculated from scratch in H3. It's helpful to keep these points in mind:

■ Each deviation subtracts the variable's mean from an observed value.
■ When the value is below the mean, the deviation is negative; when the value is above the mean, the deviation is positive.

- So, when both values are on the same side of the mean, their product is positive. When they are on different sides of the mean, their product is negative.
- The combination of the magnitudes of the deviations and the sign of their products results in an average product—a covariance.
- The covariance's sign depends on whether the products total to a positive or a negative number: whether positive deviations tend to be paired with positive deviations, or whether positive deviations tend to be paired with negative deviations.

The size of the covariance depends heavily on the measurement scales in use. If you are examining the relationship between the gross national product and national debt, the covariance will be relatively large. If your variables are family income and personal credit card debt, the covariance will be relatively small.

So, to focus on the strength of the relationship between two variables, free of the effect of the scale of measurement, divide the covariance by the product of the standard deviations of the two variables. This converts the covariance to a correlation, with a range of −1.0 to 1.0. That's interpreted much more easily. You'll find it in cell H8 of Figure 3.2, where you can see that it's identical to the correlation between these values of Height and Weight, calculated by the CORREL() function in cell H7.

> **NOTE** The P at the end of COVARIANCE.P stands for either *population* or *parameter*, as you prefer. If the values represent the full population of records that you're interested in, use COVARIANCE.P( ). If the values are a sample from a larger population, use COVARIANCE.S( ). You can think of the S as standing for either *sample* or *statistic*. In contrast to the covariance, the value returned by the CORREL( ) function is not affected by the data's status as a population or as a sample.

The SLOPE( ) Function

We're starting to get close to regression analysis, and the SLOPE() function represents a bridge between correlation and regression. Figure 3.3 shows a scatter chart of the Height values against the Weight values. It also shows what Excel terms a *trendline*, the solid diagonal line across the middle of the chart.

Figure 3.3
The closer the individual data markers to the trendline, the more accurate the estimates made by the regression equation.

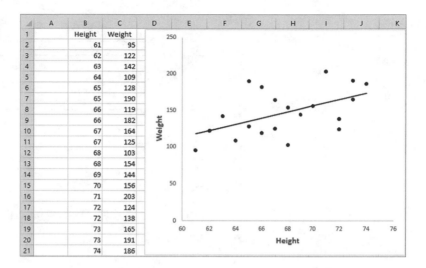

	A	B	C
1		Height	Weight
2		61	95
3		62	122
4		63	142
5		64	109
6		65	128
7		65	190
8		66	119
9		66	182
10		67	164
11		67	125
12		68	103
13		68	154
14		69	144
15		70	156
16		71	203
17		72	124
18		72	138
19		73	165
20		73	191
21		74	186

That trendline shows the general direction of the relationship between Height and Weight as measured by the values in the worksheet. It runs from the lower-left quadrant to the upper-right quadrant—that is, lower values on Height tend to be paired with lower values on Weight, and higher with higher. That's characteristic of a positive correlation between the two variables. (A negative correlation finds higher values on one variable paired with lower values on the other.) You also see this line termed a *regression line*: It displays the regression of Weight on Height.

You can use the trendline as a rough-and-ready method of predicting or forecasting one variable, given knowledge of another variable. Suppose that you wanted to estimate the weight of someone whose height is 66 inches. You could find 66 on the horizontal axis of the chart in Figure 3.3, go up from there to the trendline, and read the value on the vertical axis that corresponds to the point where 66 inches intersects the trendline. (There are other, better ways, of course, in both Excel and R, and we'll get to them shortly.)

To get that estimate, either directly or by way of the trendline, you need to know the trendline's slope—what you probably learned in middle school as the rise over the run. See Figure 3.4.

Figure 3.4

The slope makes sense only in the context of simple regression.

▲	A	B	C	D	E	F
1		Height	Weight		Correlation	
2		61	95		0.514	=CORREL(B2:B21,C2:C21)
3		62	122			
4		63	142		Slope	
5		64	109		4.239	=SLOPE(C2:C21,B2:B21)
6		65	128		4.239	=E2*(C24/B24)
7		65	190			
8		66	119			
9		66	182			
10		67	164			
11		67	125			
12		68	103			
13		68	154			
14		69	144			
15		70	156			
16		71	203			
17		72	124			
18		72	138			
19		73	165			
20		73	191			
21		74	186			
22						
23	Mean	67.8	147			
24	Standard deviation	3.776	31.138			

Excel has a worksheet function, SLOPE(), that calculates the slope for you. But it matters which variable you want to estimate, and which you want to estimate from. In this example, we're estimating Weight from Height, so Figure 3.4 uses this formula:

=SLOPE(C2:C21,B2:B21)

The syntax of the SLOPE() function is

=SLOPE(known_y's, known_x's)

Excel's documentation refers to the variable to be estimated or forecast as the *known_y's*, and the estimator or predictor variable as the *known_x's*. So if you wanted to use SLOPE() to help estimate Weight from Height, you would supply the range containing the Weight values first, and the Height values second. That's just what's done in cell E5 of Figure 3.4.

What does all this have to do with correlation? Well, the correlation helps tell you the value of the slope. Cell E6 has this formula:

=E2*(C24/B24)

That formula multiplies the correlation in cell E2 by the ratio of the standard deviation of Weight to the standard deviation of Height. That returns the original scales of measurement back into the equation. Notice that it returns the same value as the SLOPE() worksheet function in cell E5.

In fact, if your original values were what are called *z-scores*, the correlation coefficient *is* the slope. Z-scores have a standard deviation of 1.0, so multiplying the ratio of their standard deviations by the correlation results in the correlation itself as the slope of the regression line.

The INTERCEPT( ) Function

You have one more statistic to calculate in simple, single-predictor regression. That's the *intercept*. The intercept is a number that you add to what the slope tells you. The sum of those two numbers is your estimate of the y-value from the x-value: the predicted value from the predictor value.

Why the term *intercept*? Assume that the vertical axis crosses the horizontal axis at its zero point. Then, the point where the trendline intersects the vertical axis is the intercept. It's a measure of the elevation of the regression line on the chart. Clearly, you could move the regression line up or down on the chart without changing its slope. That measure of the elevation of the regression line tells you where on the chart the line is located—and therefore the value of an estimated Weight given any particular value of Height.

> **NOTE** The intercept is often termed the *constant*. Simple regression multiplies the predictor value by the slope, and the result varies according to the predictor value. Then it adds the intercept, which is a *constant* and does not vary with the value of the predictor.

Excel provides the INTERCEPT() function, which uses this syntax:

    =INTERCEPT(known_y's, known_x's)

The syntax follows the pattern used in the SLOPE() function: You enter the address of the estimated variable, the *known_y's*, followed by the address of the estimator variable, the *known_x's*.

With the results of both the SLOPE() and the INTERCEPT() functions we're in a position to estimate Weight from Height. See Figure 3.5.

Figure 3.5
Cell F8 estimates the
weight of someone who
is 60 inches tall.

▲	A	B	C	D	E	F	G
1		Height	Weight		Slope		
2		61	95		4.239	=SLOPE(C2:C21,B2:B21)	
3		62	122				
4		63	142		Intercept		
5		64	109		-140.413	=INTERCEPT(C2:C21,B2:B21)	
6		65	128				
7		65	190		Height Value	Estimated Weight	
8		66	119		60	113.935	=E2*E8+E5
9		66	182				
10		67	164				
11		67	125				
12		68	103				
13		68	154				
14		69	144				
15		70	156				
16		71	203				
17		72	124				
18		72	138				
19		73	165				
20		73	191				
21		74	186				

The approach in Figure 3.5 is to calculate the slope and the intercept separately, in cells E2 and E5. Then they are combined with a value to estimate from, 60 in cell E8, to return the estimated weight with this formula in cell F8:

=E2*E8+E5

In this case, we're using the regression equation—the slope and the intercept—to estimate the weight of a person whose height was not among the "benchmark" values: that is, the values in B2:B21 that help form the basis for the slope and the intercept. That's a typical use of a regression equation. In a very different context, you might use fiscal year (1995, 1996, and so on) as the predictor and total revenues as the predicted variable. You could use the resulting regression equation to estimate what next year's revenues will be, by plugging the value for next year (such as 2018) into the equation.

> **NOTE** Using regression with time series data as I just suggested can be tricky and requires considerable study to understand where the traps are. I mention it here only to suggest the extent of regression's applicability.

But it's also interesting to look at the values that the equation returns when you apply it to the predictor values that were used to derive the slope and intercept. See Figure 3.6.

Figure 3.6
The plotted estimates result in the regression line.

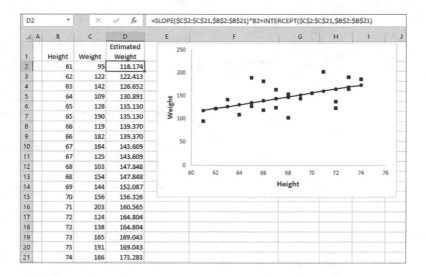

| D2 | | × ✓ fx | =SLOPE($C$2:$C$21,$B$2:$B$21)*B2+INTERCEPT($C$2:$C$21,$B$2:$B$21) |

	Height	Weight	Estimated Weight
1	Height	Weight	Estimated Weight
2	61	95	118.174
3	62	122	122.413
4	63	142	126.652
5	64	109	130.891
6	65	128	135.130
7	65	190	135.130
8	66	119	139.370
9	66	182	139.370
10	67	164	143.609
11	67	125	143.609
12	68	103	147.848
13	68	154	147.848
14	69	144	152.087
15	70	156	156.326
16	71	203	160.565
17	72	124	164.804
18	72	138	164.804
19	73	165	169.043
20	73	191	169.043
21	74	186	173.283

When you apply the calculated slope and the intercept to the original Height values, and chart the results, you get the original regression line—again, *trendline* in Excel terminology—shown in Figure 3.3. (The predicted values are shown as circles and the original values are shown as squares.)

The RSQ( ) Function

This brings us to the r-squared statistic. (Through the remainder of this book, I'll denote "r-squared" as R^2.) The R^2 statistic—both its value and the concept it represents—are central to the interpretation of any particular regression analysis, as well as regression analysis generally.

Excel offers the RSQ() function, which calculates R^2 in the context of simple regression. Interestingly, though, the RSQ() function can be valuable when you're testing the effect of adding predictors to a multiple regression equation in Excel.

Have another look at Figure 3.6. Each of the original data points, the ones that are off the regression line, is some measurable vertical distance from that regression line. That distance is called an *error of estimate*. This regression equation tells you that someone who is 68 inches tall should weigh 148 pounds. A person who stands 68 inches tall but weighs 103 pounds represents an error of estimate of 148 − 103 = 45 pounds.

Every record in your regression analysis has an error of estimate. Because there's nothing precise about predictions regarding living beings, errors of estimate are the rule. Figure 3.7 shows how those errors of measurement are calculated and used to flesh out the meaning of regression analysis.

3

Figure 3.7
Getting from errors of
estimate to R^2.

	D	E	F	G	H	I	J
	Estimated	Error of	Squared Error				
1	Weight	Estimate	of Estimate				
2	118.174	-23.174	537.030		Slope	4.239	
3	122.413	-0.413	0.171		Intercept	-140.413	
4	126.652	15.348	235.556				
5	130.891	-21.891	479.229				
6	135.130	-7.130	50.843		Sum of Squared Errors	14266.891	=SUM(F2:F21)
7	135.130	54.870	3010.669		Total Sum of Squares	19392.000	=DEVSQ(C2:C21)
8	139.370	-20.370	414.919		R^2	0.264	=1-(I6/I7)
9	139.370	42.630	1817.354				
10	143.609	20.391	415.805		R^2	0.264	=RSQ(C2:C21,B2:B21)
11	143.609	-18.609	346.284				
12	147.848	-44.848	2011.328		r	0.514	=CORREL(B2:B21,C2:C21)
13	147.848	6.152	37.849		Square of r	0.264	=I12^2
14	152.087	-8.087	65.399				
15	156.326	-0.326	0.106				
16	160.565	42.435	1800.711		Regression Sum of Squares	5125.109	
17	164.804	-40.804	1664.995		R^2	0.264	
18	164.804	-26.804	718.473				
19	169.043	-4.043	16.350				
20	169.043	21.957	482.089				
21	173.283	12.717	161.732				

There's a fair amount of calculating that's going on in Figure 3.7:

- Cells I2 and I3 return the slope and the intercept of the regression equation. These cells use the SLOPE() and INTERCEPT() functions, respectively.

- Cells D2:D21 use the slope and the intercept along with the Height values in B2:B21 to estimate each person's weight. For example, the equation in cell D2 is

=$I$2*B2+$I$3

- The differences between the actually observed weights (in C2:C21) and the estimated weights (in D2:D21) are shown in E2:E21. Each estimated weight is subtracted from each observed weight to return the error of estimate. These errors of estimate are often termed *residuals* or *deviations*.

- The raw errors of estimate in column E sum to zero (and they always do, no matter what data set you choose). Therefore, their sum is useless as a measure of the full amount of estimation error in a regression analysis. Squaring the errors takes care of that problem, and that's what's done in column F.

- Cell I6 totals the squared errors of estimate. In slightly different contexts, this total is termed the *residual sum of squares*.

- Cell I7 returns the total of the squared deviations of each Weight value from the mean of the Weight values. In those other contexts I just mentioned, this value is termed the *total sum of squares*.

- Cell I8 takes the ratio of the residual sum of squares in cell I6 to the total sum of squares in cell I7, and subtracts the result from 1.0. The result is R^2.

- Mainly to demonstrate the RSQ() function, cell I10 uses it to calculate R^2 directly. As with SLOPE() and INTERCEPT(), the arguments to RSQ() are

  =RSQ(known_y's, known_x's)

- Cell I12 shows the raw Pearson correlation between the Height and the Weight values.

- Cell I13 shows the square of the Pearson correlation. Notice that it is identical to the values in cells I8 and I10. This is where R^2 gets its name: It's the square of r, the correlation coefficient.

You can interpret R^2 as a proportion. It is the proportion of the variability in the predicted variable (here, Weight) that can be predicted from knowledge of the predictor variable (here, Height). The total amount of variability in Weight is calculated in cell I7 via Excel's DEVSQ() function. The amount of variability in Weight that *cannot* be predicted is represented by the residual sum of squares in cell I6.

So, dividing the amount of unpredicted variability by the total variability results in the proportion of the total that can't be predicted by the regression equation. And subtracting the result from 1.0 results in the proportion that *can* be predicted: R^2. Of course it's easier to get there by just squaring Pearson's r, as shown in cell I13, but that doesn't highlight the relationship between R^2 and the accuracy of the predictions.

There is a more direct way to get to R^2, via the predicted values—the other side of the coin from the errors of estimate. That's shown in cells I16 and I17. Cell I16 shows the sum of the squared deviations of each estimate from the mean of the estimates. Dividing that sum by the total sum of squares returns R^2 directly. Again, R^2 is the proportion of the total variability in the predicted variable that can be predicted by knowledge of the predictor variable.

The LINEST( ) Function

With the LINEST() function, we arrive at Excel worksheet functions that can accommodate multiple predictors. But LINEST() can also handle simple regression, of course including the Height and Weight data set we've been examining. See Figure 3.8.

Figure 3.8
The LINEST( ) function
must be array entered.

	A	B	C	D	E	F	G
					fx	{=LINEST(C2:C21,B2:B21,,TRUE)}	
1		Height	Weight				
2		61	95		=LINEST(C2:C21,B2:B21,,TRUE)		
3		62	122		4.239	-140.413	
4		63	142		1.667	113.202	
5		64	109		0.264	28.153	
6		65	128		6.466	18	
7		65	190		5125.109	14266.891	
8		66	119				
9		66	182				
10		67	164				
11		67	125				
12		68	103				
13		68	154				
14		69	144				
15		70	156				
16		71	203				
17		72	124				
18		72	138				
19		73	165				
20		73	191				
21		74	186				

In Figure 3.8, the range of cells E3:F7 shows the results of array-entering the LINEST() function. In this case, you array-enter LINEST() with these steps:

1. Select E3:F7.

2. Type =LINEST(C2:C21,B2:B21,,TRUE) but do not yet press Enter.

3. Hold down Ctrl and Shift as you press Enter.

Step 3 actually array-enters the function. Notice that the first two function arguments echo those used in the simple regression functions discussed earlier in this chapter: *known_y's*, followed by *known_x's*.

LINEST() presents the results of the three regression functions discussed earlier, SLOPE(), INTERCEPT() and RSQ(). Notice that their values, shown in Figures 3.5 and 3.7, appear in Figure 3.8 in cells E3 (slope), F3 (intercept) and E5 (R^2).

The remaining values that LINEST() returns are

- Standard error of the slope in cell E4.
- Standard error of the intercept in cell F4.
- Standard error of estimate in cell F5.
- F-ratio in cell E6.
- Degrees of freedom for the residual in cell F6.
- Regression sum of squares in cell E7. This was calculated in cell I16 of Figure 3.7.
- Residual sum of squares in cell F7. This was calculated in cell I6 of Figure 3.7.

If that were all there is to LINEST() you could probably get along without it. The statistics it reports are all available in other ways, including the standard errors of the slope and intercept.

But LINEST() is capable of returning a regression analysis based on more than one predictor variable, and therefore performs multiple regression using up to 64 predictors. Figure 3.9 shows an example, adding Age to Height and Weight.

Figure 3.9
The R^2 value has increased with the addition of another predictor variable.

F3 {=LINEST(D2:D21,B2:C21,,TRUE)}

	A	B	C	D	E	F	G	H
1		Age	Height	Weight				
2		51	61	95		=LINEST(D2:D21,B2:C21,,TRUE)		
3		43	62	122		4.390	-0.551	-124.745
4		18	63	142		1.634	0.408	111.326
5		68	64	109		0.335	27.535	#N/A
6		68	65	128		4.288	17	#N/A
7		44	65	190		6502.844	12889.156	#N/A
8		38	66	119				
9		30	66	182				
10		69	67	164				
11		55	67	125				
12		43	68	103				
13		36	68	154				
14		32	69	144				
15		37	70	156				
16		58	71	203				
17		69	72	124				
18		56	72	138				
19		52	73	165				
20		21	73	191				
21		53	74	186				

Notice in Figure 3.9 that the R^2 value is now 0.335 instead of 0.264, as in Figure 3.8. Bringing Age into the mix enables the equation to explain more of the variability in Weight than when it predicts using Height alone.

The term *slope* is not appropriate when you use multiple regression, at least not as it applies to a particular predictor variable. When you have multiple predictors, a two-dimensional chart cannot show two or more optimized predictors separately on a single horizontal axis, and so there's no single variable's slope to examine. Instead, we generally refer to *regression coefficients*. This is because regression analysis still uses them to multiply the observed predictor values, and therefore they act as coefficients in the equation. The coefficients appear in the first row of the LINEST() results.

There is one minor problem with LINEST(): It returns the regression coefficients backward. In Figure 3.9, the two predictors are in columns B and C, and Age precedes Height reading left to right. However, in the LINEST() results, the regression coefficient for Age is in cell G3 and the regression coefficient for Height is in cell F3: That is, in the LINEST() results, Height precedes Age, again reading left to right. This causes problems when you want to make use of the regression equation and multiply the original values in B2:B21 and C2:C21 by the coefficients in F3 and G3. Then, you have to multiply B2:B21 by G3 and C2:C21 by F3.

> **NOTE**
>
> There is always only one intercept, regardless of the number of predictor variables. The intercept is always in the first row and the rightmost column of the LINEST( ) results.

The regression coefficients have standard errors. The standard errors appear in the second row of the LINEST( ) results, and they appear in the same order as (and therefore directly below) their associated coefficients. You can use them to perform t-tests of the regression coefficients, by dividing each coefficient by its standard error. The result is a t-ratio that you can test in Excel using one of the T.DIST( ) worksheet functions. I discuss that usage in Functions for Statistical Inference, later in this chapter.

The standard error of estimate is found in Figure 3.9 in cell G5. Its purpose is to tell you how much variability there is in the regression equation's errors of estimate. That can inform you about how far you can expect actual observations to stray from their predicted values.

It's often said that the standard error of estimate is the standard deviation of the residuals— that is, of the differences between the actual and the estimated values of the predicted variable (here, Weight). That's a useful way to conceptualize the standard error of estimate. But don't be misled. The standard deviation of a set of raw values normally uses n or $n-1$ in its denominator. But with the standard error of estimate, you use $n-k-1$ as the denominator, where k is the number of predictor variables in the equation. A regression equation places more constraints on the degrees of freedom than is done by a simple sample of values, where the grand mean is the sole constraint. A regression equation's coefficients also act as constraints and they have to be accounted for in the degrees of freedom.

LINEST( ) provides you with a simple way to determine the degrees of freedom for the coefficient t-tests as well as the full equation's F-test. It's the value in the fourth row and second column of the results, cell G6 in Figure 3.9.

Finally, the F-ratio appears in the fourth row, first column of the LINEST( ) results, cell F6 in Figure 3.9. The F-ratio is often used as an inferential statistic, perhaps most often in the analysis of variance (ANOVA)—and with the proper coding of a predictor variable a regression analysis is identical to an ANOVA. You can test the statistical significance of an F-ratio using one of Excel's F.DIST( ) worksheet functions, discussed in the next major section along with the T.DIST( ) functions.

The F-ratio, used in that fashion, is a test of the statistical significance of the regression equation—more succinctly, it's a test of R^2. If you get an F-ratio that you regard as statistically significant, you can conclude that the equation's R^2 is significantly different from 0.0. In turn, if an F-ratio has a p-value of, say, .05, then you would get an F-ratio at least that large in only 5% of samples from a population where the R^2 is 0.0.

The TREND( ) Function

Particularly with multiple regression, it can be difficult to get the predicted values by multiplying the predictor values by the regression coefficients. (This difficulty is mainly due to the reversal of the order of the regression coefficients in the LINEST() results, discussed earlier in this chapter.) Excel's TREND() worksheet function can help out here. See Figure 3.10.

Figure 3.10
It's a good idea to use both TREND() and LINEST() in any regression analysis.

	A	B	C	D	E	F	G	H	I	J	K	L
1		Age	Height	Weight		=$K$3*B2+$J$3*C2+$L$3		=TREND(D2:D21,B2:C21)				
2		51	61	95		114.973		114.973		=LINEST(D2:D21,B2:C21,,TRUE)		
3		43	62	122		123.767		123.767		4.390	-0.551	-124.745
4		18	63	142		141.921		141.921		1.634	0.408	111.326
5		68	64	109		118.784		118.784		0.335	27.535	#N/A
6		68	65	128		123.174		123.174		4.288	17	#N/A
7		44	65	190		136.387		136.387		6502.844	12889.156	#N/A
8		38	66	119		144.080		144.080				
9		30	66	182		148.485		148.485				
10		69	67	164		131.404		131.404				
11		55	67	125		139.111		139.111				
12		43	68	103		150.108		150.108				
13		36	68	154		153.962		153.962				
14		32	69	144		160.554		160.554				
15		37	70	156		162.191		162.191				
16		58	71	203		155.020		155.020				
17		69	72	124		153.354		153.354				
18		56	72	138		160.511		160.511				
19		52	73	165		167.103		167.103				
20		21	73	191		184.170		184.170				
21		53	74	186		170.943		170.943				
22												
23						=$K$3*B24+$J$3*C24+$L$3		=TREND(D2:D21,B2:C21,B24:C24)				
24		41	70			159.989		159.989				

The instance of LINEST() in J3:L7 is there for two reasons. One is to get the regression coefficients and intercept in J3:L3 into the prediction formulas in F2:F21—just as in D2:D21 of Figure 3.7. The other reason is to get a look at the diagnostic statistics available from LINEST()—the relationship between the coefficients and their standard errors, the R^2, the F-ratio. It's unwise to use a regression equation solely to calculate predictions while ignoring those diagnostics. But you can assess the quality of the regression equation by attending to the additional statistics.

The formula in cell F24 is the same as the formula in F2, except that it points to the observed values in B24 and C24 instead of B2 and C2. In this way, you can use a regression equation developed using the data in B2:D21 to predict the weight of someone who's 41 years old and 70 inches tall: 159.989 pounds.

The TREND() function is quicker and maybe even safer. Quicker because this formula is array-entered in H2:H21:

=TREND(D2:D21,B2:C21)

whereas this one is entered in F2 and copied down into F21:

=$K$3*B2+$J$3*C2+$L$3

I say "safer" because using the regression coefficients directly in the formula risks getting the wrong coefficient multiplying the wrong variable—due to LINEST()'s idiosyncrasy in reversing the order of the coefficients. You don't run that risk using the TREND() function.

Notice that TREND() uses the familiar pattern in its arguments of *known_y's*, *known_x's*. However, its instance in H24 also specifies B24:C24 as *new_x's*. This tells Excel to calculate the regression equation using the data in B2:D21 and apply it to the predictor values in B24:C24. Although the TREND() function in H2:H21 must be array-entered, the instance in H24 can be entered normally.

Be sure to note that the predicted values in column F are identical to those in column H.

Functions for Statistical Inference

Excel provides several worksheet functions that deal with the t and the F distributions. They can be useful in various situations, including regression analysis, when you want to test the statistical significance of a regression equation or a portion thereof.

The T.DIST Functions

When you divide a regression coefficient or a regression equation's intercept by its standard error, you get what's called a *t-ratio*. You can compare a t-ratio, in combination with the regression equation's degrees of freedom, to a *t-distribution*. That comparison will tell you how likely it is that you would get a t-ratio as large as the one you did get, if the regression coefficient in the population is 0.0.

Why is that important? Consider the implications if the regression coefficient for, say, Age in the population is 0.0. Suppose that you were able somehow to include an entire population in the records that form the basis for your equation. In that case, your regression software would show a regression coefficient of 0.0 for Age. And in that case, Age as a predictor would have no effect on the estimates of the predicted variable. It wouldn't matter how old or how young someone was: If the Age coefficient is 0.0, using Age as a predictor doesn't change the equation's outcome at all. And in that case, you might as well omit Age from the equation.

> **NOTE** Then why not leave Age in the equation? If a regression coefficient of 0.0 doesn't help any, what does it harm? If you have thousands of records—if your *n* is large—then it probably does no harm. But with more typical small sample sizes, the regression equation tends to lose some stability when you include an unnecessary predictor variable. See the discussion on the adjusted R^2 later in this chapter for more information on this issue.

Using a predictor variable's t-ratio in conjunction with the t-distribution gives you some guidance regarding whether to keep a variable in the regression equation or to omit it. See Figure 3.11.

Figure 3.11
You can get all the
information needed for
a t-test of a regression
coefficient from LINEST().

	A	B	C	D	E	F	G	H
1		Age	Height	Weight				
2		51	61	95		=LINEST(D2:D21,B2:C21,,TRUE)		
3		43	62	122		4.390	-0.551	-124.745
4		18	63	142		1.634	0.408	111.326
5		68	64	109		0.335	27.535	#N/A
6		68	65	128		4.288	17	#N/A
7		44	65	190		6502.844	12889.156	#N/A
8		38	66	119				
9		30	66	182				
10		69	67	164		Height: t-ratio		
11		55	67	125		2.686	=F3/F4	
12		43	68	103				
13		36	68	154		0.992	=T.DIST(F11,$G6,TRUE)	
14		32	69	144		0.008	=T.DIST.RT(F11,$G6)	
15		37	70	156		0.016	=T.DIST.2T(ABS(F11),$G6)	
16		58	71	203				
17		69	72	124		Age: t-ratio		
18		56	72	138		-1.348	=G3/G4	
19		52	73	165				
20		21	73	191		0.098	=T.DIST(F18,$G6,TRUE)	
21		53	74	186		0.902	=T.DIST.RT(F18,$G6)	
22						0.195	=T.DIST.2T(ABS(F18),$G6)	

Figure 3.11 shows the raw data for Age, Height, and Weight that this chapter has used in its example. The LINEST() analysis of the raw data is in F2:H7.

The range F10:H15 analyzes the regression coefficient for the Height variable. The t-ratio of the coefficient, 4.39, to its standard error, 1.634, is in cell F11: 2.686.

Cell F13 compares the t-ratio of 2.686 to a t-distribution that has 17 degrees of freedom (note that an n of 20, less 2 predictors, less 1 for the grand mean, has 17 degrees of freedom, or df, as shown in cell G6). The value in cell F13, 0.992, says that 99.2% of the t-distribution with 17 df lies to the left of a t-ratio of 2.686.

Another way of putting that is to say that 100% − 99.2%, or 0.8%, of the t-distribution (with 17 df) lies to the right of a t-ratio of 2.686. You can get that value directly from Excel by using the T.DIST.RT() function, as is done in cell F14. (The *RT* tag at the end of the function name stands for *right tail*.) In other words, when the regression coefficient for Weight on Height is 0.0 in the full population, you would get a calculated coefficient of 4.39 or greater in only 0.8% of the samples you might take from that population.

At this point you must decide between two alternatives:

- Through an accident of sampling error, you happened to get one of the 0.8% of samples with a Height regression coefficient of 4.39 or greater from a population where the Height coefficient is actually 0.0.
- The regression coefficient in the population is not 0.0.

Most people would conclude that the regression coefficient in the population is not 0.0 and would retain the Height variable in the equation.

There's a third version of the T.DIST() function in Figure 3.11, in cell F15. It uses T.DIST.2T(), which returns the two-tailed version of the t-test: the probability of either a regression coefficient less than −4.39 or a regression coefficient greater than 4.39. Because the t-distribution is symmetric, that's exactly twice the probability returned by T.DIST. RT(): 0.016 in cell F15.

> **NOTE** Unlike the other T.DIST() functions, T.DIST.2T() does not accept a negative t-ratio as its first argument. To get the proper result from this function, you need to use the ABS() function around the t-ratio in case it's negative. I believe that I understand Microsoft's reason for this apparent anomaly but I disagree with it.

I'm convinced that as height increases, weight as a rule increases, and as a result I would reject the possibility of a negative regression coefficient of Weight on Height. I'd pay attention only to the 0.8% probability level reported by the T.DIST.RT() result.

You get a different outcome from testing the regression coefficient for Age. Still in Figure 3.11, you'll find that test in F17:H22. In this case, the t-ratio is −1.348, in cell F18. I'm perfectly willing to accept the possibility that in the population that this sample of 20 records came from, the greater the age the less the weight, so I'm going to pay attention to both ends of the t-distribution. The T.DIST.2T() function in F22 informs you that, from a population in which the regression coefficient of Weight on Age is 0.0, you could expect sampling error to bring about a regression coefficient of 1.348 (or larger) or −1.348 (or smaller) as much as 19.5% of the time.

It's a subjective decision, and one that should be informed by an analysis of the costs of going wrong, but if a finding could come about through random sampling error almost 20% of the time, I'm disinclined to believe it's due to something *other* than sampling error. I'd rather omit Age from the equation. But I certainly wouldn't quarrel with anyone who thought 19.5% sufficiently unusual to adopt the alternative hypothesis that the regression coefficient in the population is non-zero.

The F.DIST Functions

The approach to assessing the significance of a predictor discussed in the prior section relies on the t-distribution. A different approach, usually termed *models comparison*, compares the results of two LINEST() analyses. See Figure 3.12.

Figure 3.12
The models comparison approach usually involves the F distribution rather than the t-distribution.

| G22 | ▼ | ⋮ | × | ✓ | *fx* | =F7-F14 |

◢ A	B	C	D	E	F	G	H	I	J	K
1		Age	Height	Weight						
2	51	61	95		=LINEST(D2:D21,B2:C21,,TRUE)					
3	43	62	122		4.390	-0.551	-124.745			
4	18	63	142		1.634	0.408	111.326			
5	68	64	109		0.335	27.535	#N/A			
6	68	65	128		4.288	17	#N/A			
7	44	65	190		6502.844	12889.156	#N/A			
8	38	66	119							
9	30	66	182		=LINEST(D2:D21,C2:C21,,TRUE)					
10	69	67	164		4.239	-140.413				
11	55	67	125		1.667	113.202				
12	43	68	103		0.264	28.153				
13	36	68	154		6.466	18				
14	32	69	144		5125.109	14266.891				
15	37	70	156							
16	58	71	203							
17	69	72	124			R^2	df	"MS"	F	Prob of F
18	56	72	138		Difference in R^2	0.071	1	0.071	1.817	0.195
19	52	73	165		Residual R^2	0.665	17	0.039		
20	21	73	191							
21	53	74	186			SS	df	MS	F	Prob of F
22					Difference in SS Regression	1377.735	1	1377.7	1.817	0.195
23					Residual SS	12889.156	17	758.19		

3

The idea behind the models comparison approach is that you can create two regression equations: one with all the predictor variables and one with a subset of the predictor variables. In the current example, that could mean a model with both Height and Age, and one with Height only.

Then, statistics that reflect the quantitative difference between the two models can be assembled (quickly, by the way) and tested.

Figure 3.12 shows the two pertinent models. The "full" model is in F3:H7 and the "restricted" model, without the Age variable, is in F10:G14. The important comparison is between the two R^2 values. That comparison is in cell G18: the full model explains 7.1% more of the total variance in Weight than the restricted model, using Height alone as a predictor, does. That 7.1% value comes from subtracting the R^2 in cell F12 from the R^2 in cell F5.

We'll test that delta in the R^2 values against the residual variability in the full model. The R^2 for the full model is 0.335, so the proportion of residual variability is $1 - 0.335$, or 0.665. You'll find that in cell G19.

The degrees of freedom for the delta R^2 is 1, and for the residual is 17, just as in the full model. The "mean squares," designated as "MS", are found in I18:I19. I put them in quotes because they are not true mean squares, which are sums of squares divided by their degrees of freedom. Rather they are percentages of sums of squares—the R^2 values—divided by their degrees of freedom. The outcome is the same either way. It's just much easier to grasp the meaning of an R^2 value than to grasp that of a sum of squared deviations. But to demonstrate the equivalence, I have repeated the analysis in G22:K23 starting with sums of squares instead of R^2 values.

The ratio of the two "mean square" values in cells I18:I19 is the F-ratio, found in J18. You can test the statistical significance of the F-ratio with the F.DIST.RT() function. That's done in cell K18 with this formula:

=F.DIST.RT(J18,H18,H19)

Its value is 0.195, precisely the same as found in cell F22 of Figure 3.11. We have two analyses:

- Testing the regression coefficient for Age with its standard error and the t-distribution
- Testing the difference between the full and restricted models with the delta in R^2 and the F distribution

The conclusion in the models comparison approach is that the removal of the Age variable from the regression equation does not make a statistically significant difference, when the probability is 0.195, to the value of R^2. Therefore, *including* it in the equation will not make a significant difference.

The conclusion of the approach that uses the regression coefficient and its standard error is that the coefficient is not different from 0.0: that you would get a coefficient a large as 2.686 due to sampling error in as many as 19.5% of repeated samples from the population. Therefore leaving it in the equation does not make a meaningful difference to the equation's results.

The two conclusions have the same meaning, although they come about from different routes. They also have precisely the same numeric outcomes as measured by the statistical significance of the difference. Other things equal, it's better to have fewer predictors than more, so the decision would typically be to leave Age out of the equation.

Other Sources of Regression Analysis in Excel

Besides the worksheet functions that pertain to correlation and regression, two other features in Excel help clarify what's going on in a regression analysis. One is the Data Analysis add-in's Regression tool and the other has to do with trendlines in Excel's scatter charts.

The Regression Tool

Excel's Data Analysis add-in provides a tool for regression analysis, and it's actually not a bad way to get a reasonably rich set of results. The procedure to install the Data Analysis add-in is discussed in Chapter 2, where the focus is on the add-in's Descriptive Statistics tool. In this section, the focus is on the Regression tool but the installation procedures for the add-in are the same.

As is the case with the Descriptive Statistics tool, one principal drawback to the Regression tool is that the results it presents are not given as formulas, but as static values. This means that if you want to add to, delete from or edit the underlying data, you'll have to run the

Regression tool again in order to make sure that the results are based on the most current version of the data.

To use the Regression tool, begin by activating a worksheet with the data you want to analyze. This example will use the data in the range B2:D21 shown in Figure 3.12. Start the Data Analysis add-in by clicking its link in the Analysis group on the Ribbon's Data tab. In the Data Analysis dialog box, scroll down to find the Regression tool, select it and click OK. The dialog box shown in Figure 3.13 appears.

Figure 3.13
The plots can be an important part of regression diagnostics.

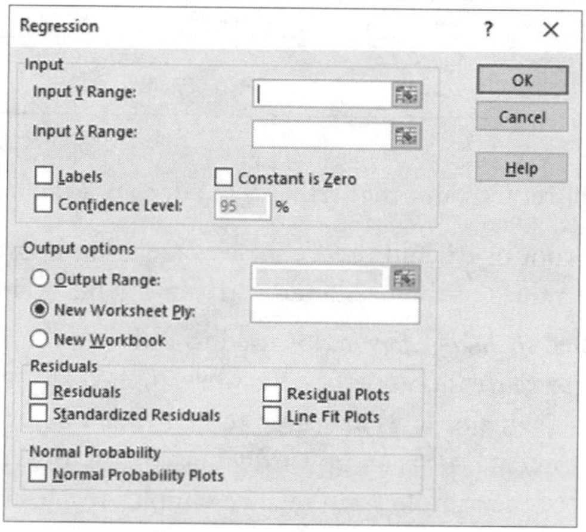

You know what to do with the dialog box shown in Figure 3.13. Just a few recommendations:

- Include variable labels in the Input Range, and use the Labels checkbox. Doing so will help keep you straight if you want to view LINEST() results in addition to the Regression tool's output—recall that LINEST() returns the coefficients in the reverse of worksheet order.

- If you specify Output Range as the location for the results, remember to click in the Output Range edit box after you choose its option button.

- Do choose the residual checkboxes. The plots they produce can inform you about the adequacy of the regression model you've chosen. I don't recommend that you choose the normal probability plot, for reasons discussed later in this section.

The results are shown in Figures 3.14 through 3.16 which assume that you chose all the available options and directed the output to a new worksheet. Figure 3.14 displays information about the regression equation itself.

Figure 3.14
This information focuses on the reliability of the regression equation.

	A	B	C	D	E	F	G	H	I
1	SUMMARY OUTPUT								
2									
3	*Regression Statistics*								
4	Multiple R	0.579							
5	R Square	0.335							
6	Adjusted R Square	0.257							
7	Standard Error	27.535							
8	Observations	20							
9									
10	ANOVA								
11		*df*	*SS*	*MS*	*F*	*Significance F*			
12	Regression	2	6502.844	3251.422	4.288	0.031			
13	Residual	17	12889.156	758.186					
14	Total	19	19392						
15									
16		*Coefficients*	*Standard Error*	*t Stat*	*P-value*	*Lower 95%*	*Upper 95%*	*Lower 95.0%*	*Upper 95.0%*
17	Intercept	-124.745	111.326	-1.121	0.278	-359.621	110.132	-359.621	110.132
18	Age	-0.551	0.408	-1.348	0.195	-1.412	0.311	-1.412	0.311
19	Height	4.390	1.634	2.686	0.016	0.942	7.838	0.942	7.838

Data that the Regression tool returns and that LINEST() does not includes the following:

- Multiple R. The square root of R^2, and the Pearson correlation between the observed values and the predicted values of the predicted variable—here, Weight.

- Adjusted R^2. The so-called *shrinkage formula* is used to estimate the value of R^2 that would be returned if these regression coefficients were applied to a new sample from the same population. The value of R^2 is expected to be lower when the original coefficients are applied to fresh data. R^2 is an upwardly biased statistic, and the degree of bias is in part a function of the sample size (smaller samples result in more bias). The shrinkage formula:

$$1 - (1 - R^2)(n-1)/(n-k-1)$$

adjusts the obtained R^2 to take account of the bias. Notice that the larger the sample size n, the less the adjustment.

- The analysis of variance (ANOVA) section shown in Figure 3.14 is similar in its intent to the ANOVA discussed earlier, in "The F.DIST() Functions" section. In this case, though, we are not using an ANOVA to compare the difference between two models, but to test one model, and specifically the difference between the obtained R^2 and 0.0. The statistic that's tested is the F-ratio, which is closely related to R^2. R^2 is the ratio of the variance explained by regression to the total variance. F is the ratio of the variance explained by regression to the unexplained variance. In Figure 3.12, the sums of squares are actually percentages of the total sum of squares, whereas the Regression tool returns the actual sum of squares. The two metrics are equivalent, though: Whether you use the actual sums of squares or the percentage of the total, the F-ratio is the same.

- The t-ratios and their probabilities shown in the final section of Figure 3.14 are not returned by LINEST(), although their building blocks (the regression coefficients and their standard errors) are. Compare the range B17:C19 in Figure 3.14 to the range F3:H4 in Figure 3.12.

- The range F17:G19 in Figure 3.14 shows the endpoints of 95% confidence intervals around each regression coefficient and the intercept. These are not provided directly by LINEST(), but each can be calculated easily from the LINEST() results. Just use T.INV() to get the 2.5% and 97.5% points in the t-distribution with 17 degrees of freedom, and multiply those two t-values by the standard error of each regression coefficient, and add the value of the coefficient itself.

- By default, the Regression tool returns the 95% confidence intervals. If you filled the Confidence Level checkbox in the Regression dialog box (see Figure 3.13) and supplied some other confidence level such as 99%, the Regression tool provides the endpoints of that confidence level as well, in the range H17:I19 of Figure 3.14.

Figure 3.15 shows the 20 original individual records in different ways.

Figure 3.15
The Predicted Weights are identical to those returned by the TREND() function.

	A	B	C	D	E	F	G
1	RESIDUAL OUTPUT					PROBABILITY OUTPUT	
2							
3	Observation	Predicted Weight	Residuals	Standard Residuals		Percentile	Weight
4	1	114.9727689	-19.97276888	-0.766836603		2.5	95
5	2	123.7672029	-1.767202937	-0.067850177		7.5	103
6	3	141.9208768	0.079123202	0.003037865		12.5	109
7	4	118.7837868	-9.783786823	-0.375639747		17.5	119
8	5	123.1738727	4.826127261	0.185294841		22.5	122
9	6	136.3869172	53.61308283	2.058426377		27.5	124
10	7	144.0802642	-25.08026419	-0.962934318		32.5	125
11	8	148.4846123	33.51538767	1.286793342		37.5	128
12	9	131.4035011	32.59649895	1.251513431		42.5	138
13	10	139.1111103	-14.1111103	-0.541783463		47.5	142
14	11	150.1077184	-47.10771843	-1.808658728		52.5	144
15	12	153.9615231	0.038476945	0.001477288		57.5	154
16	13	160.553783	-16.55378304	-0.635567698		62.5	156
17	14	162.1911514	-6.191151368	-0.237703721		67.5	164
18	15	155.0198234	47.98017659	1.842155979		72.5	165
19	16	153.3539306	-29.35393063	1.12701792		77.5	182
20	17	160.5109964	-22.51099636	-0.864289577		82.5	186
21	18	167.1032563	-2.103256347	-0.080752647		87.5	190
22	19	184.1701054	6.829894601	0.262227696		92.5	191
23	20	170.9427987	15.05720125	0.578107779		97.5	203

Figure 3.15 shows the predicted weight for each record, which Figure 3.10 shows can be calculated by applying the regression coefficients and intercept to the predictor values. Subtracting the predicted weight from the observed weight provides the residual, termed "error of estimate" in Figure 3.7. These residuals are converted to *standard residuals* in column D by dividing each residual by their standard deviation (the sample rather than the population form of the function).

The residual values are used in the plots shown in Figure 3.16. The "Probability Output" is the basis for the Normal Probability Plot, also in Figure 3.16.

Figure 3.16
The Normal Probability
plot is not a standard one.

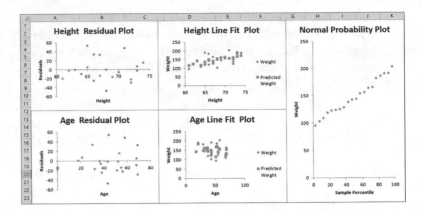

The residual plots in Figure 3.16 can be useful in diagnosing an inadequate regression model: For example, one in which a variable that's not included in the regression equation accounts for a meaningful amount of the variation in the predicted variable. It's also possible to infer that an existing predictor variable should be raised to the second or even third power and added to the regression equation. In this case, the plotted points in the two residual charts display random patterns, which is just what you'd like to see.

I would like to see a chart of the actual values of the predicted variable charted against the fitted (that is, the predicted) values, because that plot can show the effect of an inadequate model more clearly. You can create the fitted line plot easily enough by creating a scatter chart of the actual by the predicted values and calling for a linear trendline.

The normal probability plot is a nice idea, badly executed. A normal probability plot is intended to chart the actual values on the horizontal axis and their percentile positions on the vertical axis. The idea is that a normally distributed variable will appear as a straight line (instead of as an ogive, or s-shaped curve) on a normal probability plot. But for this to occur, the vertical axis must be compressed toward its middle and extended at the top and bottom. The Regression tool's normal probability plot ignores this requirement. (It would have to be done with a bar chart, which is the only two-axis chart in Excel with a category y-axis.)

Chart Trendlines

The third principal area (besides worksheet functions and the Data Analysis add-in's Regression tool) where Excel supports regression analysis is via its charts. Figure 3.17 shows an example, using the Height and Weight example from this chapter's section on simple regression.

Figure 3.17
A two-dimensional chart can show two variables only.

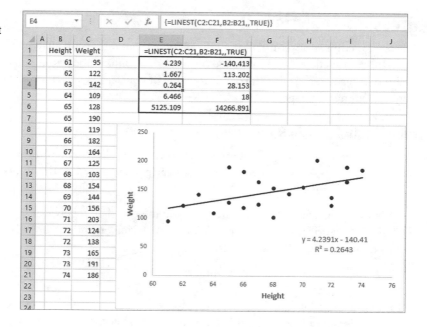

Figure 3.17 shows the same chart and trendline as Figure 3.3, but the regression equation and the R^2 value have been added. Yovu get the trendline by right-clicking one of the data markers after you have created the initial scatter chart, and choosing Add Trendline from the shortcut menu.

After creating the trendline, right-click it and choose Format Trendline from the shortcut menu. Scroll down the Format Trendline pane that appears and choose both the Display Equation on Chart and the Display R-squared Value on Chart checkboxes. Then close the Format Trendline pane.

If you intend to use the charted regression equation, be sure to verify it against the results of LINEST(). Excel regards the leftmost set of values selected on the worksheet for the chart as the predictor variable in the regression equation. So in Figure 3.17, Height is taken to be the predictor variable because it's to the left of Weight on the worksheet. This can be mildly confusing because the LINEST() function requires the predicted variable to be its first argument and the predictor variable or variables to be its second argument.

Bear in mind that although scatter charts can show the equation for multiple regression, they cannot do so when you have more than one predictor variable on the worksheet. The only way to get more than one predictor into a chart's regression equation—or, for that matter, into the chart—is by way of a polynomial trendline, which raises the (sole) predictor variable to successively greater powers: X, X^2, X^3, X^4, and so on. The polynomial trendlines generate equations with multiple predictors because there is just one underlying predictor variable—which, combined with the predicted variable, is all you can show on a two-dimensional chart.

Regression Analysis in R

R has functions that return all the information about regression analysis that Excel's worksheet functions do, plus a good bit more. The information comes back from R in a different fashion and is organized differently, of course. Let's start a comparison with the more rudimentary aspects.

Correlation and Simple Regression

Some of the following analyses are sketched earlier in this chapter in the context of Excel's function and tools. We visited correlations early on, returned by the worksheet function CORREL()—refer to Figure 3.1.

R has more than just a few ways to show you the correlation between two variables. Chapter 2 describes one, in its discussion of analyzing one numeric variable as a function of another in the same d.pizza data frame:

Desc(temperature ~ delivery_min, d.pizza)

To use the Desc function you must have loaded DescTools via the *library* command. But you can also use *cor*, a function that belongs to the *stats* package and that's therefore available when you start an R session: There's no need to load a special package. See Figure 3.18.

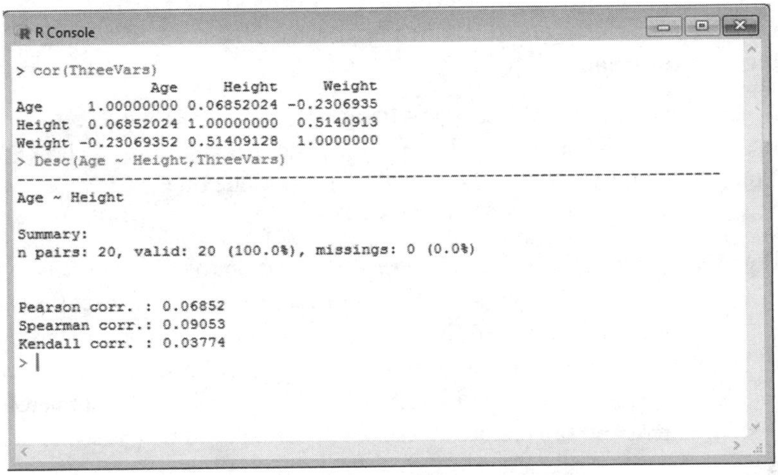

Figure 3.18
The *cor* function returns a correlation matrix if the data source has more than one numeric variable.

```
R R Console

> cor(ThreeVars)
             Age      Height      Weight
Age     1.00000000 0.06852024 -0.2306935
Height  0.06852024 1.00000000  0.5140913
Weight -0.23069352 0.51409128  1.0000000
> Desc(Age ~ Height,ThreeVars)
--------------------------------------------------------------
Age ~ Height

Summary:
n pairs: 20, valid: 20 (100.0%), missings: 0 (0.0%)


Pearson corr. : 0.06852
Spearman corr.: 0.09053
Kendall corr. : 0.03774
> |
```

The *cor* function can take several arguments, but you might supply only the name of the data source. Here, that's *ThreeVars*, which consists of the Age, Height and Weight variables analyzed repeatedly in this chapter. The quickest way to establish *ThreeVars* as a data frame is to activate the worksheet shown in Figure 3.12, select the range B1:D21, and switch to R. Enter this command in the console:

ThreeVars <– XLGetRange (header = TRUE)

The *cor* function gets you a fully populated correlation matrix, not solely the values below the main diagonal. The correlations default to Pearson product-moment correlations, but if you supply the method, you can get the Spearman correlation or Kendall's tau instead:

cor(ThreeVars, method = "kendall")

or

cor(ThreeVars, method = "spearman")

> **NOTE** Excel's Data Analysis add-in also has a Correlation tool that returns a correlation matrix. However, it does not return correlations above the matrix's main diagonal. Although that's redundant information, many matrix operations that are used in multivariate analysis require a fully populated square correlation matrix.

For comparison with *cor*, Figure 3.18 also shows the results of using the *Desc* function on two of the numeric variables in the *ThreeVars* data frame. The syntax of *Desc* requires you to specify two variables for a bivariate analysis by way of the "is a function of" tilde character (~), so you won't get a fully populated correlation matrix this way. But you will get the Pearson, Spearman and Kendall coefficients. You might regard that as helpful if the joint distribution of the two variables departs meaningfully from the bivariate normal.

Figure 3.3 shows how you can use an Excel scatter chart to show graphically the relationship between two numeric variables, and to include the regression line in the chart. Here's one way to do that in R:

With *ThreeVars* established as a data frame, enter these commands:

```
> attach(ThreeVars)
> regmodel <- lm(Weight ~ Height)
> plot(Height, Weight, pch=19)
> abline(regmodel)
```

The result appears in Figure 3.19.

Figure 3.19
The chart appears in a new window.

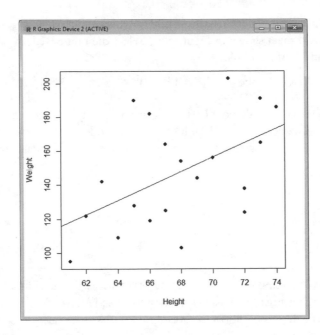

I recommend the *attach* command so that the variable names in the *ThreeVars* data frame will be in R's search path, and R will know where to find the variables named Weight and Height. Otherwise, you might wind up with labels such as ThreeVars$Weight labeling the chart's axes. If there's another data frame that's loaded and that also has Weight or Height as a variable, you can remove a data frame from the search path with the *detach* command. (I should mention that some writers deprecate the use of *attach* due to the possibility of confusing two different objects that have the same name.)

Then, use the *lm* (*l*inear *m*odel) function to calculate the slope and intercept for the relationship between the Height and Weight variables and store them in the variable I've named *regmodel*.

Use the *plot* command to create the scatter chart of Height against Weight in a new graphics window. The *pch* argument to the *plot* function specifies the type of data marker to use. It's a filled circle in Figure 3.19; specifying *pch=15* would result in filled squares.

Finally, use the *abline* function to get the slope and intercept from *regmodel*. This command also draws the line on the chart.

Bear in mind that the *plot* function places the first-named variable on the chart's horizontal axis. You'll want to make sure that you call for the correct regression line in the *abline* function—otherwise, you might not get the regression line on the chart. As a rule of thumb, that means that the variable you name *following* the tilde in the *lm* function should be the *first* one named in the *abline* function.

> **WARNING**
>
> This can get a little tricky because if you happen to use a tilde rather than a comma to separate the variable names in the *plot* function, the first-named variable is placed on the chart's vertical axis rather than its horizontal axis.
>
> Also, be aware that the graphics window has the focus after the *plot* function is complete, so you may have to click in the console before you can resume entering commands.

Figures 3.4 and 3.5 show how to pick up the slope and the intercept in simple regression using Excel worksheet functions. You can get the same information using the results of the *lm* function given earlier and repeated here:

```
> regmodel <- lm(Weight ~ Height)
> regmodel
```

Figure 3.20 shows what you see if you look inside the variable that the results of *lm* are assigned to.

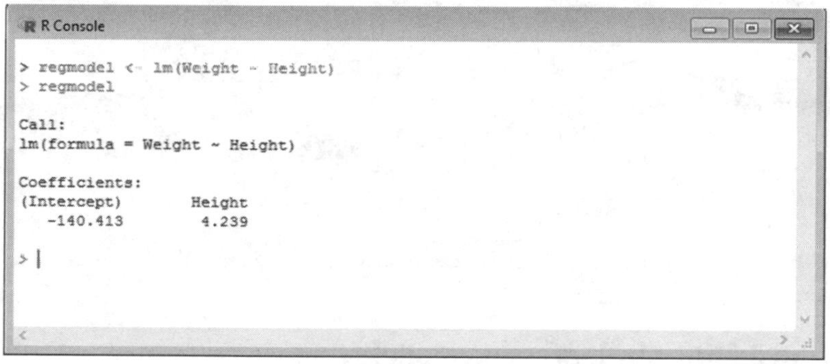

Figure 3.20
Compare these values with those returned in Figure 3.5.

```
> regmodel <- lm(Weight ~ Height)
> regmodel

Call:
lm(formula = Weight ~ Height)

Coefficients:
(Intercept)      Height
   -140.413       4.239

>
```

You can learn much more about what the *lm* function returns by using the *summary* function on, in this example, the variable named *regmodel*. More on that shortly.

Figures 3.6 and 3.7 showed how to get the predicted (also called the *fitted*) value of each record using Excel worksheet functions. In R you can use this:

```
> fitted(regmodel)
```

Figure 3.21 shows the results.

Figure 3.21
A quick way to return the predicted values without resorting to the regression equation.

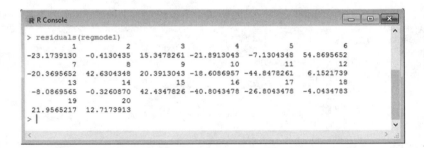

Figure 3.7 also shows the differences between the observed values of the Weight variable and the predicted values. The differences are termed *Error of Estimate* in Figure 3.7, but they are also termed *residuals*. One way to get them in R is

```
> residuals(regmodel)
```

to return the values shown in Figure 3.22.

Figure 3.22
Adding the residuals in Figure 3.22 to the estimates in Figure 3.21 gets you the original Weight observations.

```
> residuals(regmodel)
           1            2            3            4            5            6
-23.1739130   -0.4130435   15.3478261  -21.8913043   -7.1304348   54.8695652
           7            8            9           10           11           12
-20.3695652   42.6304348   20.3913043  -18.6086957  -44.8478261    6.1521739
          13           14           15           16           17           18
 -8.0869565   -0.3260870   42.4347826  -40.8043478  -26.8043478   -4.0434783
          19           20
 21.9565217   12.7173913
> |
```

Analyzing a Multiple Regression Model

Figures 3.8 and 3.9 show examples of the LINEST() function, in the context of both simple and multiple regression. Figure 3.23 shows what you get back from R's *summary* function when you apply it to a variable created by the *lm* function. The underlying data includes Height, Age and Weight, as in Figure 3.9, so you can compare directly the results of LINEST() and *lm*.

Figure 3.23
These results include
most of what LINEST( )
returns and much that it
doesn't.

```
R R Console                                                    [ - ][ □ ][ x ]
> regmodel <- lm(Weight ~ Age + Height, data = ThreeVars)
> summary(regmodel)

Call:
lm(formula = Weight ~ Age + Height, data = ThreeVars)

Residuals:
    Min      1Q  Median      3Q     Max
-47.108 -17.409  -1.935   8.887  53.613

Coefficients:
             Estimate Std. Error t value Pr(>|t|)
(Intercept) -124.7448   111.3257  -1.121   0.2781
Age           -0.5505     0.4084  -1.348   0.1953
Height         4.3901     1.6343   2.686   0.0156 *
---
Signif. codes:  0 '***' 0.001 '**' 0.01 '*' 0.05 '.' 0.1 ' ' 1

Residual standard error: 27.54 on 17 degrees of freedom
Multiple R-squared:  0.3353,    Adjusted R-squared:  0.2571
F-statistic: 4.288 on 2 and 17 DF,  p-value: 0.03105

> |
```

As you compare Excel's LINEST() results with those returned by R's *lm* function, it's helpful to keep in mind that LINEST() is live and updates automatically when you edit the underlying data. LINEST() also updates if you add records to or remove data from its precedent cells, but then you usually have to update the ranges that LINEST() is looking at. To update the results of *lm*, you have to first update the data frame and then re-run *lm* and *summary*. That may seem trivial but I find it tedious, particularly when I have to be careful about case-sensitive keywords.

That said, there's a lot of good information in Figure 3.23, starting with a restatement of the model that your call of *lm* specifies.

The first actual data that hits you are quantiles of the residuals. This listing unquestionably helps you evaluate how the residuals are distributed (symmetric? skewed?), but its positioning in the results has always struck me as odd. Sort of like starting *Macbeth* with Birnam wood coming to Dunsinane.

Next you get a matrix of information regarding the regression coefficients and the intercept. This layout is more helpful than LINEST()'s, because it associates the name of the variable with its coefficient. In LINEST() you have to infer that, and the inference is made more difficult by LINEST()'s peculiar ordering of the variables. With the coefficients themselves and their standard errors, R's results account for the first two of the five rows returned by LINEST().

The summary in Figure 3.23 goes a step further than LINEST() by calculating the t-ratio for each coefficient. Using LINEST() you have to do that yourself. R also returns the probability, based on each t-ratio and its degrees of freedom, of obtaining so large a t-ratio if the t-ratio in the population were 0.0. You can do that in Excel with the T.DIST.2T() function, but *you* have to do that. You can also infer from this discussion that *lm* returns the results of a non-directional t-test, which is surely appropriate. If you want to evaluate a directional hypothesis you can do so yourself. Probably in Excel.

Next you get a legend that explains the relationship between the number of asterisks shown by a probability level and how small that probability is. I could do without that. It strikes me as next door to p-hacking.

The legend is followed by the Residual Standard Error, which is more broadly known as the Standard Error of Estimate. (It's found in the third row, second column of the LINEST() results.) You also get the degrees of freedom for the residual, 17 in this case. It's needed to carry out various inferential tests, such as the t-tests used to assess the size of the regression coefficients. It's in LINEST()'s fourth row, second column.

The R^2 value comes next, returned by LINEST() in its third row, first column. R also provides the adjusted R^2, applying the standard shrinkage formula. In Excel you either have to calculate that yourself or resort to the Regression tool in the Data Analysis add-in.

Finally, you get the F-ratio and the degrees of freedom for the regression mean square and for the residual mean square. The F-ratio is available in LINEST()'s fourth row, first column. You also get the probability of getting an F-ratio as large or larger than the one you obtained if the R^2 in the population from which you got this sample is in fact 0.0. In Excel, you have to get the regression degrees of freedom yourself (not difficult: it's same as the number of predictor vectors) and the probability of the F-ratio. To compare the F-ratio and its probability with the Excel results, see cells E12 and F12 of Figure 3.14.

LINEST() returns the regression and the residual sums of squares in its fifth row. The summary of the *lm* function omits the sums of squares but that's not a major omission. They're useful when you're still learning about linear regression and want to explore the quantitative relationships among the various summary statistics, but they're not absolutely necessary when you already have the standard errors along with R^2 and F.

On the other hand, when you want to perform models comparison, you'll need those sums of squares. We'll look next at how R provides them.

Models Comparison in R

In multiple regression it often happens that two or more of the predictor variables are themselves correlated. That is not always true: When you have coded factors as predictors and you have an equal number of records in each factor level, you often wind up with correlations of 0.0 between the coded vectors. But when all your predictors start out as numeric variables—as is the case with Age and Height—it's typical to find that the predictors are correlated. For example, Figure 3.18 shows that the example data on Age and Height have a Pearson correlation of 0.06852.

When the predictors are correlated, you can get different results depending on which variable enters the regression equation first (more generally, with more than just two predictors, the results can change as a function of the order in which they are entered). The results that describe the full regression do not change: The overall R^2, the F-ratio, the regression coefficients and their standard errors do not vary as a function of the order in which the predictors enter the equation.

But when predictors are correlated, the variance shared by a predictor variable with the predicted variable usually does change when the order of entry changes. Figures 3.24 and 3.25 show what happens when Age enters the equation first (Figure 3.24) and when Height enters the equation first (Figure 3.25). The figures demonstrate that the overall regression statistics remain the same (compare the results of the two *summary* functions) but the sum of squares associated with each variable changes along with the order in which the variables are entered.

Figure 3.24

A sum of squares of 1032 is attributed to Age when it is entered first.

```
R R Console

> ThreeVars <- XLGetRange(header=TRUE)
> AgeFirst <- lm(Weight ~ Age + Height, data = ThreeVars)
> summary(AgeFirst)

Call:
lm(formula = Weight ~ Age + Height, data = ThreeVars)

Residuals:
    Min     1Q  Median     3Q     Max
-47.108 -17.409  -1.935   8.887  53.613

Coefficients:
             Estimate Std. Error t value Pr(>|t|)
(Intercept) -124.7448   111.3257  -1.121   0.2781
Age           -0.5505     0.4084  -1.348   0.1953
Height         4.3901     1.6343   2.686   0.0156 *
---
Signif. codes:  0 '***' 0.001 '**' 0.01 '*' 0.05 '.' 0.1 ' ' 1

Residual standard error: 27.54 on 17 degrees of freedom
Multiple R-squared:  0.3353,     Adjusted R-squared:  0.2571
F-statistic: 4.288 on 2 and 17 DF,  p-value: 0.03105

> anova(AgeFirst)
Analysis of Variance Table

Response: Weight
          Df  Sum Sq Mean Sq F value  Pr(>F)
Age        1  1032.0  1032.0  1.3612 0.25944
Height     1  5470.8  5470.8  7.2157 0.01562 *
Residuals 17 12889.2   758.2
---
Signif. codes:  0 '***' 0.001 '**' 0.01 '*' 0.05 '.' 0.1 ' ' 1
>
```

Figure 3.25
Age gets 1377.7 of the total sum of squares when it's entered second.

```
R Console                                                    ☐ ☐ ☒

> HeightFirst <- lm(Weight ~ Height + Age, data=ThreeVars)
> summary(HeightFirst)

Call:
lm(formula = Weight ~ Height + Age, data = ThreeVars)

Residuals:
    Min     1Q  Median     3Q     Max
-47.108 -17.409  -1.935   8.887  53.613

Coefficients:
              Estimate Std. Error t value Pr(>|t|)
(Intercept) -124.7448   111.3257  -1.121   0.2781
Height         4.3901     1.6343   2.686   0.0156 *
Age           -0.5505     0.4084  -1.348   0.1953
---
Signif. codes:  0 '***' 0.001 '**' 0.01 '*' 0.05 '.' 0.1 ' ' 1

Residual standard error: 27.54 on 17 degrees of freedom
Multiple R-squared:  0.3353,    Adjusted R-squared:  0.2571
F-statistic: 4.288 on 2 and 17 DF,  p-value: 0.03105

> anova(HeightFirst)
Analysis of Variance Table

Response: Weight
          Df  Sum Sq Mean Sq F value  Pr(>F)
Height     1  5125.1  5125.1  6.7597 0.01868 *
Age        1  1377.7  1377.7  1.8171 0.19534
Residuals 17 12889.2   758.2
---
Signif. codes:  0 '***' 0.001 '**' 0.01 '*' 0.05 '.' 0.1 ' ' 1
> |
```

Notice that the regression sum of squares for Age is 1032.0 when it is entered first in Figure 3.24, but 1377.7 when Age is entered second in Figure 3.25. The situation is always ambiguous when the predictor variables are correlated not only with the predicted variable (and why use them if they are not?) but also with one another.

Therefore, to minimize the effect of the ambiguity, when you have a variable that you consider a candidate for removal, it's best to enter that variable last in the full model. *Then* run the regression analysis again without that variable, for the purpose of models comparison.

Figure 3.12 shows how you might carry out the models comparison in Excel, Figure 3.26 shows how you can carry it out in R. You create two models using *lm* and then use the *anova* function to compare them.

Figure 3.26
It's best to cite the more restricted model first in the *anova* arguments when you're comparing two models.

```
R Console                                                    ☐ ☐ ☒

> FullModel <- lm(Weight ~ Age + Height, data = ThreeVars)
> HeightOnly <- lm(Weight ~ Height, data = ThreeVars)
> anova(HeightOnly, FullModel)
Analysis of Variance Table

Model 1: Weight ~ Height
Model 2: Weight ~ Age + Height
  Res.Df   RSS Df Sum of Sq      F Pr(>F)
1     18 14267
2     17 12889  1    1377.7 1.8171 0.1953
> |
```

The layout of the results in Figure 3.26 makes things a little difficult to interpret. There are seven columns:

- Model number: 1 and 2

- Degrees of freedom for the residual. Model 1 has only one predictor, Height, whereas Model 2 with two predictors has one degree of freedom fewer for the residual.

- The residual sums of squares. You can find these in earlier figures, such as cell F7 in Figure 3.8 and cell G7 in Figure 3.9.

- The difference between the degrees of freedom for the two models, $18 - 17 = 1$.

- The difference between the residual sums of squares for the two models, 1377.7. This difference is the numerator of the F-test for the models comparison. The *anova* output labels this figure *Sum of Sq*.

- Unfortunately, the *anova* function does not return the denominator of the F-ratio. You get that by dividing the residual sum of squares for Model 2, 12889, by its degrees of freedom, 17. The result, 758.186, is the denominator of the F-ratio. Divide the numerator by the denominator to get the F-ratio, 1.817.

- The final entry returned by *anova* is the probability of getting an F-ratio this large if the F-ratio in the population is 1.0. With a probability of 19.5%, an F-ratio of 1.817 isn't terribly unlikely and you might well decide to drop Age as a predictor.

Be sure to compare these findings with those based on LINEST() in Figure 3.12.

R will also return plots of residuals, although the default plots are different from those returned by Excel's Regression tool. For example, Excel creates plots of residuals by actual values for predictor variables, while R's defaults return plots of the predicted variable's residuals by its fitted values. See Figure 3.27.

Figure 3.27
A plot of Weight residuals by fitted Weight values.

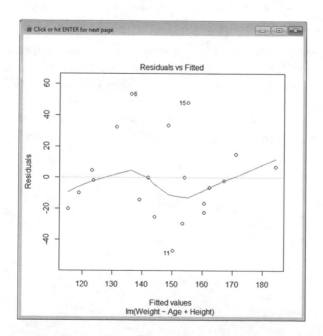

Without specifying any other plot types, you'll also get a normal quantile-quantile, a plot of fitted values by *standardized* residuals, and residuals by leverage (leverage measures the distance of an observation's value on a predictor variable from the mean of the predictor; it's closely related to *influence*).

R has a very large number of functions and packages that provide other takes on multiple regression, and probably the best way to discover them is to browse the various websites that specialize in providing alternative documentation for R. I ran across one that I had somehow missed as I was planning this chapter and it's a good one to end on:

```
>confint (FullModel, level = 0.95)
```

This function (included in the default *stats* package) returns the upper and lower bounds of the regression coefficients and intercept for whatever model is in the FullModel variable. (FullModel is created earlier in this chapter by the *lm* function). You get the results shown in Figure 3.28.

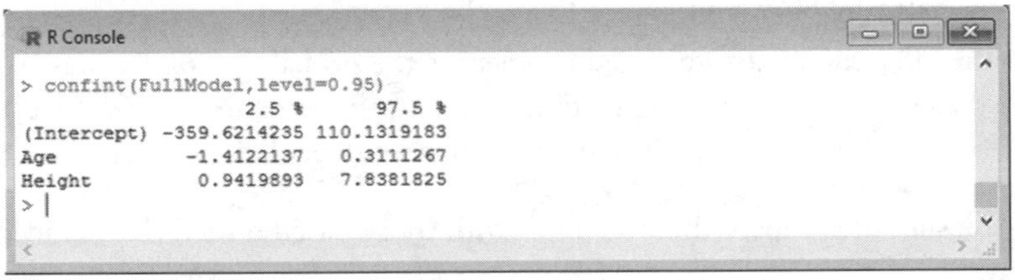

Figure 3.28
If a confidence interval for a regression coefficient spans 0.0, there's an argument for omitting it from the equation.

```
R R Console

> confint(FullModel,level=0.95)
                  2.5 %      97.5 %
(Intercept) -359.6214235 110.1319183
Age           -1.4122137   0.3111267
Height         0.9419893   7.8381825
> |
```

You might want to compare these results with the ones shown in Figure 3.14.

It's probably obvious that you can specify other sizes of confidence interval such as 0.90 and 0.99 by altering the *level* argument. In this case, the 95% confidence interval for Age spans zero.

It is rational to decide that this confidence interval for the Age coefficient is one of the 95% of the confidence intervals that captures the population value of the regression coefficient. It is considerably less rational to decide that this is one of the 5% of confidence intervals that don't capture the population value, and that the regression coefficient therefore is not 0.0. This outcome echoes the results discussed earlier in this chapter when we tested the Age variable via a t-test and also, in the material on models comparison, via an F-test.

Analysis of Variance and Covariance in Excel and R

You can think of an analysis of variance (ANOVA) that employs just one factor—sex, for example, or political affiliation or type of medication used—as one step beyond t-tests in complexity and one step below ANOVAs with two or more factors. A t-test is limited to the comparison of two group means—men and women, say, or Republicans and Democrats. But ANOVAs are designed to assess the differences between three or more group means, such as Republicans, Democrats, and Libertarians. ANOVAs can also accommodate more than just one factor in the same analysis, so you could simultaneously study the *joint* effects of sex and type of medication on a given disease. We'll look at both single- and multiple-factor analyses in this chapter, and we'll also take a look at a valuable extension of ANOVA, the analysis of covariance.

As did Chapter 3, this chapter examines those topics in both the context of Excel and that of R. These analyses are somewhat more complex than those I discuss in earlier chapters. As such, they tend to highlight the usage differences between Excel and R:

- Excel is often the better choice when you are learning what makes a type of analysis tick, and when you want a look inside the analysis to see what happens on the way from the raw data to the probability estimate.

- R is often the better choice when you're sure of how a given function does its work with your data, and when you want access to reference distributions such as q that Excel doesn't offer.

Single-Factor Analysis of Variance

Both Excel and R have various ways of handling designs with no more than one factor. In Excel, it's a matter of deciding which approach you want to use:

- The traditional approach to ANOVA, which involves the calculation of different sums of squares, via several different worksheet functions.
- The ANOVA: Single Factor tool in the Data Analysis add-in.
- The regression approach, which relies on the worksheet function LINEST() to generate all the results.

Each approach has advantages and drawbacks:

- With one factor only, the traditional approach is quicker than the regression approach. It returns live worksheet functions rather than the static values returned by the Data Analysis tool, so you can easily edit the underlying data and see immediately whether that makes a difference to the outcome.
- Using the Single Factor tool in the Data Analysis add-in returns descriptive statistics that the traditional approach makes you enter worksheet functions to get at. But it's static, and if even one value in the underlying data changes, perhaps to correct a typo, you have to run the tool over again.
- The regression approach requires that labels such as "Male" and "NSAID" be recoded to numeric values that LINEST() can deal with. As such, it can be tedious to set up. But when that's done, you can get a much richer set of information than is possible either from the traditional approach or from the ANOVA: Single Factor tool. Furthermore, the regression approach is the only way in Excel to deal with factorial designs (those that have more than one factor) when the number of observations in each design cell are not uniformly equal. (My bias is probably apparent: I prefer the regression approach because it can accommodate more designs and because it provides more information.)

Using Excel's Worksheet Functions

Figure 4.1 shows how you might carry out an ANOVA with one factor and three levels of that factor.

Figure 4.1
Things are simplest when each group has the same number of observations.

B15		f_x	=DEVSQ(B11:E11)*8		
	A	B	C	D	E	F
1	Group	1	2	3	4	
2		4	2	6	10	
3		3	2	6	10	
4		5	6	11	4	
5		4	10	5	6	
6		5	1	4	5	
7		11	3	7	6	
8		5	7	10	8	
9		2	2	10	10	
10						
11	Mean	4.875	4.125	7.375	7.375	
12	Sum of Squares	50.875	70.875	47.875	41.875	
13						
14		SS	df	MS	F	p
15	Between groups	68.375	3	22.7917	3.0173	0.0465
16	Within Groups	211.5	28	7.5536		
17	Total	279.875	31			

A one-factor ANOVA with an equal number of observations in each cell is probably the quickest and easiest to construct. A couple of intermediate calculations are needed:

The mean of each group in B11:E11. For example, in cell B11:

=AVERAGE(B2:B9)

You also need the sum of the squared deviations (more often termed *sum of squares*) within each group. Excel's DEVSQ() function is convenient for that. The sums of squares are in B12:E12, and the formula used in cell B12 is

=DEVSQ(B2:B9)

The DEVSQ() function subtracts the mean of the arguments from each value, squares the result, and totals the squares.

Now, to get the ANOVA's sum of squares based on differences between groups, Figure 4.1 uses this formula in cell B15:

=DEVSQ(B11:E11)*8

The Sum of Squares Between involves multiplication by 8, the number of cases in each group. The reason is that the difference between the group mean and the grand mean is taken 8 times for each group, once for each observation. Because in this example the difference between the group mean and the grand mean is constant for each group, it's simpler to multiply the sum of the squared differences by the number of observations in the group.

The Sum of Squares Within is just the total of the sum of squares within for each group. The formula in cell B16 is

    =SUM(B12:E12)

The remainder of the ANOVA table is completed as you'd expect. The degrees of freedom between is the number of groups minus 1. The degrees of freedom within is the total count, less the degrees of freedom between, less 1. Each Mean Square (MS) is a sum of squares divided by its degrees of freedom. And the F-ratio is the ratio of the MS Between to the MS Within. You get the probability of observing an F-ratio at least this large with this formula in cell F15:

    =F.DIST.RT(E15,C15,C16)

Using the ANOVA: Single Factor Tool

The worksheet function approach is pretty quick, and the formulas recalculate automatically if you find it necessary to edit the underlying data. Figure 4.2 shows how to analyze the same data set using the ANOVA: Single Factor tool in the Data Analysis add-in.

Figure 4.2
The tool's results run from cell A11 to G24.

	A	B	C	D	E	F	G
1	Group	**1**	**2**	**3**	**4**		
2		4	2	6	10		
3		3	2	6	10		
4		5	6	11	4		
5		4	10	5	6		
6		5	1	4	5		
7		11	3	7	6		
8		5	7	10	8		
9		2	2	10	10		
10							
11	Anova: Single Factor						
12	SUMMARY						
13	*Groups*	*Count*	*Sum*	*Average*	*Variance*		
14	1	8	39	4.875	7.267857		
15	2	8	33	4.125	10.125		
16	3	8	59	7.375	6.839286		
17	4	8	59	7.375	5.982143		
18							
19	ANOVA						
20	*Source of Variation*	*SS*	*df*	*MS*	*F*	*P-value*	*F crit*
21	Between Groups	68.375	3	22.7917	3.0173	0.0465	2.9467
22	Within Groups	211.5	28	7.5536			
23							
24	Total	279.875	31				

It's easy enough to run the Single Factor tool. You do need to start by arranging the data as shown in Figure 4.2, in the range B1:E9.

> **NOTE** You could transpose the range of the raw data, turning it 90 degrees counterclockwise. The Single Factor tool can accommodate that arrangement. However, it's an unconventional way to lay out a data set in Excel.

Then take these steps.

1. Click Data Analysis in the Analyze group on the Ribbon's Data tab.
2. Choose ANOVA: Single Factor from the list box.
3. Drag through the worksheet range that contains the raw data, including the column labels (here, they're in B1:E1).
4. Fill the Labels in First Row check box.
5. If you want, adjust the default .05 level of significance to something else, such as 0.1 or 0.01.
6. Click the Output Range options button. Click in its edit box, and then click the cell where you'd like the output to begin.
7. Click OK.

The Alpha box has an effect only on the F Crit value in the output (*F Crit* is short for *critical F-ratio*). That value tells you the minimum F-ratio necessary to reject the hypothesis of no difference between the group means at the level of significance—the alpha level—that you choose. Although your choice of alpha level is of great importance, the value you enter in the Alpha box is related only to the reported F Crit value.

> **NOTE** You can get the F Crit value yourself with this formula, which uses the default alpha of 0.05 and the degrees of freedom reported in cells C21 and C22 of Figure 4.2:
>
> =F.INV.RT(0.05,C21,C22)

The ANOVA: Single Factor tool returns the results shown in the range A11:G24 in Figure 4.2. Notice that the ANOVA table returns precisely the same results as do the worksheet functions shown in Figure 4.1.

Using the Regression Approach to ANOVA

Linear regression analysis and the analysis of variance both test for the statistical significance of differences between the means of several groups. Both types of analysis do so by means of F-tests. Both types are based on the general linear model. The basic difference between the two types is that traditional ANOVA calculates and makes use of sums of squared deviations—sums of squares. Regression analysis also makes use of sums of squares, but it does so principally as a route to calculating R^2 values and therefore percentages of shared variance.

Figure 4.3 shows how you might analyze the data used in Figures 4.1 and 4.2 using Excel's main regression function, LINEST().

Figure 4.3
The raw data must be arranged in the form of a list.

	A	B	C	D	E	F	G	H	I	J	K	L
	Score	Group	Group Vector 1	Group Vector 2	Group Vector 3			=LINEST(A2:A33,C2:E33,,TRUE)				
1	Score	Group	Vector 1	Vector 2	Vector 3							
2	4	1	1	0	0			1.438	-1.813	-1.063	5.938	
3	3	1	1	0	0			0.842	0.842	0.842	0.486	
4	5	1	1	0	0			0.244	2.748	#N/A	#N/A	
5	4	1	1	0	0			3.017	28	#N/A	#N/A	
6	5	1	1	0	0			68.375	211.500	#N/A	#N/A	
7	11	1	1	0	0							
8	5	1	1	0	0			SS	df	MS	F	p
9	2	1	1	0	0		Between groups	68.375	3	22.792	3.017	0.0465
10	2	2	0	1	0		Within Groups	211.5	28	7.554		
11	2	2	0	1	0		Total	279.875	31			
12	6	2	0	1	0							
13	10	2	0	1	0							
14	1	2	0	1	0							
15	3	2	0	1	0							
16	7	2	0	1	0							
17	2	2	0	1	0							
18	6	3	0	0	1							
19	6	3	0	0	1							
20	11	3	0	0	1							
21	5	3	0	0	1							
22	4	3	0	0	1							
23	7	3	0	0	1							
24	10	3	0	0	1							
25	10	3	0	0	1							
26	10	4	-1	-1	-1							
27	10	4	-1	-1	-1							
28	4	4	-1	-1	-1							

In Excel, regression analysis requires that the raw data be in a list (or in a formal table), with different variables occupying different columns, and different records occupying different rows. That's usually the way you want your data laid out anyway—in fact, the layout used in Figure 4.2 is mandated by the ANOVA tool, not by Excel itself. Several coding methods are available to show the group that each record belongs to. The method used in Figure 4.3 is called *effect coding*, principally because it results in regression coefficients that equal the effect of belonging to a particular group vis-à-vis the grand mean.

The codes in columns C, D, and E place each record in the proper group, according to these rules:

- Records in Group 1 get a 1 in Group Vector 1 (Column C) and a 0 in the other two group vectors.
- Records in Group 2 get a 1 in Group Vector 2 (Column D) and a 0 in columns C and E.

- Records in Group 3 get a 1 in Group Vector 3 (Column E) and a 0 in Group Vectors 1 and 2.
- Records in Group 4 get a −1 in all three vectors.

With those codes in place, you're in a position to use LINEST() to regress the Score variable onto the three Group vectors. This formula is *array*-entered into the range H2:K6 in Figure 4.3:

   =LINEST(A2:A33,C2:E33,,TRUE)

It's straightforward to assemble the ANOVA table from the LINEST() results. The most important portion for ANOVA purposes is the results' fifth row, which shows the regression sum of squares and the residual sum of squares. These are the values for Sum of Squares Between and Sum of Squares Within in the ANOVA table. LINEST() also returns the residual degrees of freedom (cell I5) and the F-ratio itself (cell H5).

LINEST() also returns other useful statistics. The R^2 value, shown in cell H4, expresses the proportion of the variability in the Score variable that's attributable to variability in the Group variable. The combination of the regression coefficients in row 2 with their standard errors in row 3 is useful for multiple comparisons, which help you pinpoint which of the mean differences is or are responsible for a significant F-ratio. (With effect coding, used in this example, the Dunnett procedure might be an apt choice of multiple comparison method.)

Single-Factor ANOVA Using R

R has plenty of functions in both the base and the contributed packages that return an ANOVA. This chapter looks at a couple of them to illustrate a single-factor ANOVA. It looks at others to handle more complex designs.

Setting Up Your Data

Let's start our discussion of ways to run an ANOVA in R by looking at how to set up the data frame. So far in this chapter the labels that are used to distinguish between the groups have not had any meaningful effect on the analysis results. To make a point, I chose the numbers 1, 2, 3, and 4 to label the four groups.

The nature of the labels has no effect on how Excel's worksheet functions bring about the analysis. If you use the ANOVA: Single Factor tool in the Data Analysis add-in *and* include the group labels as part of the input range, the tool uses them in the output of the descriptive statistics (see the range A14:A17 in Figure 4.2). But again, the labels have no effect on the analysis itself.

Some care is needed when you want to create a data frame in R as the data source for an ANOVA. If you continue to use numbers—1, 2, 3, and 4—to identify group membership, R interprets them as values belonging to a numeric variable. (So would Excel if, for example, you forgot to fill the Labels in First Row check box.) But the important point is that R relies on what it knows about a data frame's variables to define the analysis.

In Chapter 2, for example, you saw how the Desc function in the DescTools package relies on knowing that *delivery_min* is a numeric variable when it encounters this command:

> Desc(temperature ~ delivery_min, d.pizza)

Because information in the data frame tells Desc that both *temperature* and *delivery_min* are numeric variables, Desc knows to return correlations and, if asked for a plot, a scatter chart.

But if you populate a data frame in R using numeric values to label the groups, as in column B of Figure 4.3, R assumes that the variable is numeric. And when you tell an R function to return an ANOVA that analyzes Score by Group, the function thinks that Group is a numeric covariate rather than a factor with character values. Therefore, it gets 1 degree of freedom rather than 3, and the significance tests are all wrong.

This represents a downside to R's approach of choosing methods of analysis by referring to the nature of the variables you identify in a function's arguments. In Excel, and in many applications whose use is specifically statistical, the user identifies the variables *and the analysis* of interest. In many cases, R uses information about the variables in data frames to inform its choice of analysis. You need to be careful of that to avoid problems like the one shown in Figure 4.4.

Figure 4.4
The function assumes that Group is *intended* as a numeric variable.

```
R R Console
> SingleFactorExample <- XLGetRange(header=TRUE, stringsAsFactors=TRUE)
> SingleFactorResults <- aov(Score ~ Group, data = SingleFactorExample)
> summary(SingleFactorResults)
            Df Sum Sq Mean Sq F value Pr(>F)
Group        1  46.23   46.23   5.935  0.021 *
Residuals   30 233.65    7.79
---
Signif. codes:  0 '***' 0.001 '**' 0.01 '*' 0.05 '.' 0.1 ' ' 1
> |
```

The *aov* function is one of the various functions in R that take a data frame as an argument and return an analysis of variance. But as the data frame is designed in Figure 4.4, there's a snag. Notice in Figure 4.4 that R's *aov* function considers the Group variable to be a numeric predictor—a covariate—rather than a factor with four levels.

You can handle this problem in any of several ways. Here are two:

- Create a new variable in R with the same numeric values but that R treats as a factor
- Replace the numeric values in Excel with characters (such as A, B, C, and D) before you import the data into R

You could use code such as the following to create a new variable in R, one that *aov* would treat as a factor rather than a covariate:

```
> GroupFactor <- as.factor(SingleFactorExample$Group)
> SingleFactorResults <- aov(Score ~ GroupFactor, data = SingleFactorExample)
> summary(SingleFactorResults)
```

This approach uses the numeric values in the Group variable as levels in the new GroupFactor variable. It calculates the sum of squares and degrees of freedom correctly, given that Group is regarded as a factor with levels rather than as a covariate.

Arranging for the ANOVA Table

Figure 4.5 shows how the analysis should go, with the Group variable recast in Excel so that it has character values rather than numbers to distinguish its four levels.

Figure 4.5
The function assumes that Group is *intended* as a factor.

```
R R Console
> SingleFactorExample <- XLGetRange(header=TRUE, stringsAsFactors=TRUE)
> SingleFactorResults <- aov(Score ~ Group, data = SingleFactorExample)
> SingleFactorResults
Call:
   aov(formula = Score ~ Group, data = SingleFactorExample)

Terms:
                    Group Residuals
Sum of Squares     68.375   211.500
Deg. of Freedom        3        28

Residual standard error: 2.748376
Estimated effects may be unbalanced
> summary(SingleFactorResults)
            Df Sum Sq Mean Sq F value Pr(>F)
Group        3  68.38  22.792   3.017 0.0465 *
Residuals   28 211.50   7.554
---
Signif. codes:  0 '***' 0.001 '**' 0.01 '*' 0.05 '.' 0.1 ' ' 1
>
```

Notice that the results shown in Figure 4.5 treat Group as a factor with four levels and therefore three degrees of freedom, rather than as a covariate with 1 degree of freedom as depicted in Figure 4.4. The difference is due to changing the raw data values from 1, 2, 3, and 4 for the four group labels to A, B, C, and D. The XLGetRange function obtains the data from the selected range of the active Excel worksheet and places it in a data frame, here named *SingleFactorExample*.

The results of applying the *aov* function to the variables Score and Group in the SingleFactorExample data frame appear in Figure 4.5, as SingleFactorResults. But the layout is inconvenient. You're given the sum of squares due to the factor Group and the residual sum of squares, as well as the degrees of freedom for each source of variation. And for some reason you're given what linear regression terms the standard error of estimate (see Figure 4.3, cell I4.) Given the sums of squares and the degrees of freedom, you can assemble the full ANOVA table.

But you shouldn't have to do that, and this is where the *summary* function can come into play. The second analysis shown in Figure 4.5 shows what happens to the contents of SingleFactorResults when you deploy the *summary* function. That function behaves differently, depending on the object that you supply as an argument. In the case of the results produced by the *aov* function, the *summary* function reformats the contents of SingleFactorResults as a typical ANOVA table, with a row for each source of variation, and columns for degrees of freedom, sums of squares, mean squares, the F-ratio and the F-ratio's probability.

Another of R's functions that return an ANOVA table is the *Anova* function, part of the *car* package. To use that function, you first need to install the *car* package (*car* is an acronym for Companion for Applied Regression) and then load it using *library*. You'll also need to call the *lm* function as part of *Anova*'s arguments (see the second statement in Figure 4.6). Compare the results of *Anova* in Figure 4.6 to the results of *aov* in Figure 4.5.

Figure 4.6
With *Anova*, you don't need to use *summary* to get the ANOVA table.

```
R R Console                                                    □ ▣ ✕

> SingleFactorExample <- XLGetRange(header=TRUE,stringsAsFactors=TRUE)
> SingleFactorResults <- Anova(lm(Score ~ Group, SingleFactorExample))
> SingleFactorResults
Anova Table (Type II tests)

Response: Score
          Sum Sq Df F value  Pr(>F)
Group     68.375  3  3.0173 0.04647 *
Residuals 211.500 28
---
Signif. codes:  0 '***' 0.001 '**' 0.01 '*' 0.05 '.' 0.1 ' ' 1
> summary(SingleFactorResults)
     Sum Sq             Df            F value          Pr(>F)
 Min.   : 68.38   Min.   : 3.00   Min.   :3.017   Min.   :0.04647
 1st Qu.:104.16   1st Qu.: 9.25   1st Qu.:3.017   1st Qu.:0.04647
 Median :139.94   Median :15.50   Median :3.017   Median :0.04647
 Mean   :139.94   Mean   :15.50   Mean   :3.017   Mean   :0.04647
 3rd Qu.:175.72   3rd Qu.:21.75   3rd Qu.:3.017   3rd Qu.:0.04647
 Max.   :211.50   Max.   :28.00   Max.   :3.017   Max.   :0.04647
                                  NA's   :1       NA's   :1
> |
```

Notice in Figure 4.6 that the *Anova* function returns the ANOVA table directly. If you apply the summary function to the results, you get a table of specific quantiles found among the data in the ANOVA table. The takeaway is that you need to know, usually from experience, when you should apply the summary function to a set of results and when you need not.

After you get a result like those shown in Figures 4.5 and 4.6, with an F-ratio that's improbable if the null hypothesis is true, you might want to look at the group means. As shown in Chapter 2, R's *DescTools* package has a function, *Desc*, that returns descriptive statistics by factor level. See Figure 4.7.

Figure 4.7
The Desc function returns the descriptive statistics behind the ANOVA.

```
R Console                                                              ─ ▫ ✕
> options(scipen = 10)
> Desc(Score ~ Group, SingleFactorExample)
--------------------------------------------------------------------------
Score ~ Group

Summary:
n pairs: 32, valid: 32 (100.0%), missings: 0 (0.0%), groups: 4


             A        B        C        D
mean      4.875    4.125    7.375    7.375
median    4.500    2.500    6.500    7.000
sd        2.696    3.182    2.615    2.446
IQR       1.250    4.250    4.250    4.250
n             8        8        8        8
np      25.000%  25.000%  25.000%  25.000%
NAs           0        0        0        0
0s            0        0        0        0

Kruskal-Wallis rank sum test:
  Kruskal-Wallis chi-squared = 8.2064, df = 3, p-value = 0.04193
> |
```

The difference in means between Groups A and B and Groups C and D is probably responsible for the size of the F-ratio, but you would need to run a multiple comparisons procedure to verify that impression. (You can read more on that later in this chapter in the Multiple Comparison Procedures in Excel and R section.) In the meantime, the question of different standard deviations (equivalently, different variances) in different groups comes up when the group sizes are unequal. In this case, the group counts are equal (and the variances are fairly close to one another) so that issue isn't a matter of concern.

The Single-Factor ANOVA with Missing Values

It's normal for fairly small, tightly controlled experiments, where the effect being tested is manipulated by the experimenter, to have an equal number of records in each design cell. That's the case with the data set that the prior section looked at: Each of the four groups has eight observations.

Often, however, you have at least a few differences among cell sizes. These differences can come about for reasons that have nothing to do with the effect that's being studied, and then again they might. That distinction can become critical in factorial designs—those with two or more factors. But even in single-factor designs you need to be alert to situations in which the cell sizes are very different *and* the group variances are also very different.

When *larger* groups have larger variances, you tend to get an overestimate of the residual variation, leading to an F-test that's more conservative than the central F-distribution would indicate. Similarly, when the larger groups have *smaller* variances, your F-test is more liberal. The report of the group sizes and standard deviations that the *Desc* function provides can warn you if one of those situations has come about. (Fortunately, the differences in the probability statements are insubstantial unless the differences between variances and the differences among cell sizes are on the order of 3 to 1 or greater.)

Apart from that problem, there's no basic adjustment to the calculation of the F-ratio needed when the cell sizes are unequal in a single-factor analysis. See Figure 4.8.

Figure 4.8
The cell sizes are no longer identical.

| B15 | ▼ | : | ✕ | ✓ | f_x | =(B13-$F$13)^2*B12 |

◢	A	B	C	D	E	F
1		Group 1	Group 2	Group 3	Group 4	
2		4	2	6	10	
3		3	2	6	10	
4		5	6	11	4	
5		4	10	5	6	
6		5	1	4	5	
7		11	3	7	6	
8		5	7	10	8	
9		2		10		
10						
11		Group 1	Group 2	Group 3	Group 4	Grand mean
12	Count	8	7	8	7	
13	Mean	4.875	4.429	7.375	7	5.933
14	Sum of Squares	50.875	65.714	47.875	34	
15	Squared Mean Deviations	8.961	15.850	16.627	7.964	
16						
17		SS	df	MS	F	p
18	Between groups	49.40238	3	16.467	2.157	0.1173
19	Within Groups	198.4643	26	7.633		
20	Total	247.8667	29			

Figure 4.8 uses the worksheet function approach to the ANOVA calculations. The raw data is identical to that used by prior examples in this chapter, except that one record is deleted from Group B and another from Group D.

Because of the unequal group sizes, the squared deviations of each group mean from the grand mean have to be calculated separately, with each squared deviation multiplied by its group size. (With equal group sizes, the group n's are a constant and the sums of squares between groups can be calculated with just one formula.)

Apart from that, the calculations are identical to those used in the single-factor, equal-n design. In this case, removing those two records from the data set decreases the size of the F-ratio and therefore increases its probability of occurrence in a central F-distribution. The same analysis appears in Figure 4.9, which shows the results of using the Data Analysis add-in's ANOVA: Single Factor tool on the same data set.

Figure 4.9
The results in the ANOVA table are identical to those returned by the worksheet functions.

	A	B	C	D	E	F	G
1		Group 1	Group 2	Group 3	Group 4		
2		4	2	6	10		
3		3	2	6	10		
4		5	6	11	4		
5		4	10	5	6		
6		5	1	4	5		
7		11	3	7	6		
8		5	7	10	8		
9		2		10			
10							
11	Anova: Single Factor						
12							
13	SUMMARY						
14	Groups	Count	Sum	Average	Variance		
15	Group 1	8	39	4.875	7.267857		
16	Group 2	7	31	4.429	10.95238		
17	Group 3	8	59	7.375	6.839286		
18	Group 4	7	49	7	5.666667		
19							
20	ANOVA						
21	Source of Variation	SS	df	MS	F	P-value	F crit
22	Between Groups	49.402	3	16.467	2.157	0.1173	2.9752
23	Within Groups	198.464	26	7.633			
24	Total	247.867	29				

And the regression approach agrees, as shown in Figure 4.10. The net is that whether you use worksheet functions, the ANOVA: Single Factor tool, or the regression approach, you get the same results, both with equal and with unequal cell sizes. Furthermore, with one small exception in the calculation of the sum of squares between groups using worksheet functions, the presence of unequal cell sizes makes no difference to the way you go about obtaining the figures in the ANOVA table.

Figure 4.10
The results in the ANOVA table are identical to those returned by the worksheet functions.

	A	B	C	D	E	F	G	H	I	J	K	L
			Group	Group	Group							
1	Score	Group	Vector 1	Vector 2	Vector 3		=LINEST(A2:A31,C2:E31,,TRUE)					
2	4	Group 1	1	0	0		1.455	-1.491	-1.045	5.920		
3	3	Group 1	1	0	0		0.856	0.895	0.856	0.506		
4	5	Group 1	1	0	0		0.199	2.763	#N/A	#N/A		
5	4	Group 1	1	0	0		2.157	26	#N/A	#N/A		
6	5	Group 1	1	0	0		49.402	198.464	#N/A	#N/A		
7	11	Group 1	1	0	0							
8	5	Group 1	1	0	0			Sum of		Mean		
9	2	Group 1	1	0	0			Squares	df	Squares	F	Prob of F
10	2	Group 2	0	1	0		Regression	49.402	3	16.467	2.157	0.117
11	2	Group 2	0	1	0		Residual	198.464	26	7.633		
12	6	Group 2	0	1	0							
13	10	Group 2	0	1	0							
14	1	Group 2	0	1	0							
15	3	Group 2	0	1	0							
16	7	Group 2	0	1	0							
17	6	Group 3	0	0	1							
18	6	Group 3	0	0	1							
19	11	Group 3	0	0	1							
20	5	Group 3	0	0	1							
21	4	Group 3	0	0	1							
22	7	Group 3	0	0	1							
23	10	Group 3	0	0	1							
24	10	Group 3	0	0	1							
25	10	Group 4	-1	-1	-1							
26	10	Group 4	-1	-1	-1							
27	4	Group 4	-1	-1	-1							

The Factorial ANOVA

A factorial ANOVA is one that uses two or more factors simultaneously. That is, a simple 2-by-2 factorial design might examine the effects of two different medications on males and on females. The term "factorial" is a typical example of misleading statistical jargon. There's nothing non-factorial about a single-factor design. But the field of statistics has decided over the years to reserve the term "factorial" for designs with two or more factors.

An experimental design that's the basis for a factorial ANOVA has plenty to recommend it. It's the only way to assess the *joint* effect of two or more factors: For example, does Medication A work better with men than with women? Than Medication B for either sex?

Another advantage is that you can often get more statistical power from a factorial design. Some of the variance in the dependent variable will be attributed to the second factor instead of to the error term, and that will tend to increase the value of the F-ratio. And you often get more information about two or more factors from one set of subjects—and from the associated costs—than from running multiple single-factor experiments with multiple groups of subjects.

Excel is perfectly capable of analyzing factorial designs. Worksheet functions alone can handle balanced designs (those with equal or proportional cell sizes) and the Data Analysis add-in includes a tool for two-factor designs with equal cell sizes. You may need to use regression analysis for unbalanced factorial designs in Excel, but R has various functions that handle balanced and unbalanced factorial designs. The remainder of this section steps through some of your options.

Balanced Two-Factor Designs in Excel

Excel's worksheet functions can return a traditional two-factor analysis for balanced designs, using sums of squares between and within groups to arrive at an ANOVA table. Figure 4.11 lays out the calculations with a new data set, one with four treatment groups and the two sexes.

Figure 4.11
The ANOVA table calls out two main effect (Group and Sex) and one interaction effect.

I17 =DEVSQ(B11:E11)*2*4

	A	B	C	D	E	F	G	H	I	J	K	L	M
1		Group 1	Group 2	Group 3	Group 4		Marginal Means						
2	Female	4	2	6	10		5.875						
3		3	2	6	10								
4		5	6	11	4								
5		4	10	5	6								
6	Male	5	1	4	5		6.000						
7		11	3	7	6								
8		5	7	10	8								
9		2	2	10	10								
10													
11	Marginal Means	4.875	4.125	7.375	7.375		5.9375						
12													
13	Cell Means	4	5	7	7.5								
14		5.75	3.25	7.75	7.25						ANOVA table		
15									SS	df	MS	F	p
16	Cell Sums	2.00	44.00	22.00	27.00			Sex	0.125	1	0.125	0.015	0.903
17	of Squares	42.75	20.75	24.75	14.75			Group	68.375	3	22.792	2.763	0.064
18								Sex by Group	13.375	3	4.458	0.540	0.659
19	Interaction	0.660	0.879	0.098	0.035			Within	198.000	24	8.250		
20	Sums of Squares	0.660	0.879	0.098	0.035			Total	279.875				

The preparations for a two-factor ANOVA are, as you might expect, somewhat more involved than for a single-factor analysis. You have an additional factor to account for, as well as the *interaction* (the usual term for the joint effect of the two factors). Here's a walkthrough of what you need:

- Marginal means. In Figure 4.11, the marginal means for the Sex factor are in cells G2 (the mean for all females in the sample) and G6 (the mean for all males in the sample). The marginal means for Group are in the range B11:E11. The grand mean is in cell G11. All these means are calculated using Excel's AVERAGE() function.
- The eight cell means are in B13:E14, again calculated with the AVERAGE() function.
- The sum of squares within each cell are in B16:E17. For example, the sum of the squared deviations from the mean of females in Group 1 is returned in cell B16 with this formula:

  =DEVSQ(B2:B5)

■ The range B19:E20 accumulates a different sort of sum of squares. From each cell mean is subtracted the marginal mean for both the sex and the group that define the cell. Then the grand mean is added, and the result is squared. For example, the formula in cell B19 is

=(B13-G2-B11+G11)^2

With those preliminary calculations in place we can assemble the ANOVA table. The hard part is the sums of squares, described below.

■ The sum of squares between for the Sex factor, in cell I16, uses this formula:

=DEVSQ(G2:G6)*4*4

In words: Get the sum of squares for the mean values of females and males by means of the DEVSQ() function. Multiply that by the number of observations in each level of Sex. Here, that's 16: Four levels of Group times four females in each level.

■ The sum of squares between for the Group factor, in cell I17, uses this formula:

=DEVSQ(B11:E11)*2*4

Use DEVSQ() to get the sum of squared deviations of the Group means. Multiply that by the number of observations in each level of Group. Here, that's 8: Two levels of Sex times four observations in each level.

■ The sum of squares for the interaction of Sex with Group, in cell I18, is easy given the spadework done in the range B19:E20. Just multiply the sum of the cells in that range by the number of observations in each design cell:

=4*SUM(B19:E20)

■ The sum of squares within groups in cell I19 is also easy:

=SUM(B16:E17)

It's just the sum of the sums of squares within each of the eight groups.

■ The total sum of squares is, as usual, the sum of the squared deviations of all the observations from the grand mean. You can test that value if you'd like by getting the total of the sum of squares for each main effect (here, Sex and Group) plus the sum of squares for the interaction, plus the sum of squares within. Here it is in Excel syntax:

=SUM(I16:I19)

The remainder of the ANOVA table is as you probably expect. The degrees of freedom for each main effect is its number of levels minus 1. The degrees of freedom for the interaction is the product of the degrees of freedom for each factor involved in the interaction. And the degrees of freedom within groups is the number of observations, minus the degrees of freedom for the main effects and the interaction, minus 1.

The mean squares for the main effects, the interactions, and within groups are the effect's sum of squares divided by its degrees of freedom. And the F-ratio for each effect is the mean square for the effect divided by the mean square within. You can get the probability associated with each F-ratio using the F.DIST.RT() function. For example:

=F.DIST.RT(L18,J18,$J$19)

for the probability of the F-ratio associated with the mean square for the interaction. Cell L18 contains the F-ratio in question, J18 contains the degrees of freedom for the interaction, and J19 contains the degrees of freedom for the mean square within.

Now, this all probably seems unnecessarily complicated, and as far as I'm concerned it is—particularly as compared to structuring a single-factor ANOVA using Excel's worksheet functions. You've probably been through it before, and I've inflicted it on you mainly as a reminder of all the steps involved. It's a good idea for a student to go through those steps as part of a statistics class, but that's enough already. Another way in Excel is to use the ANOVA: Two Factor with Replication tool in the Data Analysis add-in.

Balanced Two-Factor Designs and the ANOVA Tool

The Data Analysis add-in, besides its ANOVA: Single Factor tool, has two two-factor tools. The one named ANOVA: Two Factor with Replication is intended for the sort of balanced, two-factor design discussed in the prior section. The one named ANOVA: Two Factor Without Replication provides the traditional method of repeated measures analysis. The term *replication* as used by those two tools simply means that each design cell has more than one observation.

Start the two-factor ANOVA tool by selecting it from the list box you get when you select Data Analysis on the Ribbon's Data tab. You get the dialog box shown in Figure 4.12.

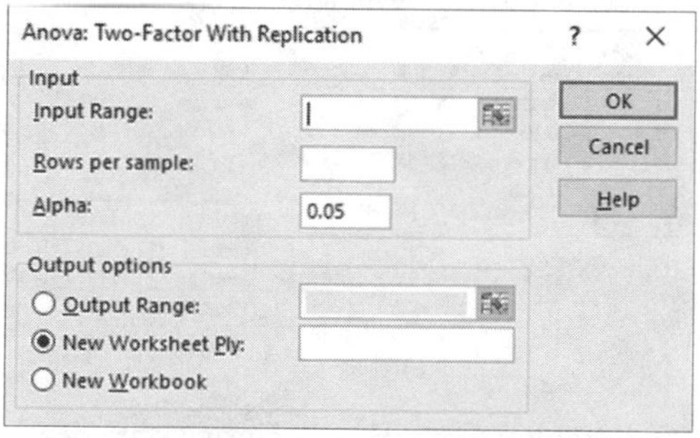

Figure 4.12
This dialog box requires some care in the layout of the raw data.

Figure 4.13 shows how to lay out the data for use with the ANOVA: Two Factor with Replication tool. The data set is otherwise identical to the one used in the prior section.

Figure 4.13
You need to include the labels in B1:E1, A2 and A6.

	A	B	C	D	E
1		Group 1	Group 2	Group 3	Group 4
2	Female	4	2	6	10
3		3	2	6	10
4		5	6	11	4
5		4	10	5	6
6	Male	5	1	4	5
7		11	3	7	6
8		5	7	10	8
9		2	2	10	10

You might have noticed that there's no Labels in First Row check box in the dialog box shown in Figure 4.12. That's because you don't have a choice: The Input Range you specify must include both row and column labels. That means, as the data is laid out in Figure 4.13, you must specify the range A1:E9 as the Input Range.

You must also specify the number of rows that represent each level of the factor that occupies rows in your input data. In this case, there are four rows for females and four rows for males, so you would enter 4 in the Rows Per Sample edit box.

After you specify the location where you want the output to start, click OK to run the tool. You get results that look much like Figure 4.14.

Figure 4.14
I have rearranged the output to get it all in one figure.

	A	B	C	D	E	F	G	H	I	J	K	L	M	N
1		Group 1	Group 2	Group 3	Group 4				Anova: Two-Factor With Replication					
2	Female	4	2	6	10									
3		3	2	6	10				SUMMARY	Group 1	Group 2	Group 3	Group 4	Total
4		5	6	11	4				Female					
5		4	10	5	6				Count	4	4	4	4	16
6	Male	5	1	4	5				Sum	16	20	28	30	94
7		11	3	7	6				Average	4	5	7	7.5	5.875
8		5	7	10	8				Variance	0.667	14.667	7.333	9	8.517
9		2	2	10	10									
10									Male					
11	ANOVA								Count	4	4	4	4	16
12	Source of Variation	SS	df	MS	F	P-value	F crit		Sum	23	13	31	29	96
13	Sample	0.125	1	0.125	0.015	0.903	4.260		Average	5.75	3.25	7.75	7.25	6
14	Columns	68.375	3	22.792	2.763	0.064	3.009		Variance	14.250	6.917	8.25	4.917	10.133
15	Interaction	13.375	3	4.458	0.540	0.659	3.009							
16	Within	198	24	8.250					Total					
17	Total	279.88	31						Count	8	8	8	8	
18									Sum	39	33	59	59	
19									Average	4.875	4.125	7.375	7.375	
20									Variance	7.268	10.125	6.839	5.982	

Usually you'll find the ANOVA table below the descriptive statistics, but I have moved it to take advantage of the available space. Compare the ANOVA table in Figure 4.14 with that in Figure 4.11 to see that they return precisely the same results, but the approach illustrated in Figures 4.12 through 4.14 is much faster.

On the other hand, neither approach can accommodate unequal cell sizes. And the Data Analysis' ANOVA tool cannot accommodate covariates. In either case you must resort to the regression approach (and that's what the applications that are specifically designed for statistical analysis do with unbalanced factorial designs). The next section looks at how you can use the regression approach to handle both balanced and unbalanced two-factor designs.

Using Regression with Two-Factor ANOVA Designs

Recall from an earlier section of this chapter, "Using the Regression Approach to ANOVA," that you need to undertake a major restructuring of the raw data to use regression analysis with a single-factor design in Excel. The same is true, redoubled, with a factorial design. See Figure 4.15.

Figure 4.15
This design calls for seven predictor variables, not just three as in Figure 4.3.

	A	B	C	D	E	F	G	H	I	J	K	L	M	N
		Group 1	Group 2	Group 3	Group 4		Score	S1	G1	G2	G3	Sex by G1	Sex by G2	Sex by G3
2	Female	4	2	6	10		4	1	1	0	0	1	0	0
3		3	2	6	10		3	1	1	0	0	1	0	0
4		5	6	11	4		5	1	1	0	0	1	0	0
5		4	10	5	6		4	1	1	0	0	1	0	0
6	Male	5	1	4	5		2	1	0	1	0	0	1	0
7		11	3	7	6		2	1	0	1	0	0	1	0
8		5	7	10	8		6	1	0	1	0	0	1	0
9		2	2	10	10		10	1	0	1	0	0	1	0
10							6	1	0	0	1	0	0	1
11							6	1	0	0	1	0	0	1
12							11	1	0	0	1	0	0	1
13							5	1	0	0	1	0	0	1
14							10	1	-1	-1	-1	-1	-1	-1
15							10	1	-1	-1	-1	-1	-1	-1
16							4	1	-1	-1	-1	-1	-1	-1
17							6	1	-1	-1	-1	-1	-1	-1
18							5	-1	1	0	0	-1	0	0
19							11	-1	1	0	0	-1	0	0

To run the two-factor ANOVA using regression techniques, it's necessary to recast the raw data as an Excel list (or, if you prefer, an Excel table) instead of as a matrix as in the range B2:E9 of Figure 4.15. The list appears in Figure 4.15 in the range G2:N33. Making that conversion looks like a lot of work, and in fact some is required, but it's nowhere near as much as it looks. I show you a painless way to do it shortly, in Figure 4.17.

First, though, have a look at the results in Figure 4.16.

Figure 4.16
The LINEST() function returns only a test of the overall regression equation.

| L9 | ▼ : × ✓ fx | =RSQ($A$2:$A$33,C2:C33-TREND(C2:C33,$B2:B33)) |

	I	J	K	L	M	N	O	P	Q	R
1			=LINEST(A2:A33,B2:H33,,TRUE)							
2		-0.313	0.938	-0.813	1.438	-1.813	-1.063	-0.063	5.938	
3		0.879	0.879	0.879	0.879	0.879	0.879	0.508	0.508	
4		0.293	2.872	#N/A	#N/A	#N/A	#N/A	#N/A	#N/A	
5		1.418	24	#N/A	#N/A	#N/A	#N/A	#N/A	#N/A	
6		81.875	198.000	#N/A	#N/A	#N/A	#N/A	#N/A	#N/A	
7										
8			S1	G1	G2	G3	Sex by G1	Sex by G2	Sex by G3	Within
9	% of Variance		0.04%	8.93%	7.62%	7.88%	1.43%	2.98%	0.37%	70.75%
10										
11			% of Variance	SS	df	MS	F	Prob of F		
12	Sex		0.04%	0.125	1	0.125	0.015	0.903		
13			8.93%							
14			7.62%							
15	Group		7.88%	68.375	3	22.79	2.763	0.064		
16			1.43%							
17			2.98%							
18	Sex by Group		0.37%	13.375	3	4.458	0.540	0.659		
19	Within		70.75%	198.000	24	8.25				
20										

The LINEST() results shown in Figure 4.16 are based on the list that's in the range G2:N33 of Figure 4.15. It's also in Figure 4.16, in columns A through H, but to save space I've started Figure 4.16 with column I.

> **NOTE** It's possible to tell what's going on in most of the figures in this book by examining them. There's so *much* going on in Figure 4.16 that, if you haven't done so already, I urge you to visit the publisher's website and download the Excel workbooks that accompany this book. It will be much easier to follow the discussion of Figure 4.16 if you have the actual worksheet open in your computer.

Notice first that the LINEST() function in Figure 4.16 reports on the full regression equation: how well Sex and Group jointly predict the variable Score. The only apparent points of agreement between Figure 4.14 and the LINEST() results in J2:Q6 of Figure 4.16 are as follows:

- The regression sum of squares in cell J6 equals the total of the sums of squares for the main and interaction effects in B13:B15 of Figure 4.14.

- The residual sum of squares in cell K6 equals the sum of squares within, in B16 of Figure 4.14.

So LINEST() provides you descriptive and inferential information about the full regression. That's often enough when you're investigating only one predictor variable: Then, the entire equation is about the sole predictor. But in a multiple-factor situation, or one in which you have one factor and a covariate, you want to know whether each factor has a significant effect by itself, and whether the interaction of the effects is significant. Those individual analyses are hidden inside the omnibus F-ratio that LINEST() returns.

Those individual analyses begin in cell K9, which contains this formula:

=RSQ(A2:A33,B2:B33)

It returns 0.04%. That's the percent of the variance in the outcome variable Score in column A that's shared with the Sex vector in column B. Recall that Excel's RSQ() function returns the R^2 between two individual variables. As you'll see, the remaining analyses in K9:R9 make extensive use of this function, even though we're working here with multiple regression.

There's only one vector for Sex because it has just two values, 1 and –1. That's not the case for the Group variable, which—with four possible values—has three vectors in columns C, D, and E.

The formula for the first variable, Sex, is special because it's the first variable that we're considering. That means that no other variable has entered the equation before Sex, so we don't have to account for one. But when the first Group variable, G1, enters the equation, we have to account for the Sex vector, and we do so with this equation in cell L9:

=RSQ($A$2:$A$33,C2:C33-TREND(C2:C33,$B2:B33))

Take first the fragment at the end of the formula:

TREND(C2:C33,B2:B33)

It returns the result of predicting the values in column C, or the G1 vector, from the values in column B, the Sex vector.

Next, subtract from the G1 vector the results of predicting the G1 vector from the Sex vector:

C2:C33-TREND(C2:C33,B2:B33)

The latter fragment returns the residuals in G1: the result of subtracting the predicted G1 values from the actual G1 values. (R's *residuals* function returns residuals too, but you still have to fit the model first, just as Excel's TREND() function does.)

Finally, the full formula in cell L9 returns the R^2 between Score, in column A, with the residuals—what's left over in G1 after predicting the G1 vector from the Sex vector.

That's important because the two predictor vectors, Sex and G1, are correlated. They share variance. So do the Score variable and S1, and so do the Score variable and G1.

We want to be sure that when we add G1 to the regression equation, joining Sex as a predictor variable, we don't attribute variance in Score to G1 if it has already been attributed to Sex. Therefore when we calculate the R^2 of Score with G1, we do so with that portion of G1 that cannot be predicted by Sex. Getting the R^2 of Score with the *residuals* of G1 ensures that we're working with unique variance, and not with variance in Score that we've already associated with Sex.

The remaining values in the range M9:Q9 of Figure 4.16 follow the pattern established in cell L9. Here's L9 once again:

    =RSQ($A$2:$A$33,C2:C33-TREND(C2:C33,$B2:B33))

and here's M9:

    =RSQ($A$2:$A$33,D2:D33-TREND(D2:D33,$B2:C33))

You can get the formula for cell M9 simply by dragging cell L9 one column to the right. When you do so, here's what happens to the formula:

The outcome variable, Score, remains in place as $A$2:$A$33, the first argument to RSQ(). The current variable, G2, is found in D2:D33 and that address adjusts correctly as you drag the main formula one cell to the right.

The range address of the variable(s) already in the regression equation changes from this:

    $B2:B33

to this:

    $B2:C33

as the formula is dragged to the right. The dollar sign of course anchors the first column at B and broadens the address to include column C. The point is that when we are adding the G2 vector to the equation, we want its residual values that result from regressing G2 on Sex *and* G1, which are found in columns B and C. By doing so, we ensure that the residuals of G2 are independent of both predictors that are already in the equation: Sex and G1. The R^2 for Score with G2, then, is unambiguous and shares no variance with either Sex or G1.

The same process is carried out through cell Q9, where the final effect-related R^2 is found with this formula:

    =RSQ($A$2:$A$33,H2:H33-TREND(H2:H33,$B2:G33))

which calculates the R^2 between Score and the final interaction vector, Sex by G3.

> **NOTE** Another term for the values in the range L9:Q9 is *squared semipartial correlations.*

It remains only to calculate the percentage of within cell variance, which is the amount of variance in Score that's left after associating available variance with Sex, G1, G2, . . . Sex by G3. The within cell R^2 is calculated most easily by this formula in cell R9:

=1-SUM(K9:Q9)

Notice that, as a check, you can take the sum of the R^2 values in cells K9:Q9 and multiply by the total sum of squares for Score, which is 279.875. The result, 81.875, is identical to the regression sum of squares returned by LINEST() in cell J6. Similarly, the 70.75% within cell variance proportion in cell R9, multiplied by 279.875, returns 198, the residual sum of squares reported by LINEST() in cell K6.

A minor layout problem remains. The way that the R^2 values were derived depended on combining the mixed reference addressing in the RSQ() formulas and the arrangement of the predictor vectors into Excel's list format. So while the R^2 values are left in row 9, traditional ANOVA tables are laid out with different sources of variation in different rows, not different columns.

It's easy enough to overcome this difficulty with Excel's TRANSPOSE() function. Given the layout in Figure 4.16, just array-enter this formula, using Ctrl + Shift + Enter, in K12:K19:

=TRANSPOSE(K9:R9)

Then accumulate the R^2 values for each effect into column L and multiply the results by the total sum of squares for Score. For example, here's the formula for cell L15:

=SUM(K13:K15)*DEVSQ(A2:A33)

The remainder of the ANOVA table is completed as usual, dividing the sums of squares by the degrees of freedom to get mean squares, and dividing the effect mean squares by the within mean square to get the F-ratios.

Finally, let's have a look at an efficient way to populate the vectors for Sex and Group that form the basis for the regression analysis. See Figure 4.17.

Figure 4.17
The LINEST() function requires numbers rather than text as factor levels.

	A	B	C	D	E	F	G	H	I	J	K	L	M	N	O
	Score	Sex	Group	Sex	G1	G2	G3	Sex x G1	Sex x G2	Sex x G3					
2	4	Female	A	1	1	0	0	1	0	0		Female	1		
3	3	Female	A	1	1	0	0	1	0	0		Male	-1		
4	5	Female	A	1	1	0	0	1	0	0					
5	4	Female	A	1	1	0	0	1	0	0		A	1	0	0
6	2	Female	B	1	0	1	0	0	1	0		B	0	1	0
7	2	Female	B	1	0	1	0	0	1	0		C	0	0	1
8	6	Female	B	1	0	1	0	0	1	0		D	-1	-1	-1
9	10	Female	B	1	0	1	0	0	1	0					
10	6	Female	C	1	0	0	1	0	0	1					
11	6	Female	C	1	0	0	1	0	0	1					
12	11	Female	C	1	0	0	1	0	0	1					
13	5	Female	C	1	0	0	1	0	0	1					
14	10	Female	D	1	-1	-1	-1	-1	-1	-1					
15	10	Female	D	1	-1	-1	-1	-1	-1	-1					
16	4	Female	D	1	-1	-1	-1	-1	-1	-1					
17	6	Female	D	1	-1	-1	-1	-1	-1	-1					
18	5	Male	A	-1	1	0	0	-1	0	0					
19	11	Male	A	-1	1	0	0	-1	0	0					

F2   fx   =VLOOKUP($C2,$L$5:$O$8,3)

The idea is to use Excel's VLOOKUP() function to convert possibly text values such as "Male" and "D" to numeric values so that LINEST() can deal with them, and at the same time use the rules of effect coding to put 1s, 0s and −1s where they belong in the vectors that LINEST() will use as the predictor variables.

> **NOTE** You can use some coding system other than effect coding, such as dummy coding (1s and 0s only) or orthogonal coding (the codes depend on a variety of factors). Take care, though, with orthogonal coding: You don't want to convert vectors that are in fact correlated into uncorrelated vectors. You'll just mislead yourself.

Begin by setting up a key range (which Excel terms a *table_array*). There are two in Figure 4.17: in L2:M3 and in L5:O8. The first pertains to the Sex factor and the second to the Group factor.

You'll use the VLOOKUP() function to find an existing value such as "Female" in L2:L3 and return the associated value in M2:M3. So this formula in cell D2:

    =VLOOKUP(B2,$L$2:$M$3,2)

returns 1. The value "Female" in B2 is compared with the values in L2:L3 and it finds the value in L2. It looks one column to the right and finds a 1 in cell M2 (the second column in $L$2:$M$3), which it returns into cell D2.

Similarly, this formula:

    =VLOOKUP($C2,$L$5:$O$8,2)

in cell E2 looks for the value "A" from cell C2 in L5:L8. It returns the value 1, which it finds in cell M5 (M is the second column in L5:O8). The formulas in F2:G2 follow the same pattern but reference the third and fourth columns in the key table. So the formula in cell F2 is

    =VLOOKUP($C2,$L$5:$O$8,3)

and in G2 the formula is

    =VLOOKUP($C2,$L$5:$O$8,4)

Now just copy and paste the formulas in D2:G2 down through the final row of data.

All that remains is to create the interaction vectors. They are the products of the main effect vectors, so the formula in H2 is

    =$D2*E2

Copy and paste it two columns to the right, and then down through the end of the data set, to complete the coding process for the predictor vectors.

Analyzing Balanced Factorial Designs with R

The procedures that the previous section discusses have to do with analyzing a two-factor design that has an equal number of observations in each design cell—that is, four males and four females in Group A, four males and four females in Group B, and so on. I'm sure that as you read through that section, it seems like a lot of work to set up the coded vectors and then to assemble the RSQ() formulas that determine the R^2 values, vector by vector.

All I can say is that it goes a lot faster after you've been through it once or twice and understand the purpose of each step. The reasons to do all that include actually seeing everything that goes on from the time you start laying the data out until you derive the probability of the final F-ratio. If you're learning this material for the first time, or reviewing it after a long layoff, there's nothing like seeing the actual step-by-step calculations.

It can also happen that something in an ANOVA table takes you by surprise. You can't always come up with the explanation if all you have at hand is the raw data and the F-ratios. Then it's good to be able to refer to the unabridged analysis.

But speed has a lot going for it too, and there's no doubt that if you know what's going on in R, you can finish a lot faster that way than someone who knows what's going on in Excel.

R has various ways to put together a multi-factor ANOVA table given the proper data frame: one with two or more factors and a numeric outcome variable.

Things can get confusing because some of R's functions that appear to perform ANOVA calculations really don't: They just take the results of another R function and rearrange them to conform to a traditional ANOVA table.

It can also be confusing to see the results of different R functions and notice that they all return the same results. You'll see evidence of that in this section, but it's because the analysis discussed here pertains to balanced designs. When we look at unbalanced designs, before the end of this chapter, the differences between the R functions will be clearer.

We start with the *aov* function, which you've already seen in the context of a single-factor ANOVA. See Figure 4.18.

4

Figure 4.18
The *aov* function calculates its own ANOVA.

```
R Console

> TwoFactor <- XLGetRange(header=TRUE,stringsAsFactors=TRUE)
> aovResults <- aov(Score ~ Sex * Group, data=TwoFactor)
> aovResults
Call:
    aov(formula = Score ~ Sex * Group, data = TwoFactor)

Terms:
                    Sex   Group Sex:Group Residuals
Sum of Squares    0.125  68.375    13.375   198.000
Deg. of Freedom       1       3         3        24

Residual standard error: 2.872281
Estimated effects may be unbalanced
> summary(aovResults)
            Df Sum Sq Mean Sq F value Pr(>F)
Sex          1   0.13   0.125   0.015  0.903
Group        3  68.38  22.792   2.763  0.064 .
Sex:Group    3  13.38   4.458   0.540  0.659
Residuals   24 198.00   8.250
---
Signif. codes:  0 '***' 0.001 '**' 0.01 '*' 0.05 '.' 0.1 ' ' 1
> |
```

The data set used in Figure 4.18 (and also in Figures 4.19 and 4.20) is the same one used in Figures 4.11 through 4.17. The range A1:C33 of Figure 4.17 is the active range at the point that R's XLGetRange function runs, as shown in Figure 4.18. To ensure that R will treat the Sex and the Group variables as factors, the XLGetRange function includes the *stringsAsFactors* argument with a value of TRUE. (The default value of *stringsAsFunctions* is FALSE. Given the argument's history in R, that's not as odd as it seems at first.)

> **TIP** A quick way to check on the status of the variables in a data frame is to use R's *str* function (*str* for *structure*). For example:
>
> ```
> > str(TwoFactor)
> ```

If you compare the sums of squares, degrees of freedom, mean squares, F-ratios and probability levels shown in Figure 4.18 with those in Figures 4.11, 4.14, and 4.16, you'll see that they're identical.

The *aov* function is part of the *stats* package. That package loads automatically when you start R, so you can call *aov* as soon as you've made your data set available. Furthermore, *aov* calculates the values for the ANOVA table, so it's the only function you need to carry out a balanced multiple-factor ANOVA.

Notice that R creates the data frame named *TwoFactor* by importing it from the selected range on an active Excel worksheet, by means of the XLGetRange function. To use that function you need to have loaded the package DescTools.

The *aov* function is one of those that do not automatically format its results as a traditional ANOVA table. Figure 4.18 shows the contents of the object named *aovResults*, which consist of the ANOVA table's building blocks. Given the sum of squares and degrees of freedom for each effect, it's straightforward to assemble the ANOVA table. That's what the *summary* function does when applied to *aovResults*.

Notice also that Figure 4.18 does not specify the interaction between the two main effects. The interaction is implied by the use of the * operator. You can specify each term for *aov* using this syntax:

aovResults <– aov(Score ~ Sex + Group + Sex:Group, data = TwoFactor)

in which the interaction is specified using the : operator. That expression is equivalent to the one that appears in Figure 4.18:

aovResults <– aov(Score ~ Sex * Group, data = TwoFactor)

Figure 4.19 shows a different way of getting to the same result.

Figure 4.19
The *Anova* function relies on functions such as *lm* to do the ANOVA calculations.

```
> TwoFactorResults <- Anova(lm(Score ~ Sex + Group + Sex:Group, data=TwoFactor))
> TwoFactorResults
Anova Table (Type II tests)

Response: Score
            Sum Sq Df F value  Pr(>F)
Sex          0.125  1  0.0152 0.90306
Group       68.375  3  2.7626 0.06402 .
Sex:Group   13.375  3  0.5404 0.65922
Residuals  198.000 24
---
Signif. codes:  0 '***' 0.001 '**' 0.01 '*' 0.05 '.' 0.1 ' ' 1
>
```

To use the *Anova* function you need to have first loaded the *car* package. Once *lm* has made the necessary calculations, the *Anova* function reformats the results and displays the ANOVA table shown in Figure 4.19. Notice that *Anova* does not show the column for the mean squares, but they're easy enough to calculate yourself, and you can get the F-ratios from the sums of squares and degrees of freedom anyway.

The *Anova* results hint at how you can use the function in more complicated situations, when the design is unbalanced and you don't have the same number of observations in each design cell. In that case, there are three standard ways to calculate the sums of squares, known unhelpfully as Type I, Type II, and Type III. When the design is balanced, as in Figure 4.19, the methods are equivalent and the Type II approach requires less calculation—therefore, it's accurate if unnecessary to mention Type II in the results.

Notice that the *Anova* function specifically calls out the interaction between the main effects using the : operator. You could imply it using *Sex * Group* instead.

One more alternative: The *anova* function is available in the *stats* package.

> **NOTE**
>
> The *Anova* function, shown in Figure 4.19 and part of the *car* package, uses an uppercase A in its name.
> The *anova* function is part of the *stats* package and its name is lowercase throughout.

Figure 4.20 shows how to call the *anova* function as well as its results.

Figure 4.20
The *anova* function appears to behave in the same way as does *Anova*.

```
R R Console                                                          _ □ ✕

> lmresults<-lm(Score ~ Sex * Group, data=ThreeVars)
> anova(lmresults)
Analysis of Variance Table

Response: Score
          Df  Sum Sq Mean Sq F value  Pr(>F)
Sex        1   0.125  0.1250  0.0152 0.90306
Group      3  68.375 22.7917  2.7626 0.06402 .
Sex:Group  3  13.375  4.4583  0.5404 0.65922
Residuals 24 198.000  8.2500
---
Signif. codes:  0 '***' 0.001 '**' 0.01 '*' 0.05 '.' 0.1 ' ' 1
> |
```

Both the *Anova* and *anova* functions reformat the results of the *lm* function (in these examples) to show the traditional ANOVA table. It may appear that the two functions are identical, apart from the facts that they belong to different packages and that the *Anova* results omit a column for the mean squares.

But there's an important difference between the *anova* and *Anova* functions. The next section discusses that difference, which is due to unequal numbers of observations in design cells and correlations between coded vectors.

Analyzing Unbalanced Two-Factor Designs in Excel and R

As background for the three types of sums of squares that R analyzes, it's useful to take a brief detour into how coding vectors are correlated with one another. Here are the outcomes you can expect to find, assuming you use a standard coding system such as effect coding or dummy coding:

For multiple-factor designs in which each design cell contains the same number of observations, vectors that belong to one factor have a correlation of 0.0 with vectors that belong to a different factor or interaction. See Figure 4.21.

Figure 4.21
Each design cell has four observations.

	A	B	C	D	E	F	G	H	I	J	K
1	Prefer-ence	Party	College	Party Vector	Education Vector	Interaction Vector			Party Vector	Education Vector	Interaction Vector
2	48	Rep	Yes	1	1	1		Party Vector	1		
3	47	Rep	Yes	1	1	1		Education Vector	0	1	
4	46	Rep	Yes	1	1	1		Interaction Vector	0	0	1
5	45	Rep	Yes	1	1	1					
6	47	Dem	Yes	-1	1	-1					
7	46	Dem	Yes	-1	1	-1					
8	50	Dem	Yes	-1	1	-1					
9	51	Dem	Yes	-1	1	-1					
10	48	Rep	No	1	-1	-1					
11	51	Rep	No	1	-1	-1					
12	54	Rep	No	1	-1	-1					
13	53	Rep	No	1	-1	-1					
14	51	Dem	No	-1	-1	1					
15	49	Dem	No	-1	-1	1					
16	51	Dem	No	-1	-1	1					
17	52	Dem	No	-1	-1	1					

Figure 4.21, like Figure 4.16, shows a balanced two-factor design. It contains four design cells, defined by college-no college and Democrat-Republican. Each design cell has four observations.

Notice the correlation matrix in the range H1:K4. It shows the correlations between the vectors that represent Party affiliation, College graduation, and the interaction of those two factors. All the correlations are 0.0.

Now have a look at Figure 4.22.

Figure 4.22
The design cells have different numbers of observations.

	A	B	C	D	E	F	G	H	I	J	K
1	Prefer-ence	Party	College	Party Vector	Education Vector	Interaction Vector			Party Vector	Education Vector	Interaction Vector
2	48	R	Y	1	1	1		Party Vector	1		
3	47	R	Y	1	1	1		Education Vector	0.043	1	
4	46	R	Y	1	1	1		Interaction Vector	0.149	-0.289	1
5	47	D	Y	-1	1	-1					
6	46	D	Y	-1	1	-1					
7	50	D	Y	-1	1	-1					
8	51	D	Y	-1	1	-1					
9	48	D	Y	-1	1	-1					
10	51	R	N	1	-1	-1					
11	54	R	N	1	-1	-1					
12	51	D	N	-1	-1	1					
13	49	D	N	-1	-1	1					
14	51	D	N	-1	-1	1					
15	52	D	N	-1	-1	1					

In Figure 4.22, the numbers of observations per design cell varies from two to four. The coding method is the same one used in Figure 4.21. But now the correlation matrix for the vectors shows that the correlations between the vectors are non-zero.

With equal design cell sizes, the coded vectors are *orthogonal* to one another. The correlations are all 0.0, and therefore there can be no variance shared by the vectors. They are independent of one another.

When two coded vectors are independent of one another—when they are orthogonal—the order in which they enter the regression equation makes no difference to the amount of variance they share with the outcome variable. If education level is independent of party affiliation, then the variance that education shares with the outcome variable must also be independent of the variance that affiliation shares with the outcome measure. Figure 4.23 illustrates this concept.

Figure 4.23
The design cells have *equal* numbers of observations.

	A	B	C	D	E	F	G	H	I
C19			f_x	=RSQ($A$2:$A$17,C2:C17-TREND(C2:C17,$B2:B17))					
1	Prefer-ence	Party Vector	Education Vector	Interaction Vector		Prefer-ence	Education Vector	Party Vector	Interaction Vector
2	48	1	1	1		48	1	1	1
3	47	1	1	1		47	1	1	1
4	46	1	1	1		46	1	1	1
5	45	1	1	1		45	1	1	1
6	47	-1	1	-1		47	1	-1	-1
7	46	-1	1	-1		46	1	-1	-1
8	50	-1	1	-1		50	1	-1	-1
9	51	-1	1	-1		51	1	-1	-1
10	48	1	-1	-1		48	-1	1	-1
11	51	1	-1	-1		51	-1	1	-1
12	54	1	-1	-1		54	-1	1	-1
13	53	1	-1	-1		53	-1	1	-1
14	51	-1	-1	1		51	-1	-1	1
15	49	-1	-1	1		49	-1	-1	1
16	51	-1	-1	1		51	-1	-1	1
17	52	-1	-1	1		52	-1	-1	1
18									
19		1.43%	48.03%	6.91%			48.03%	1.43%	6.91%

In Figure 4.23, the Party and the Education vectors are orthogonal: The correlation between the vectors is 0.0. Therefore, the vectors share the same amount of variance with the outcome variable regardless of which vector enters the regression equation first. Notice that the Party vector shares 1.43% of its variance with the outcome variable when it's entered first (in cell B19) and when it's entered second (in cell H19). The same is true for the Education vector, which shares 48.03% of its variance with the outcome whether it's entered second (cell C19) or first (cell G19).

Contrast that with the situation shown in Figure 4.24, where the design is unbalanced and the Party and Education vectors are therefore correlated (at 0.043; see Figure 4.22).

Figure 4.24
The percentages of shared variance change depending on which vector enters the equation first.

	A	B	C	D	E	F	G	H	I	J
H17		▾	:	✕	✓	f_x	=RSQ($F$2:$F$15,H2:H15-TREND(H2:H15,$G2:G15))			
	Prefer-	Party	Education	Interaction		Prefer-	Education	Party	Interaction	
1	ence	Vector	Vector	Vector		ence	Vector	Vector	Vector	
2	48	1	1	1		48	1	1	1	
3	47	1	1	1		47	1	1	1	
4	46	1	1	1		46	1	1	1	
5	47	-1	1	-1		47	1	-1	-1	
6	46	-1	1	-1		46	1	-1	-1	
7	50	-1	1	-1		50	1	-1	-1	
8	51	-1	1	-1		51	1	-1	-1	
9	48	-1	1	-1		48	1	-1	-1	
10	51	1	-1	-1		51	-1	1	-1	
11	54	1	-1	-1		54	-1	1	-1	
12	51	-1	-1	1		51	-1	-1	1	
13	49	-1	-1	1		49	-1	-1	1	
14	51	-1	-1	1		51	-1	-1	1	
15	52	-1	-1	1		52	-1	-1	1	
16										
17		0.25%	52.89%	10.01%			53.11%	0.03%	10.01%	

In Figure 4.24, notice that the Party vector shares more variance with the outcome variable when it is entered first (0.25% versus 0.03%). The same is true of the Education vector (53.11% versus 52.89%). Those aren't large differences, but they can easily increase to meaningful amounts given another data set.

The problem has to do with *ambiguity*. When factors such as Party Affiliation and College Degree are correlated, the amount of variability in the outcome variable that should be assigned to each variable becomes ambiguous. When the factors are orthogonal, there's no ambiguity: A factor's shared variance with the outcome is the same regardless of its order of entry in the regression equation.

But a large enough amount of shared variance can cause you to decide that, say, differences in party affiliation make a reliable difference to attitudes—that is, that the difference is "statistically significant." And in that case, the amount of shared variance should not depend on what might be a random decision concerning which variable first enters the regression equation. The decision should be based on a rational choice, and that's where sums of squares of Types I, II, and III come into play.

I take that issue up in the next section, but first think a bit more about what causes unequal cell sizes. One cause of an unbalanced design is a relationship in the population from which the data is sampled. Studies that are repeated over the years show a relationship between respondents' sex and party preference. In recent years women have been more likely to report that they are Democrats than that they are Republicans. A good random sample from that population would follow that pattern. You would have the choice of working with unequal cell sizes or selectively discarding observations until you achieved a balanced design.

The trouble with discarding observations in the interest of equal cell sizes is that it results in what Kerlinger and Pedhazur (Holt, Rinehart, and Winston, 1973) termed *dismemberment of reality*. Discarding observations artificially removes genuine correlations between factors and, therefore, changes the amount of variation in the outcome variable

4

that's shared with the factors. One result is that the sample is no longer representative of the population from which it was taken.

Note that this concern does not apply to a true experiment, in which the effect of research interest is applied as a result of random assignment to groups. In an experiment that administered one of two medications to 50 males and 50 females, you're entirely justified in randomly assigning 25 subjects of each sex to one of two treatments. A preference for one medication instead of another is not something that subjects bring to the study, the way that they do political preference. Rather, it's something that's under the joint control of random assignment and the design of the experiment.

Dealing with the Ambiguity

Three generally accepted ways of dealing with ambiguity in the allocation of shared variance exist:

- *Type I*. This approach is also variously termed *a priori ordering*, *hierarchical* and *sequential*. Under this approach, you assume responsibility for deciding on the order in which the factors enter the regression equation. You generally have some reason grounded in theory for specifying that order.

- *Type II*. Also termed the *experimental design* and *classic experimental* approach. This approach runs the analysis more than just once, and the order in which the factors enter the analysis varies. With Factor A and Factor B, you would analyze the data once with Factor B entering the equation *after* Factor A, and once with Factor B entering the analysis *before* Factor A. In both analyses, the interaction enters the analysis after the main effects. This approach ensures that each main effect is evaluated after the other main effect has entered the analysis, and therefore variance that it shares with the outcome measure is unique to that factor.

- *Type III*. This approach is similar to Type II, except that the main effect that's evaluated enters the analysis after both the other main effect(s) and after the interactions that include it.

Using the sequential approach with these two factors, party affiliation and college education, doesn't make a lot of sense. You would probably want to apply the Type II or Type III method instead. The time to consider using the Type I, a priori ordering or sequential approach is when you have good reason to believe that one factor causes another, or at least precedes the other factor in time.

For example, suppose that the two factors in the present example were not party affiliation and college education but party affiliation and sex. There is ample evidence that, in the 2010's and in the population of the United States, females tend to identify as Democrats more than they do as Republicans, and a good sample from the population would not only reflect that tendency but express it in unequal cell sizes and correlations between the coded vectors that represent the factors.

In that sort of situation it makes sense to enter the sex factor before the affiliation factor. Sex, as it's mediated through social attitudes, may have an effect on a person's decision to affiliate with a particular political party, but party registration can have no causal effect on a person's sex. So allot to the Sex factor all the variance that it shares uniquely with the outcome variable, plus variance that it shares with both the outcome variable and the Party factor. Do so by entering the Sex factor first.

But the variables used in the actual example of Figure 4.24, Education and Party Affiliation, do not operate in a causal fashion—or if they do, the evidence is not as clear as with Sex and Party Affiliation. You would have difficulty making a strong case either that Education determines choice of Party, or that choice of Party determines level of education.

If you nevertheless decided to use the Type I sequential approach, you could go about it as shown in Figure 4.25.

Figure 4.25
The sequential approach is probably a bad idea if you aren't sure of the nature of the relationship between the factors.

G7 =G2*$G$4

	A	B	C	D	E	F	G	H	I	J	K	
1	Prefer-ence	Party Vector	Education Vector	Inter-action			Party	Education	Interaction	Residual		
2	48	1	1	1		% of Variance	0.25%	52.89%	10.01%	36.85%		
3	47	1	1	1								
4	46	1	1	1		Total SS	77.21					
5	47	-1	1	-1								
6	46	-1	1	-1			Party	Education	Interaction	Residual		
7	50	-1	1	-1		SS	0.19	40.84	7.73	28.45		
8	51	-1	1	-1								
9	48	-1	1	-1								
10	51	1	-1	-1		> summary(aov(Preference ~ Party * College, data=unbal))						
11	54	1	-1	-1								
12	51	-1	-1	1			Df	Sum Sq	Mean Sq	F value	Pr(>F)	
13	49	-1	-1	1		Party	1	0.19	0.19	0.068	0.80027	
14	51	-1	-1	1		College	1	40.84	40.84	14.355	0.00355	**
15	52	-1	-1	1		Party:College	1	7.73	7.73	2.72E+00	0.13026	
16						Residuals	10	28.45	2.85			

Figure 4.25 shows four groups of subjects with different cell sizes. I have created the coded vectors in B2:D15, but to save space I have removed the text values for the factors such as *Republican* and *Yes*. The range G2:J2 contains the sort of analysis last used in Figure 4.24, which determines the percentage of variance that each vector shares with the outcome, exclusive of variance shared by vectors that are already in the regression equation. So, if you had good reason to suppose that Party Affiliation in some fashion determined whether a subject earned a college degree, you might enter Party first and note that it shares 0.25% of its variance with the outcome measure (see cell G2).

If you prefer to think in terms of sums of squares, you'll find them in G7:J7. Those values are just the percentages in G2:J2 times the total sum of squares in cell G4. Those sums of squares also ease the comparison of the analysis according to Excel with the analysis according to R, in the range G13:K16. (The data for that analysis was picked up from the range A1:C15 in Figure 4.22.) Notice that the sums of squares reported by R are the same as those calculated in G7:J7.

You can get R's analysis from either the *aov* or the *anova* functions in the *stats* package. I have shown the syntax for the *aov* function starting in cell F10 of Figure 4.25. You can control the order in which the factors enter the analysis when you call *aov*. For example, to force the College Education factor to enter the analysis before the Party Affiliation factor, you could use this:

```
> summary(aov(Preference ~ College * Party, data=unbal))
```

I should reiterate that this sequential approach to allocating the sums of squares (or, equivalently, the percentages of shared variance) would be a poor choice for this data. There's no compelling theoretical reason to give either factor priority over the other. Probably either the Type II or Type III approach would be a better choice. See Figure 4.26 for an example of using Type II, the classic experimental approach.

Figure 4.26

Excel is not a convenient application if you want to vary the order in which factors enter a regression equation.

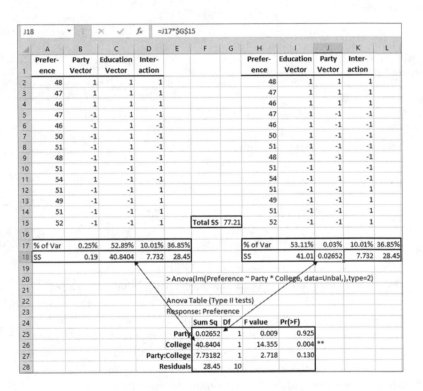

Figure 4.26 highlights one reason that Excel, for all its useful tools, can present problems that an application such as R doesn't. To conform with the approach required by the Type II method of allocating sums of squares, you need to arrange the underlying data in two different ways: In this example, one arrangement has the Party vector entering the analysis first (in the range A1:D15), and the other arrangement has the Education vector entering first (in the range H1:K15). The reason is that worksheet functions such as LINEST() and TREND() require that the predictor variables be in contiguous columns and in left-to-right order. (Figure 4.26 uses the TREND() function in the formulas for the

squared semipartial correlations, in C17:D17 and J17:K17.) In contrast, an application such as R enables you to automatically vary the order in which variables enter the analysis in the syntax. For example:

> Anova(lm(Preference ~ Party * College, data=Unbal,),type=2)

The *type=2* argument informs R that it is to treat first the Party factor, then the College factor, as the final main effect to enter the analysis. If you prefer, you could use *type = "II"* instead of *type=2*.

Notice that the function that's called is *Anova*, with its first letter capped. It's a different function than *anova*. The *anova* function does not take a *type* argument, and it's part of the *stats* package. The *Anova* function accepts a *type* argument and it's part of the *car* package, so you'll need to install that package before you can use *Anova*.

The results returned by R in Figure 4.26 are in the range E22:I28.

In Figure 4.26, the percentages of shared variance in B17:E17 and in I17:L17 are multiplied by the total sum of squares in cell G15 to return the sum of squares for each effect, first with Party entered first and then with Education entered first. Note these two points:

- The sum of squares for Education, when entered after Party, is shown in cell C18. It's identical to the sum of squares for Education returned by R's *Anova* function in cell F26.
- The sum of squares for Party, when entered after Education, is shown in cell J18. It's identical to the sum of squares for Party returned by R's *Anova* function in cell F25.

Notice that the sum of squares associated with Party in Figure 4.26 is identical that shown in Figure 4.25, cells H7 and H14. This is because the sequential analysis in Figure 4.25 happened to enter Party as the second vector in the equation, whereas in Figure 4.26 Party is entered second as part of the Type II routine. Again, the analysis is run twice, once with Party and once with Education as the second variable in the equation.

Keep in mind that the principal advantage of the *Anova* function compared to *aov* or *anova* is that it's more convenient to specify *type=2* in *Anova* than to run *aov* or *anova* twice, altering the order that you call for the factors.

Since 1969, a substantial collection of papers has been written about these different methods of allocating sums of squares in unbalanced factorial designs. That year is when a paper by Overall and Spiegel cataloged the three methods discussed here. This is a book about R and Excel, not about the disputes you can find in that literature, so I'm limiting the discussion to how R (and other statistical packages such as SAS) labels the types of allocation. The third type is often called Type III, and you can call for it using the *Anova* function, where you specify *type=3* or *type="III"*. (Type II is the default). Under this method of allocation, the two-factor example that this section examines enters each effect of interest after *both* the other effects: the other main effect and the interaction effect. Usually this means that you have already tested the interaction and found it statistically significant.

Therefore you would want to account for, say, Party and the Party:Education interaction before allocating a portion of the sum of squares to the Education main effect. (An appreciable amount of the disputes in the literature concerning these topics has centered on whether a significant interaction means that you should not examine the main effects, or whether you may do so.)

Figure 4.27 shows Type III in both the Excel and the R context.

Figure 4.27
With this data set, and particularly with the weak interaction between the two main effects, you would ordinarily choose the Type II approach.

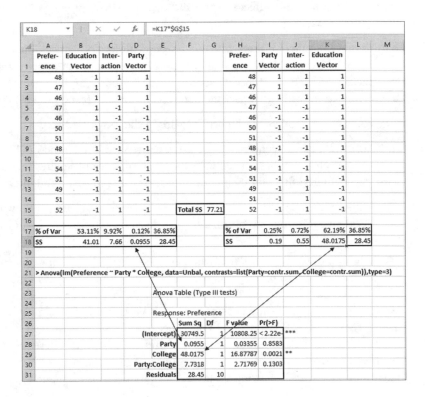

In Figure 4.27, the data is laid out in A1:D15 so that Party follows Education and the interaction, and in H1:K15 so that Education follows Party and the interaction. The idea behind Type III is that a significant interaction may be allocated so much of the available variance in the outcome measure that a main effect—here, Party or Education—cannot be attributed with enough variance to have a significant F-ratio. From this point of view, a significant interaction makes it difficult or even impossible to sensibly interpret the meaning of a main effect that's involved in the interaction. This point of view has plenty of adherents, as well as plenty of others in disagreement.

The squared semipartial correlations for a model in which Party enters last and in which Education enters last are in the usual place in Figure 4.27, C17:D17 and J17:K17. The associated sums of squares are one row down, in C18:D18 and J18:K18. The sum of squares for Party in D18 is identical to that for Party in R's Type III results, in cell F28, and for Education in K18 the value is identical to R's result in F29. The sum of squares for the interaction in F30 is identical to its sum of squares for the Type II analysis in Figure 4.26, where the interaction always enters the analysis last.

My own point of view regarding the interpretation of main effects in the presence of a significant interaction isn't especially pertinent here. I do want to point out that deriving the percentages of explained variance via squared semipartial correlations, and converting the percentages to sums of squares, is often enlightening to someone who is studying these topics for the first time or is returning to them after a lengthy period. The R results are not particularly helpful for developing an understanding of the logic behind the procedures.

But R can be a *lot* faster.

Specifying the Effects

The *aov*, *anova* and *Anova* functions (and any function that bases its results on the *lm* function) recognize three operators that can help you define the effects that you want the function to analyze.

It's helpful in discussing these operators to distinguish between *main effects* and *interactions*. In a factorial design, one in which two or more factors are analyzed simultaneously, each factor by itself represents a main effect, while the joint effect of two or more factors is termed an interaction. So, in an experiment in which Sex, Drug and Patient Ethnicity are used as factors, each factor is a main effect. The joint effect of, say, Sex and Drug is one of the possible interactions in this design, and represents differences between the effect of Drug A on Males, Drug A on Females, Drug B on Males, and Drug B on Females.

With just two main effects, matters are handled pretty easily. There are only two factors and one interaction (say, Sex, Drug, and Sex by Drug) to account for. R functions offer these ways to specify all the available main effects and interactions:

```
> Results <- aov(Score ~ Sex + Drug + Sex:Drug, data = TwoWay)
> summary(Results)
```

In this case, each of the available main and interaction effects are called out separately in the formula. You will get three rows in the resulting ANOVA table for the two main effects and their interaction. The plus sign is used as an operator to separate individual effects, and the colon is used as an operator to request the interaction of the main effects that the colon separates.

Here's a quicker way:

```
> Results <- aov(Score ~ Sex * Drug, data = TwoWay)
> summary(Results)
```

Here, the asterisk replaces the plus sign as the operator. The asterisk in this context tells the function to *cross* the effects to the left of the asterisk with the effects to the right of the asterisk: That is, to include the named effects as main effects and to include interactions between them. Again, the ANOVA table will include Sex, Drug, and the Sex by Drug interaction as sources of variation.

In a factorial design with just two factors, there's not much to choose from between this command:

```
> Results <- aov(Score ~ Sex + Drug + Sex:Drug, data = TwoWay)
```

and this command:

```
> Results <- aov(Score ~ Sex * Drug, data = TwoWay)
```

Both formulas return the same set of results, and there's only a tiny time saving from using the asterisk instead of the plus signs and the colon. But what if you have three main effects? Suppose you add Ethnicity to the factors? Now you have seven sources of variation:

- Three main effects: Sex, Drug, and Ethnicity
- Three two-way interactions: Sex by Drug, Sex by Ethnicity, and Drug by Ethnicity
- One three-way interaction: Sex by Drug by Ethnicity

That's starting to be a lot of effects to specify individually. You can get them all using the asterisk:

```
> Results <- aov(Score ~ Sex*Drug*Ethnicity, data = ThreeWay)
> summary(Results)
```

The main effects are called out and their two- and three-way interactions are implied by the asterisks.

The combination of the plus sign and the colon comes into its own when you want to tailor the sources of variation that appear in the ANOVA table. Suppose that you ran the full three-way analysis and found that the only significant effects were Sex and the interaction of Drug and Ethnicity. If you wanted to pool the sums of squares and the degrees of freedom for the other five effects into the Residual term, you could do so with these commands:

```
> Results <- aov(Score ~ Sex + Drug:Ethnicity, data = ThreeWay)
> summary(Results)
```

The only effects that would appear as sources of variation in the ANOVA table would be Sex and the Drug by Ethnicity interaction.

Multiple Comparison Procedures in Excel and R

Suppose that you analyze data from a survey of attitudes toward a proposed bond issue. The respondents are selected randomly and consist of several hundred men and women. You run either a traditional ANOVA or a regression analysis with coded vectors and find a significant F-ratio for the difference in the means of the two groups. Because there are only two groups involved, you know exactly the source of the significant mean difference: It's between the men's mean and the women's.

Now suppose that you analyze a similar survey, but instead of one group of men and another of women you have three groups of registered voters who self-identify as Republicans, Democrats or Independents. Again you get a significant F-ratio, but this time it's not obvious whether all three means are significantly different, or just two—and if so, which two? Or is one mean significantly different from the *average* of the other two?

This is the sort of situation that a set of procedures, collectively known as *multiple comparisons*, are intended to address. They help you pinpoint which of a set of means are significantly different, as opposed to the so-called *omnibus* F-test, which does not distinguish between specific group means. A variety of multiple comparisons tests exists because they are designed for different situations. For example:

- You specify the comparisons you want to make before you see the outcomes of the experiment, or you wait until you've seen the results.

- You restrict the comparisons to those that are statistically independent of one another (that is, orthogonal contrasts), or you don't restrict yourself to those contrasts.

- You want your alpha level to apply to individual contrasts, or you want it to apply to all the contrasts that you test.

Another distinction is the type of statistic that the multiple comparison procedure returns. The F-ratio, the t-ratio, and the studentized range or q statistic are each used. Excel is limited here, because although it provides you access to the chi-square, binomial, Poisson, t, F and other distributions, it does not offer the q-distribution. That's a shame because one of the most frequently used multiple comparison methods, Tukey's HSD or Honest Significant Difference, uses the q as its reference distribution.

Let's start with Tukey's technique.

Tukey's HSD Method

You can use this technique in Excel, but you do have to resort to outside information. Excel's F.INV() and T.INV() functions return an F-ratio and a t-ratio if you supply a probability and degrees of freedom, but Excel has no Q.INV() function—or Q.DIST() function for that matter. So although you can do most of the calculations to use the HSD method in Excel, you need to look up the q value elsewhere (the appendix of an intermediate level statistics book is often a good place to look).

Figure 4.28 shows how things work out in Excel.

Figure 4.28
Preliminary calculations: The HSD procedure requires some data from the ANOVA.

	A	B	C	D	E	F	G	H	I	J	K	L
1	Score	Group	Grp Vector 1	Grp Vector 2		=LINEST(A2:A34,C2:D34,,TRUE)						
2	22	Grp 1	1	0		-1.606	-2.333	24.8				
3	23	Grp 1	1	0		0.514	0.514	0.36				
4	27	Grp 1	1	0		0.665	2.086	#N/A				
5	22	Grp 1	1	0		29.756	30.000	#N/A				
6	22	Grp 1	1	0		258.970	130.545	#N/A				
7	23	Grp 1	1	0								
8	22	Grp 1	1	0		Anova: Single Factor						
9	22	Grp 1	1	0								
10	22	Grp 1	1	0		SUMMARY						
11	20	Grp 1	1	0		Groups	Count	Sum	Average	Variance		
12	22	Grp 1	1	0		Grp 1	11	247	22.455	2.873		
13	23	Grp 2	0	1		Grp 2	11	255	23.182	0.364		
14	23	Grp 2	0	1		Grp 3	11	316	28.727	9.818		
15	23	Grp 2	0	1								
16	25	Grp 2	0	1								
17	23	Grp 2	0	1		ANOVA						
18	23	Grp 2	0	1		Source of Variation	SS	df	MS	F	P-value	F crit
19	23	Grp 2	0	1		Between Groups	258.970	2	129.485	29.756	0.000	3.316
20	23	Grp 2	0	1		Within Groups	130.545	30	4.352			
21	23	Grp 2	0	1								
22	23	Grp 2	0	1		Total	389.515	32				

Figure 4.28 shows the results of a traditional ANOVA on data in the range A1:B34. The data set has one factor only and the results of running the Data Analysis add-in's ANOVA Single Factor tool appear in F8:L22. (The data was first laid out as shown in Figure 4.2.)

Columns C and D contain effect-coded vectors to represent group membership, and along with the Score variable in column A they are run through the LINEST() worksheet function, with the results shown in F2:H6. Note that the omnibus F-ratio is returned by both LINEST() in cell F5 and by the ANOVA tool in cell J19. We'll need the Mean Square Within, returned by the ANOVA tool in cell I20, for the HSD procedure. It is not returned by LINEST() but is easily calculated by dividing the residual sum of squares in cell G6 by the residual degrees of freedom in cell G5.

The F-ratio, although statistically significant by most people's lights, does not identify which group means are responsible for its magnitude. For that we have to go to Figure 4.29.

Figure 4.29
Preliminary calculations: The HSD procedure requires some data from the ANOVA.

	E22	▼	:	×	✓	f_x	=B17-B$21		
	A	B	C	D	E	F	G
1	Anova: Single Factor						
2	SUMMARY						
3	*Groups*	*Count*	*Sum*	*Average*	*Variance*		
4	Grp 1	11	247	22.455	2.873		
5	Grp 2	11	255	23.182	0.364		
6	Grp 3	11	316	28.727	9.818		
7							
8	ANOVA						
9	*Source of Variation*	*SS*	*df*	*MS*	*F*	*P-value*	*F crit*
10	Between Groups	258.970	2	129.485	29.756	0.000	3.316
11	Within Groups	130.545	30	4.352			
12	Total	389.515	32				
13							
14	SQRT(MS_w/n)	0.629		$_{.95}q_{3,30}$	3.486		
15							
16						p < .05?	
17	Grp 2 - Grp 1	0.727		=B17/$B$14	1.156	N	
18	Grp 3 - Grp 1	6.273		=B18/$B$14	9.973	Y	
19	Grp 3 - Grp 2	5.545		=B19/$B$14	8.817	Y	
20							
21	Half of .95 interval	2.193		Comparison	Lower limit	Upper limit	
22				Grp 1 - Grp 2	-1.466	2.920	
23				Grp 1 - Grp 3	4.080	8.466	
24				Grp 2 - Grp 3	3.353	7.738	

Figure 4.29 repeats for convenience the ANOVA table from Figure 4.28. We'll divide the differences between each pair of group means by the value in cell B14. That value is the square root of the Mean Square Within from the ANOVA table, divided by the number of observations per cell. So the formula in cell B14 is

=SQRT(D11/B4)

It's at this point that we need to resort to an external source of information. This example assumes that alpha has been set to 0.05, so we look up the 95th percentile of the q-distribution for three groups and a total of 30 degrees of freedom, corresponding to the residual or within degrees of freedom in the ANOVA. The tabled figure is 3.486 (see cell E14).

Back to Excel. The range B17:B19 contains the differences between the means of the three groups. Divide each difference by cell B14 to reach the three q values in cells E17:E19. Any of those three values whose absolute value exceeds the critical q value of 3.486 is considered a significant difference at the 0.05 alpha level. In this case, the mean of Group 3 is significantly different from the means of Groups 1 and 2.

One useful feature of the HSD method is that you can place simultaneous confidence intervals around the mean differences. In Figure 4.29, that's done in the range A21:F24. In cell B21 you calculate half the width of the 95% confidence interval by multiplying the value in cell B14 by the q value you looked up in a table, in cell E14. Cells E22:F24 add/subtract half of the confidence interval to/from the calculated mean differences, thus establishing the values that define each confidence interval.

4

So, for example, a 95% confidence interval around the difference between the means of Groups 1 and 2 runs from −1.466 to 2.920. The confidence interval spans 0.0, so one cannot say with 95% confidence that there's a reliable difference between the group means. The other two confidence intervals do *not* span zero, so you can conclude that the means are significantly different at 95% confidence.

That's a fair amount of work. Let's see how you might handle it in R. See Figure 4.30.

Figure 4.30
You can run the ANOVA and the Tukey multiple comparison with just two or three function calls.

```
> model <- aov(Score ~ Group, data = mcdata)
> summary(model)
             Df Sum Sq Mean Sq F value   Pr(>F)
Group         2  259.0  129.48   29.76 7.56e-08 ***
Residuals    30  130.6    4.35
---
Signif. codes:  0 '***' 0.001 '**' 0.01 '*' 0.05 '.' 0.1 ' ' 1
> TukeyHSD(model, ordered = FALSE, conf.level = 0.95)
  Tukey multiple comparisons of means
    95% family-wise confidence level

Fit: aov(formula = Score ~ Group, data = mcdata)

$Group
                diff       lwr      upr     p adj
Grp 2-Grp 1 0.7272727 -1.465550 2.920096 0.6951715
Grp 3-Grp 1 6.2727273  4.079904 8.465550 0.0000002
Grp 3-Grp 2 5.5454545  3.352631 7.738278 0.0000021

>
```

Start by establishing the model for the data. The *aov* function is handy for this:

```
model <- aov(Score ~ Group, data = mcdata)
```

Just to verify the initial analysis, you might want to use this command to display the results of calling *aov*:

```
summary(model)
```

Finally, call the *TukeyHSD* function:

```
TukeyHSD(model, ordered = FALSE, conf.level = 0.95)
```

The arguments used here are

- *model*. The name of the object that you saved the results of *aov* into.
- *ordered = FALSE*. If you set this argument to TRUE, the *TukeyHSD* function presents the groups in ascending order of their outcome variable means. In this particular case, the *ordered* argument has no effect because the data comes to the function already ordered in that way.

■ *conf.level = 0.95.* The type of confidence interval you want the function to calculate. Here, it's a 95% confidence interval. Equivalently, *conf.level* is 1.0 − alpha, where alpha is the probability of rejecting a true null hypothesis you're willing to tolerate.

The *TukeyHSD* function returns, for each pair of group means, these results:

■ The difference between the means

■ The lower bound of the requested confidence interval

■ The upper bound of the requested confidence interval

■ The probability of observing a q statistic as large as the one calculated if the difference between the means in the population is 0.0

The reason that the fourth column in the results, the probability for a given contrast, is labeled *p adj* is that the Tukey HSD method uses what's generally termed a *familywise* error rate: Thus, if you set alpha to 0.05 (and therefore the confidence level to 0.95), then the probability is 5% that you would suffer a Type I error in one or more of the contrasts that you test. Other methods such as the Newman-Keuls, discussed in the next section, use a contrast-based error rate. In that case, an error rate of, say, 5% applies to each contrast that you test. Other things being equal, a contrast-based error rate declares more contrasts as significant (and therefore has more Type I errors) than a family-based error rate.

The *p adj* values represent an attempt to distribute the family-based error rate among the individual contrasts.

The Newman-Keuls Method

Another multiple comparisons procedure, Newman-Keuls, is closely related to Tukey's HSD method in at least two ways:

■ The Newman-Keuls method relies on the q-distribution, as does the HSD.

■ Both methods deal with *ranges* of group means, starting by testing the largest observed difference and stopping when a mean difference is not deemed significant at the chosen alpha level.

A major difference between the two methods is that while the Tukey HSD method uses a family-based error rate, the Newman-Keuls approach uses a contrast-based error rate.

Figure 4.31 shows how the Newman-Keuls works out in the Excel context.

4

Figure 4.31
The critical value of q changes as the number of means from which the contrasts are selected changes.

C20 =B20/$B$17

	A	B	C	D	E	F	G
1	Anova: Single Factor						
2							
3	SUMMARY						
4	*Groups*	*Count*	*Sum*	*Average*	*Variance*		
5	Grp 1	11	247	22.455	2.873		
6	Grp 2	11	255	23.182	0.364		
7	Grp 3	11	316	28.727	9.818		
8							
9							
10	ANOVA						
11	*Source of Variation*	*SS*	*df*	*MS*	*F*	*P-value*	*F crit*
12	Between Groups	258.970	2	129.485	29.756	0.000	3.316
13	Within Groups	130.545	30	4.352			
14							
15	Total	389.515	32				
16							
17	Standard error	0.629					
18							
19		Mean difference	q	Critical q			
20	Grp 3 - Grp 1	6.273	9.97	$_{.95}q_{3,30}$	3.486		
21	Grp 3 - Grp 2	5.545	8.82	$_{.95}q_{2,30}$	2.888		
22	Grp 2 - Grp 1	0.727	1.16	$_{.95}q_{2,30}$	2.888		

4

Figure 4.31 repeats the results of the ANOVA: Single Factor tool: Again, it's a handy way to get at the group means and the Mean Square Within. That value, which here is 4.352, is divided by the number of observations per group, and the square root of the result is taken in cell B17.

That value is divided into the difference between each pair of means, and the result is compared to the critical value for *q*, shown in E20:E22. If the absolute value of the ratio exceeds the critical value, then the contrast between the group means is significant at the chosen alpha level.

Be sure to notice that the critical value of *q* changes as a function of the number of means available for the contrasts. For the first contrast, we choose the largest difference in the three contrasts, which will always be the largest mean minus the smallest mean. (And here the Tukey HSD test is always identical to the Newman-Keuls.) So, to get the critical value of q, we look to the tabled value of q for 3 (groups) and 30 df, or groups × $(n-1)$.

Once that contrast is judged significant, as it is here, we move to the sets of two contrasts. We have finished choosing among three means and now are choosing among two means (Group 1 versus Group 2 and Group 2 versus Group 3). So the critical value for *q* is adjusted to take account of the smaller number of means, as shown in the range D20:E22 in Figure 4.31.

In this case, Tukey's HSD test and the Newman-Keuls return the same results in the sense that Group 3's mean is significantly different from the means of Groups 1 and 2, and that Groups 1 and 2 do not differ significantly from one another.

R gets you to the same conclusion with, perhaps, less effort. See Figure 4.32.

Figure 4.32
You'll need to install the *GAD* package before you can use this function.

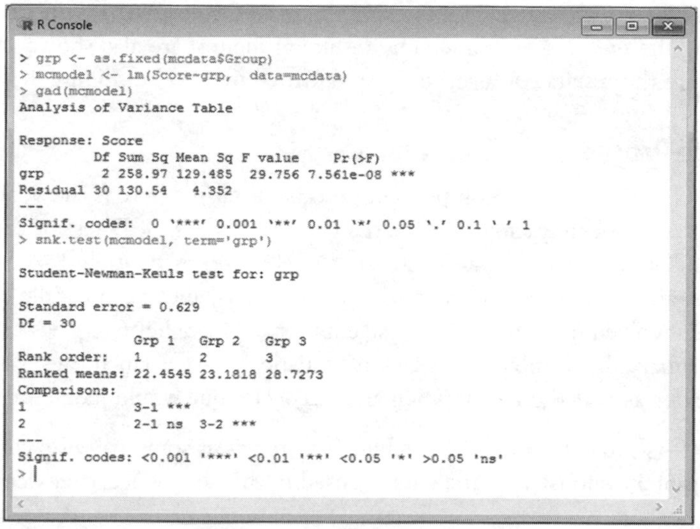

```
R R Console
> grp <- as.fixed(mcdata$Group)
> mcmodel <- lm(Score~grp, data=mcdata)
> gad(mcmodel)
Analysis of Variance Table

Response: Score
          Df Sum Sq Mean Sq F value    Pr(>F)
grp        2 258.97 129.485  29.756 7.561e-08 ***
Residual  30 130.54   4.352
---
Signif. codes:  0 '***' 0.001 '**' 0.01 '*' 0.05 '.' 0.1 ' ' 1
> snk.test(mcmodel, term='grp')

Student-Newman-Keuls test for: grp

Standard error = 0.629
Df = 30
              Grp 1   Grp 2   Grp 3
Rank order:     1       2       3
Ranked means: 22.4545 23.1818 28.7273
Comparisons:
1             3-1 ***
2             2-1 ns   3-2 ***
---
Signif. codes: <0.001 '***' <0.01 '**' <0.05 '*' >0.05 'ns'
> |
```

The *GAD* package is needed to run this function. It is specifically coded to handle designs with factors that are either fixed or random, and crossed or nested. These distinctions have implications for the proper sum of squares to use in building an ANOVA's F-ratios. As a result, if you want to use its *snk.test* function to perform a Newman-Keuls multiple comparison, you'll need first to inform the package whether your grouping variable is fixed or random. You can do that here with this statement:

```
grp <- as.fixed(mcdata$Group)
```

which causes R to establish grp as a fixed factor with the same values as are found in the original Group variable. Group is the factor in the prior section's discussion of the Tukey HSD test, and is found in the *mcdata* data frame.

Then generate the model for Score as a function of Group, using the *stats* package's *lm* function:

```
mcmodel <- lm(Score~grp, data=mcdata)
```

and have a look at the fitted model by means of the *GAD* function:

```
gad(mcmodel)
```

If all looks well in the ANOVA table, you can proceed to run the Newman-Keuls test with this command:

```
snk.test(mcmodel, term='grp')
```

This runs the Newman-Keuls test, using the fixed factor *grp* that you arranged for after importing the *mcdata* data frame. The results of the test are also shown in Figure 4.32. Notice that the results conform to those returned by Excel in Figure 4.31.

Using Scheffé Procedure in Excel and R

The final multiple-comparison procedure to be discussed here is the Scheffé. It is at the same time considerably more flexible than either Tukey's HSD test or the Newman-Keuls and considerably less powerful (in the statistical sense) than either. It can be used on a post hoc basis, after you've seen your experimental results, and it can handle comparisons that are more involved than simple pairwise contrasts. The Scheffé test has other advantages, but its primary disadvantage is its lack of statistical power, which causes it to declare many comparisons as non-significant when another technique would judge them significant.

Figure 4.33 shows how to use the Scheffé test to assess some pairwise contrasts and one more complex contrast with the data set used in this section's earlier examples.

Figure 4.33
The Scheffé procedure begins by defining the interesting contrasts.

F2 =MMULT(B2:D2,$B$11:$B$13)

	A	B	C	D	E	F	G	H	I
1		Grp 1	Grp 2	Grp 3		ψ	$S_ψ$	Ratio	Critical F
2	Grp 3 - Grp 1	-1	0	1		6.273	0.889	7.052	2.575
3	Grp 3 - Grp 2	0	-1	1		5.545	0.889	6.234	
4	Grp 2 - Grp 1	-1	1	0		0.727	0.889	0.818	
5	(Grp 3 + Grp 1)/2 - Grp 2	0.5	-1	0.5		2.409	0.770	3.127	
6									
7	MS_W	4.352							
8	Confidence level	95%							
9							95% Confidence Interval		
10		Mean	n				Lower bound	Upper bound	
11	Grp 1	22.455	11			Grp 3 - Grp 1	3.982	8.563	
12	Grp 2	23.182	11			Grp 3 - Grp 2	3.255	7.836	
13	Grp 3	28.727	11			Grp 2 - Grp 1	-1.563	3.018	
14						(Grp 3 + Grp 1)/2 - Grp 2	0.425	4.393	

The matrix of contrasts in the range B2:D5 of Figure 4.33 defines four contrasts. A group mean's weight is defined by the number in the matrix. So, the contrast defined by the first row in the matrix is Group 3 (1) minus Group 1 (–1). The fourth contrast is defined as the average of Group 1 (0.5) and Group 3 (0.5) minus Group 2 (–1). The weights in a given contrast must sum to zero. (You'll also see the term *coefficient* or *contrast coefficient* used synonymously with *weight*.)

The range B11:B13 contains the actual group means. They are multiplied by the weights for each contrast and the products are totaled. Because of the way that the data is laid out, I find it convenient to use Excel's MMULT() function to take care of the multiplying and adding. For example, this is the formula that cell F2 uses:

```
=MMULT(B2:D2,$B$11:$B$13)
```

That formula's result, which is usually termed *psi*, is the sum of the products of the contrast weights and the associated group means. In the case of the first contrast in row 2, psi is Group 3's mean less Group 1's mean, or 6.273. The psi value for the fourth contrast, in row 5, is the average of the means of Groups 1 and 3, less the mean of Group 2.

The standard errors of psi, found in G2:G5, are calculated using formulas of this sort, which is used in cell G2:

=SQRT($B$7*MMULT(B2:D2^2,1/$C$11:$C$13))

In words:

■ The squares of the contrast weights in B2:D2
■ Times the inverses of the number of observations per cell in C11:C13
■ Those quantities summed (the products and their sums are the combined effects of the MMULT() function)
■ Times the Mean Square Within in cell B7, from the ANOVA
■ And the square root of that quantity

> **NOTE** With an equal number of observations per design cell, the standard error of any contrast is constant with respect to any other contrast that employs the same weights.

4

In column H, the ratio of each psi to psi's standard error is formed.

Each ratio in column H is compared to a critical value, shown in cell I2 of Figure 4.33. For this data, the formula in cell I2 is

=SQRT(2*F.INV.RT(1-B8,2,30))

Both instances of the numeral 2 in the formula represent the degrees of freedom for the factor—here, Group. The design has three levels of the factor Group, so its degrees of freedom equals 2. The numeral 30 is the degrees of freedom associated with the Mean Square Within, also from the ANOVA table.

The formula's reference to the F-distribution returns a value from the F-distribution that's based on 2 and 30 degrees of freedom. The 1–B8 fragment returns 0.05 here: It is 1.0 minus the confidence level specified in cell B8. So the F.INV.RT() function returns the F-ratio that cuts off 5% of the right tail of the F-distribution that has 2 and 30 degrees of freedom.

I find it convenient to think in terms of the distribution's right tail, but that's a personal preference. You can get the same result if you prefer to think of the 95% of the distribution to the *left* of the critical value. Then you could use this formula instead:

=SQRT(2*F.INV(B8,2,30))

To determine whether the mean difference that's defined by a given contrast is significant at the level specified in the F.INV() function, compare the ratio of the absolute value of psi to its standard error with the critical value. If the ratio is greater than the critical value, the contrast is deemed significant. With the analysis in Figure 4.33, you would conclude that the contrasts in rows 2, 3, and 5 represent significant differences.

The next step is to put confidence intervals around the values of psi. For each psi, you subtract (lower bound) and add (upper bound) the product of the contrast's standard error and the critical value in cell I2. For example, the formula in cell G11 is

    =F2-G2*$I$2

and in cell H11 the formula is

    =F2+G2*$I$2

A confidence interval that spans 0.0, such as the one defined by cells G13 and H13, judges the associated contrast as not significantly different from 0. The confidence intervals echo the findings of the comparisons of the psi ratios with the critical value, but they bring additional information to the analysis.

The confidence intervals reported by Tukey's HSD method and by Scheffé's procedure are *simultaneous* confidence intervals, and that reflects the family-wise error rates adopted by the two methods. The confidence interval associated with a given contrast, such as the mean of Group 1 minus the mean of Group 2, does *not* have a probability associated with it.

Assume that the alpha you select is 0.05 and that the confidence intervals you create are therefore 95% intervals. It is *not* true that, say, the confidence interval on contrast 1 contains the population value of that contrast 95% of the times that you run this study.

But it *is* true to state that all the confidence intervals created in this study capture the population's values of the contrasts in 95% of the times you run the study.

It's also worth noting that for strictly pairwise comparisons, Tukey's HSD test is more powerful than Scheffé's test. Compare the 95% confidence intervals in Figure 4.33 with those reported in Figure 4.29. Those created using Tukey's method are narrower, therefore less likely to span zero, therefore more powerful statistically.

As usual, things are easier, if terser, in R. See Figure 4.34.

Figure 4.34
Defining the contrast matrix can get a little tricky.

```
R Console

> model <- aov(Score ~ Group, data = mcdata)
> summary(model)
            Df Sum Sq Mean Sq F value    Pr(>F)
Group        2  259.0  129.48   29.76 0.0000000756 ***
Residuals   30  130.6    4.35
---
Signif. codes:  0 '***' 0.001 '**' 0.01 '*' 0.05 '.' 0.1 ' ' 1
> conmat <- matrix( c(-1,0,1,0,-1,1,-1,1,0,0.5,-1,0.5),ncol=4)
> conmat
     [,1] [,2] [,3] [,4]
[1,]   -1    0   -1  0.5
[2,]    0   -1    1 -1.0
[3,]    1    1    0  0.5
> ScheffeTest(model, contrasts=conmat)

  Posthoc multiple comparisons of means : Scheffe Test
    95% family-wise confidence level

$Group
                    diff     lwr.ci   upr.ci      pval
Grp 3-Grp 1    6.2727273  3.9821234 8.563331 0.00000043 ***
Grp 3-Grp 2    5.5454545  3.2548506 7.836058 0.00000386 ***
Grp 2-Grp 1    0.7272727 -1.5633312 3.017877    0.7185
Grp 1,Grp 3-Grp 2 2.4090909 0.4253697 4.392812    0.0145 *

---
Signif. codes:  0 '***' 0.001 '**' 0.01 '*' 0.05 '.' 0.1 ' ' 1

> |
```

The *DescTools* package includes a function, *ScheffeTest*, that calculates and assesses the contrasts between group means according to your specifications. Figure 4.34 shows the process. Before you begin, you need two items:

- A data frame with, at a minimum, a factor and a numeric variable. As in earlier examples, the factor here is named Group and the numeric variable is named *Score*. The data frame itself is named *mcdata*.
- The package *DescTools* must be loaded via the *library* function.

The commands in Figure 4.34 establish a linear model, named *model,* via the *aov* function. You usually want to see the results returned by *aov*, and you do so using the *summary* function.

Next, define the contrasts. You can use any of several ways to do so, but the one I prefer combines the *c* function with the *matrix* function. The *c* function combines values into a vector or list, and the *matrix* function turns that vector or list into a matrix. So, to store the contrast weights in a matrix similar to that shown in the range B2:D5 of Figure 4.33, you can use a statement such as this:

```
conmat <- matrix( c(-1,0,1,0,-1,1,-1,1,0,0.5,-1,0.5),ncol=4)
```

where *conmat* is an object that contains the matrix. To see what the result is, simply enter the object's name, *conmat*, at the command prompt, as shown in Figure 4.34.

Notice that the *matrix* function includes an argument that specifies the number of columns that the result matrix is to contain. Here, that's four columns. In most writing that you see regarding multiple comparisons, it's typical to show the matrix of contrast weights or coefficients with each contrast in a different row and each factor level in a different column.

Probably to take advantage of some efficiencies in the coding of the functions, the *ScheffeTest* function wants the transpose of that matrix. Compare the matrix shown in the range B2:D5 of Figure 4.33 with the one shown in Figure 4.34. The rows and columns are exchanged. So, for example, the first three arguments passed to the *c* function turn out to be the values in the first *column* of the eventual matrix. That may seem counterintuitive, but you'll want to keep it in mind, whatever method you choose to populate the matrix.

At this point it's time to use the *ScheffeTest* function:

```
ScheffeTest(model, contrasts=conmat)
```

As shown in Figure 4.34, you get back the value of each contrast—typically, the differences between means on a pairwise basis, plus any more complex contrasts that return the difference between combinations of means. You also get the lower and upper bounds of confidence intervals placed on the contrast values. The default is a 95% confidence interval, but you can specify a different confidence level using function calls such as this:

```
ScheffeTest(model, contrasts=conmat, conf.level = .90)
```

or this:

```
ScheffeTest(model, contrasts=conmat, conf.level = .99)
```

Be sure to compare the 95% confidence intervals shown in Figure 4.34 with those shown in Figure 4.33, to verify that they are identical.

Analysis of Covariance in Excel and R

Let's finish this chapter with a look at an analysis of covariance (ANCOVA). As you likely know, having come this far, ANCOVA adds a numeric variable to an ANOVA, so that you wind up explaining variability in an outcome variable according to one or more factors (such as Sex and Treatment) *and* according to a numeric covariate (such as Age or Unit Price).

Done using traditional techniques that involve sums of squares and within-cell cross products, ANCOVA is tedious and error prone. Except when I'm demonstrating its pitfalls, I never do ANCOVA using those traditional techniques. I much prefer the regression approach.

ANCOVA Using Regression in Excel

When you add a covariate to an ANOVA with one or more factors, you have at least two ends in mind:

- You hope to use the relationship between the covariate and the outcome measure to help equate the factor levels on the outcome variable. Even with random selection and assignment of subjects, two or more groups might not start out on the same footing. You might be able to use the correlation between the covariate and the outcome measure to give random assignment an assist. This is termed ANCOVA's *bias reduction* function.

■ It often happens that a useful fraction of the outcome measure's variance can be attributed to the covariate instead of to the Within Cell error term. When the Within Cell mean square is reduced, the F-ratio is increased—and the result is a more sensitive F-test. This is termed ANCOVA's *power enhancement* function.

As a practical matter, ANCOVA is able to increase statistical power over ANOVA more reliably than it can reduce bias.

When you add a covariate to a factor-only ANOVA, you are actually adding more than just the covariate—at least, initially. The covariate might interact with the factor, just as two factors, Sex and Treatment, might interact. It's necessary to test that covariate-factor interaction and test its statistical significance. Figure 4.35 shows how this works out in the Excel context.

Figure 4.35
This worksheet uses the models comparison approach to test the factor-covariate interaction.

J21   × ✓ *fx*   =J16*(H13+I13)

Main data (columns A–F):

Outcome	Covariate	Group Vector 1	Group Vector 2	Covariate by Group Vector 1	Covariate by Group Vector 2
77	18	1	0	18	0
80	23	1	0	23	0
80	18	1	0	18	0
81	22	1	0	22	0
77	19	1	0	19	0
78	21	1	0	21	0
80	23	0	1	0	23
79	20	0	1	0	20
82	24	0	1	0	24
81	21	0	1	0	21
83	25	0	1	0	25
83	26	0	1	0	26
83	26	-1	-1	-26	-26
85	28	-1	-1	-28	-28
82	24	-1	-1	-24	-24
84	27	-1	-1	-27	-27
83	27	-1	-1	-27	-27
82	23	-1	-1	-23	-23

=LINEST(A3:A20,B3:F20,,TRUE)

0.09	-0.09	-1.73	1.18	0.54	68.67
0.18	0.19	4.26	4.16	0.13	3.16
0.841	1.10	#N/A	#N/A	#N/A	#N/A
12.65	12	#N/A	#N/A	#N/A	#N/A
77.14	14.63	#N/A	#N/A	#N/A	#N/A

=LINEST(A3:A20,B3:D20,,TRUE)

0.16	-0.72	0.54	68.66
0.35	0.50	0.13	2.90
0.836	1.04	#N/A	#N/A
23.86	14	#N/A	#N/A
76.76	15.01	#N/A	#N/A

Source	R² Delta	R² Delta	df	MS Delta	F	Prob of F
Gp by X	=H4-H11	0.004	2	0.0021	0.156	0.856
Within	=1-H4	0.159	12	0.0133		
Total	=J16+J17	0.164				

Source	SS Delta	df	MS Delta	F	Prob of F
Gp by X	0.38	2	0.19	0.156	0.856
Within	14.63	12	1.22		
Total	15.01				

4

To save space, Figure 4.35 omits the factor (Groups 1, 2, and 3) and uses the two effect-coded vectors to represent the factor. The figure also includes two vectors that represent the factor-covariate interaction. It's simple enough to populate those two vectors: They are simply the products of the covariate with each of the two-factor vectors.

With the outcome variable, the covariate, the factor vectors, and the factor-covariate interactions in place, we can run LINEST() on the full model. The LINEST() results appear in Figure 4.35, in H2:M6. The R^2 for this model, 0.841, appears in cell H4.

A more restricted model, which regresses the outcome measure on the covariate and the factor only, omitting the factor-covariate interaction vectors, appears in H9:K13. The R^2 for this model, 0.836, appears in cell H11.

So, we can predict $0.841 - 0.836 = 0.005$, or 0.5%, more of the variance in the outcome measure by including the factor-covariate interaction in the model. This proportion of shared variance is tested by way of an F test in the range H16:N18, where it turns out to be insignificant. That analysis, using sums of squares instead of proportions of variance, is repeated in the range I21:N23 (with, of course, the same result).

So we need not worry about a factor-covariate interaction and can proceed with the analysis of the effects of the covariate and the factor as main effects. That ANCOVA appears in Figure 4.36.

Figure 4.36
This worksheet uses the models comparison approach to test the factor's main effect.

| K15 | | × ✓ fx | =H15-$I$3*(I15-$I$18) | | | | | | | | | | |

	A	B	C	D	E	F	G	H	I	J	K	L	M	N
1	Group	Outcome	Covar	Group Vector 1	Group Vector 2									
2	1	77	18	1	0		=LINEST(B2:B19,C2:E19,,TRUE)				=LINEST(B2:B19,C2:C19,,TRUE)			
3	1	80	23	1	0		0.16	-0.72	0.5401	68.66		0.67	65.61	
4	1	80	18	1	0		0.35	0.50	0.13	2.90		0.08	1.88	
5	1	81	22	1	0		0.84	1.04	#N/A	#N/A		0.81	1.04	
6	1	77	19	1	0		23.86	14	#N/A	#N/A		69.23	16	
7	1	78	21	1	0		76.76	15.01	#N/A	#N/A		74.55	17.23	
8	2	80	23	0	1									
9	2	79	20	0	1		Source	SS Formula	Unique SS	df	MS	F	Prob of F	
10	2	82	24	0	1		Between	=G7-L7	2.21	2	1.11	1.03	0.3817	
11	2	81	21	0	1		Within	=H7	15.01	14	1.07			
12	2	83	25	0	1		Total	=M7	17.23	16				
13	2	83	26	0	1									
14	3	83	26	-1	-1			Outcome	Covariate		Adjusted Outcome			
15	3	85	28	-1	-1		Mean, Grp 1	78.83	20.17		80.39			
16	3	82	24	-1	-1		Mean, Grp 2	81.33	23.17		81.27			
17	3	84	27	-1	-1		Mean, Grp 3	83.17	25.83		81.67			
18	3	83	27	-1	-1		Grand Mean	81.11	23.06					
19	3	82	23	-1	-1									

In the models comparison shown in Figure 4.36, the range G3:J7 contains LINEST() results for the regression of the outcome variable on both the covariate and the factor. The range L3:M7 contains the results for the regression of the outcome variable on the covariate only.

The difference between the two models as measured by the sums of squares is in cell I10, which contains the difference in the regression sums of squares of the two models. The remainder of the range G10:M12 tests the statistical significance of that difference, which is due solely to the absence of the factor from the LINEST() analysis in L3:M7.

The analysis in G10:N12 tests the differences between the means of the three groups, *adjusted* so that they represent what they would have been if the three groups had started out with the same means on the covariate. The analysis tells us that the adjusted means do not differ significantly.

You can find both the observed and the adjusted means in the range H15:K17 of Figure 4.36. The adjusted means are calculated using a combination of the group mean on the outcome measure, the regression coefficient for the covariate, and the difference between the group mean on the covariate and the covariate's grand mean. For example, the adjusted mean for Group 1, in cell K15, is calculated with this formula:

=H15−$I$3*(I15−$I$18)

In words:

- Get the difference between Group 1's mean on the covariate (I15) and the covariate's grand mean ($I$18).
- Multiply that difference by the regression coefficient for the covariate ($I$3).
- Subtract the result from the observed mean of the outcome measure for Group 1 (H15).

> **NOTE** You can use the same regression coefficient in your calculation of the adjusted means for all three groups because you rejected the hypothesis of a non-zero interaction between the factor and the covariate. Had you found that you needed to retain that hypothesis, you would have had to resort to other techniques to arrive at the adjusted means.

Notice that the adjusted means are much closer together than the original means on the outcome measure. Evidently the three groups started out with considerable differences on both the covariate and the outcome measure, and the differences on the outcome measure shrank when the groups were equated on the covariate.

ANCOVA in R

Up to now, this book has shown the commands needed to get a particular analysis largely by means of screenshots of the R console. This section shows the commands to carry out an ANCOVA because the use of several functions requires some explanation, and because although the ANCOVA itself can be carried out with a minimum number of commands, arranging for the adjusted means is more tedious.

This example assumes that you have already established the raw data in an Excel worksheet, made the worksheet active and selected the data on the worksheet. This is just as shown, and with the same data as shown, in Figure 4.36, if the range A1:C19 were selected.

In preparation to import the data in A1:C19 of Figure 4.36 into R, load the *DescTools* package.

```
> library(DescTools)
```

Import the data into a data frame named *InputData*:

```
> InputData <- XLGetRange(header=T)
```

With so many commands, you'd like to avoid the necessity of repeating the data frame name each time a variable is named (for example, *InputData$Group*) or repetitively specifying the data frame's name as a separate argument (for example, *data = InputData*). Therefore, you can use the *attach* function to put the data frame into R's search path. Use *detach* later to remove the data frame from the search path.

```
> attach(InputData)
```

Establish Group as a factor. I use the *factor* function rather than *XLGetRange*'s *stringsAsFactors* argument because the Group values as stored in Excel are integers, not strings:

```
> GroupFactor <- factor(Group)
```

You need to get each group's unadjusted (that is, observed) mean on the outcome variable. One good way to do that is to use the *tapply* function, which takes as its arguments the name of the variable to be summarized (here, *Outcome*), the values of the variable that establishes the groups (here, *GroupFactor*) and the type of summary you want (here, that's the mean):

```
> Unadjusted <- tapply(Outcome, list(GroupFactor), mean)
```

So here are the unadjusted group means of the outcome variable:

```
> Unadjusted
```

R responds with 78.8 for Group 1, 81.3 for Group 2 and 83.2 for Group 3. Now use the *lm* function to fit the data to a linear model and store it in an object named *AncovaModel*.

```
> AncovaModel <- lm(Outcome ~ Covar * GroupFactor)
```

Use the *anova* function to format the model in *AncovaModel* as a traditional analysis of variance table and store the result in *AncovaTable*:

```
> AncovaTable <- anova(AncovaModel)
> AncovaTable
```

Here's what the table looks like:

Analysis of Variance Table

Response: Outcome					
	Df	Sum Sq	Mean Sq	F value	Pr(>F)
Covar	1	74.548	74.548	61.1342	4.75E-06
GroupFactor	2	2.215	1.107	0.9081	0.4293
Covar:GroupFactor	2	0.382	0.191	0.1564	0.8569
Residuals	12	14.633	1.219		

Notice that the *lm* function was called with the *Covar* and the *GroupFactor* variables connected by an asterisk. That operator informs R that you want not only those two effects, but their interaction as well. Therefore the model as represented in the ANCOVA table includes the interaction effect. You can see that the interaction is quite weak and not even close to statistical significance. Be sure to compare the finding for the factor-by-covariate interaction with Excel's analysis of the same effect, in the range I21:N23 of Figure 4.35.

Once you have dismissed the interaction from consideration, you might re-run the ANCOVA without the interaction effect. To do so, just replace the asterisk in the *lm* function with a plus sign:

```
> AncovaModel <- lm(Outcome ~ Covar + GroupFactor)
> AncovaTable <- anova(AncovaModel)
> AncovaTable
```

And here's what the table looks like, omitting the factor-by-covariate interaction:

Analysis of Variance Table

Response: Outcome					
	Df	**Sum Sq**	**Mean Sq**	**F value**	**Pr(>F)**
Covar	1	74.548	74.548	69.5109	8.44E-07
GroupFactor	2	2.215	1.107	1.0326	0.3817
Residuals	14	15.015	1.072		

If you compare these results with those shown in Figure 4.36, you see agreement where you would expect it: for example, the sum of squares for the Covar effect in cell L7, the sum of squares for the GroupFactor effect in cell I10, the sum of squares within in cell I11. But it's difficult to make a direct comparison because LINEST(), which is used extensively in Figure 4.36, does not report sums of squares for each effect, just for the overall regression. You need to break out the R^2 values for each effect using squared semipartial correlations, and move from them to sums of squares, to make a direct comparison with R's results. See Figure 4.37.

4

Figure 4.37
Compare the effect sums of squares with those returned by the combination of R's *lm* and *anova* functions.

E22 =RSQ($B$2:$B$19,E2:E19-TREND(E2:E19,$C2:D19))

	A	B	C	D	E	F	G	H
1	Group	Outcome	Covar	Group Vector 1	Group Vector 2			
2	1	77	18	1	0			
3	1	80	23	1	0			
4	1	80	18	1	0			
5	1	81	22	1	0			
6	1	77	19	1	0			
7	1	78	21	1	0			
8	2	80	23	0	1			
9	2	79	20	0	1			
10	2	82	24	0	1			
11	2	81	21	0	1			
12	2	83	25	0	1			
13	2	83	26	0	1			
14	3	83	26	-1	-1			
15	3	85	28	-1	-1			
16	3	82	24	-1	-1			
17	3	84	27	-1	-1			
18	3	83	27	-1	-1			
19	3	82	23	-1	-1			
20								
21			Covar	Group Vector 1	Group Vector 2	Within	Total	
22		R^2 for vector	0.812	0.022	0.003			
23		R^2 for effect	0.812		0.024	0.164		
24		Sum of Squares	74.548		2.215	15.015	91.778	

Figure 4.37 derives the R^2 values and, from them, the sums of squares for each vector that enters the regression equation. The R^2 values are based on squared semipartial correlations, most recently seen in this chapter in Figure 4.27. The squared correlations represent percentages of shared variance, and the associated sums of squares are calculated by multiplying the R^2 values by the total sum of squares of the outcome variable.

Using this approach, it's easy to verify that Excel and R return the same results. Compare the sums of squares in R's output, given in the Analysis of Variance table earlier in this section, with the sums of squares in row 24 of Figure 4.37.

We still need to get the group means on the outcome measure, this time adjusted for the relationship between the covariate and the outcome measure.

Start by establishing a new variable that contains the factor levels:

```
> PredictionGroups <- factor(c(1,2,3))
```

> **NOTE** The *c* function combines its arguments into a vector or list of values. In this case, the result is then turned into a factor.

Establish another variable that contains three instances of the grand mean of the covariate:

```
> PredictionCovariates <- rep(mean(Covar), 3)
```

As used here, the *rep* function replicates the mean of the variable Covar three times.

Establish a new data frame named *PredictionBasis*, with the names of the variables used to build the *lm* model (*GroupFactor* and *Covar*) but with the values just created in Prediction-Groups and PredictionCovariates.

```
> PredictionBasis <- data.frame(GroupFactor = PredictionGroups,
  Covar = PredictionCovariates)
```

Now we have a data frame with the grand mean of the covariate assigned to each of the three groups:

```
> PredictionBasis
```

	GroupFactor	Covar
1	1	23.05556
2	2	23.05556
3	3	23.05556

Now apply the regression coefficient for the covariate found in the *lm* model to the values established in PredictionBasis, and store the results in AdjustedMeans:

```
> AdjustedMeans <- predict(AncovaModel, PredictionBasis)
> AdjustedMeans
```

R responds with 80.4 for Group 1, 81.3 for Group 2 and 81.7 for Group 3. Compare these means with those returned by Excel, shown in K15:K17 of Figure 4.36.

> **NOTE** The *predict* function works with a variety of models, not solely those produced by the *lm* function. As used here, the first argument is a model produced by *lm* and the second argument is a data frame with values that *predict* uses in conjunction with the specific model to return predicted values. For more information, check the (terse) documentation available by means of this command:
>
> ```
> > ??predict.lm
> ```

4

Logistic Regression in Excel and R

5

Chapter 4 includes a substantial amount of material on regression analysis of a particular sort: the assessment of the reliability of differences in the means of different groups. When that sort of question is at issue, it's typical that you have a variable such as cholesterol level, measured on a numeric scale, that quantifies an outcome. You also have one or more variables, usually termed *factors*, under which you aggregate your measurements: men and women, for example, or medication and placebo. These factors are generally measured on a nominal scale, although they are coded as numeric values when you use regression to analyze the data.

You might also include a covariate such as age, measured on a numeric scale, along with your factors. In this way you can ask, for example, if there's a difference in mean cholesterol level for those who took a medication versus those who took a placebo, controlling for the subject's age.

It's entirely possible, and it's frequently a good idea, to turn those roles around. Then you might ask how well knowledge of a subjects' cholesterol levels, along with the subjects' ages, predict whether a medication or a placebo was used.

That sort of problem—analyzing an outcome with a few nominal values at most—was handled for much of the 20th century by means of a multivariate technique called *discriminant function analysis*, and that technique is still in widespread use, for good reason. But a different technique, *logistic regression*, has come into more frequent use since the 1950s. As used now, logistic regression depends on odds, logarithms, and maximum likelihood techniques to predict a binomial variable such as Buy/Don't Buy or Male/Female using factors or covariates, or both, as predictors.

It is also possible to use logistic regression to predict the relative frequency of occurrence among more than two alternatives. Variables measured on a Yes/No or Male/Female scale, for example, with just two alternatives are termed *binomial* variables. Other variables, such as Train/Plane/Car or Ford/Toyota/GM/Audi, are termed *multinomial* variables.

Excel handles binomial logistic regression fairly easily, and this chapter reviews the procedures involved. The tools are bread-and-butter formulas and functions such as odds, probabilities and logarithms, all given an assist from Excel's Solver add-in.

Multinomial logistic regression is a good bit more complex and (although Excel is perfectly capable of handling it) the benefits of using Excel as the platform are not usually worth the difficulties involved in, for example, laying out the data properly.

Therefore, this chapter does not demonstrate multinomial logistic regression in the Excel context. R, however, offers a function named *mlogit* that can handle both binomial and multinomial logistic regression. This chapter demonstrates how to use *mlogit*. Because *mlogit* is a complicated function to apply, I also demonstrate R's *glm* function which, although it does not perform multinomial logistic regression, does handle the binomial situation with more straightforward syntax than does *mlogit*.

Problems with Linear Regression and Nominal Variables

Excel has no LOGISTIC() function. Unless you develop a user defined function yourself, you cannot enter a single worksheet function such as LINEST() and expect to get the results that normally come back from a logistic regression analysis.

But Excel has three capabilities needed to perform a logistic regression analysis:

- It can calculate logarithms.
- It can calculate the probability of a chi-squared value.
- It can call on an add-in called Solver.

Let's look at the reasons that these three capabilities are important.

It's entirely possible to run a standard linear regression analysis on a data set that has a categorical (or nominal) variable as its predicted variable. To do so you would need to code the nominal values, such as Buy versus Doesn't Buy, or Win versus Lose, as numeric values such as 0 and 1.

Furthermore, you can use numeric variables as predictors (just as you might use Height as a predictor of Weight). And you can use coded nominal variables, such as 1 to represent New York and −1 to represent Los Angeles, as discussed in Chapter 4.

Just because you *can* use linear regression—thus, something such as Excel's LINEST() function—on a nominal predicted variable doesn't mean you should do so. You frequently use the basic results of a linear regression analysis to extend its reach: for example, to put confidence intervals around predicted values, or to make an inference about whether the R^2 in the population from which you drew your sample might in fact be 0.0.

In ordinary linear regression, you subtract predicted values from observed values to arrive at residuals. But when you use linear regression to predict a *nominal* variable, the residuals don't conform the usual assumptions that we make about the residuals. Those assumptions include a normal distribution, and homogeneous variances at different values of the predictor. The next section discusses how violating those assumptions can create problems when you use linear regression to predict a binomial variable.

Problems with Probabilities

Again, with the proper coding you can certainly run a linear regression analysis that predicts a binomial variable. But you might not be able to put confidence in the subsequent inferences that you're accustomed to making after the regression analysis is complete. Those inferences often assume that the residuals are normally distributed and have at least roughly the same variances.

When residuals meet those assumptions, you have more confidence in setting confidence intervals around predicted values. Residuals at different points along the predictor variable's axis have homogeneous variances, and you can compare confidence intervals constructed at different points on that axis. This is just another way of saying that the standard error of estimate is the same at one point on that axis as it is at some other point on the axis.

Furthermore, those confidence intervals may well depend on the use of the normal distribution or the closely related t-distribution. But if you construct a histogram of the frequency of different residual values from a binary predicted variable, you find that the chart looks nothing remotely resembling a normal curve.

Figures 5.1 and 5.2 illustrate another sort of problem with predicted variables that are measured on a binominal scale.

Figure 5.1
The predictor might meaningfully take on much larger values but the predicted variable might not.

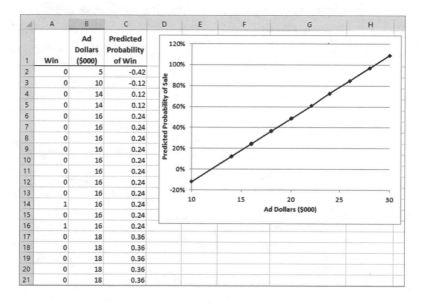

Figure 5.1 shows what might happen if you predict a nominal variable (here, a binomial variable) from a numeric variable using standard linear regression. The actual nominal variable might be whether a political candidate won a given voting district, recoded so that a Win is a 1 and Loss is a 0. The predictor variable might be dollars spent in each district on political ads.

Coding the predicted variable as 1 and 0 is tantamount to using regression to predict probabilities of winning a district. Although the observed data show either a 1, or 100%, for an actual win and 0, or 0%, for an actual loss, the regression equation predicts values running from 0 to 1 depending on the number of ad dollars spent.

As usual, plotting the predicted outcomes against the observed predictors results in a straight line (and it's identical to the linear trendline that Excel would chart if you plotted actual outcome against the predictor variable). Notice that as the ad dollars exceed $28,000, the probability of winning exceeds 100%. And as the ad dollars fall below $13,000, the probability of winning becomes negative.

Mathematically that's not an issue. There's no arithmetic prohibition against a percentage less than 0% or greater than 100%. Logically, it's another story. If you're running the show as the communications director for a candidate for statewide office, you want results that make better sense than predicted outcomes of a –28% chance of winning this district, or a 112% chance of winning that one.

> **NOTE** This sort of logical anomaly is one reason that some people—wrongly in my view—adopt the regression approach that forces the constant, or intercept, to equal 0. The argument is that if you're regressing, for example, plot yield against acreage, then the predicted yields should be zero when the acreage is zero. But if the model is appropriate and if the data is accurate, regression analysis will put the constant near to zero anyway, without distorting the other relationships implied by the regression equation.

Now compare Figures 5.1 with 5.2.

Figure 5.2
Maximum likelihood techniques bend the curve where necessary.

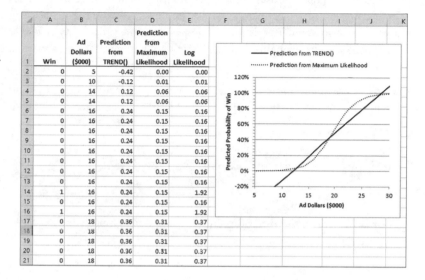

	Win	Ad Dollars ($000)	Prediction from TREND()	Prediction from Maximum Likelihood	Log Likelihood
2	0	5	-0.42	0.00	0.00
3	0	10	-0.12	0.01	0.01
4	0	14	0.12	0.06	0.06
5	0	14	0.12	0.06	0.06
6	0	16	0.24	0.15	0.16
7	0	16	0.24	0.15	0.16
8	0	16	0.24	0.15	0.16
9	0	16	0.24	0.15	0.16
10	0	16	0.24	0.15	0.16
11	0	16	0.24	0.15	0.16
12	0	16	0.24	0.15	0.16
13	0	16	0.24	0.15	0.16
14	1	16	0.24	0.15	1.92
15	0	16	0.24	0.15	0.16
16	1	16	0.24	0.15	1.92
17	0	18	0.36	0.31	0.37
18	0	18	0.36	0.31	0.37
19	0	18	0.36	0.31	0.37
20	0	18	0.36	0.31	0.37
21	0	18	0.36	0.31	0.37

Linear regression normally returns a straight line of the sort shown in Figure 5.1. But that's not useful for some types of data. One example is that of various sorts of time measures, such as the amount of learning time required to master a particular task. The appropriate regression equation might incorporate both a strictly linear component, say x minutes, plus a quadratic component, say x^2. The result would often be a curvilinear trendline, even though the analysis technique is standard linear regression.

But in this case we're not deriving the relationship between a predicted variable and different powers of a predictor. We're using highly educated trial-and-error methods to find the coefficients that maximize the likelihood that predicted values will come as close as possible to the observed values.

The methods in play calculate odds and the ratios of odds to one another. They are conceptually similar to multiple regression, but the math is very different—for example, calculations are based not on correlations and squared semipartial correlations, but on probabilities and odds.

And there's the big difference between R and Excel. The difference exists in a variety of analyses, but I find that it's clearest when I contrast the results of a logistic regression done in Excel with one done in R. Both applications return the same equation coefficients. Both return the same log likelihood. Both return the same value for McFadden's pseudo-R^2.

But in Excel, you can *see* how you got there. In R, all you can see is the destination. Depending on what you're after, the choice of platform is pretty clear.

5

Using Odds Instead of Probabilities

The concept of odds is closely related to that of probabilities. At a basic level, odds are a ratio of complementary probabilities. For example, suppose the probability that you will go to a grocery store tomorrow is 0.75 or 75%. Then the probability that you will *not* do so is 0.25 or 25%. The probability that you will go is three times greater than the probability that you will not go, and the odds you will go are 3 to 1.

A couple of formulas summarize the relationship between probabilities and odds pretty succinctly. Assume that *P* stands for *probability* and *O* stands for *odds*. Then:

$$O = P / (1 - P)$$

Or, revisiting the grocery store example:

$$3 = 0.75 / (1 - 0.75) = 0.75 / 0.25$$

It's just as easy to go the other direction, from odds to a probability:

$$P = O / (1 + O)$$

Back to the grocery store:

$$.75 = 3 / (1 + 3) = 3 / 4$$

Why is this relationship useful in the context of logistic regression? Because it deals with one of the problems caused by predicting probabilities: Winding up with a probability greater than 100%.

Have another look at Figure 5.2. The dotted line represents predicted probabilities, but they are probabilities that are calculated from the associated odds. The prediction equation predicts the odds of a win based on the number of advertising dollars spent in a district, and those odds can follow the number of dollars spent as high as they'll go.

Once the odds have been predicted—perhaps as high as 10,000 to 1, but they could be infinitely higher—they are converted back to probabilities using the formula just given. And no matter how high the odds, the associated probability cannot be greater than 100%.

Of course, the higher the odds, the closer the probability gets to 100%, but it will never be greater than 100%. Figure 5.3 may give you a sense of how odds and probabilities work to keep the probability between 0% and 100%.

Figure 5.3
The nonlinear relationship between probability and odds keeps the probability within its proper range.

B2		:	×	✓	f_x	=A2/(1+A2)	
	A		B			C	D
1	**Odds**		**Probability**				
2	0.0001		0.01%				
3	0.001		0.10%				
4	0.01		0.99%				
5	0.1		9.09%				
6	1		50.00%				
7	10		90.91%				
8	100		99.01%				
9	1,000		99.90%				
10	10,000		99.99%				
11							

Using the Logarithms of the Odds

It's helpful to convert probabilities to odds in order to solve the problem of predicting probabilities greater than 100%. But odds don't help you in the same way at the other end of the scale, where relatively small predictor values might want to return probabilities less than 0%.

The numerator of the formula for odds is a probability value. To repeat:

$$O=P/(1-P)$$

We don't want to deal with a probability that's less than 0%, and that implies that we won't deal with an odds less than 0. If the probability in the numerator of the equation is positive, then the odds must also be positive. How then do we allow the solution of the equation to follow the predictor values down and return a negative predicted value, without allowing a negative probability?

The answer is to work with the *logarithms* of the odds. If it's been a while: A logarithm is a power to which you raise a base number in order to return another number. Suppose that the base number is 2.718. Then, the logarithm of the number 10 is 2.302. That is, using Excel syntax:

$$10 = 2.718 \wedge 2.302$$

The number 2.718 is the *base*, and it's used in what are called *natural logarithms*. More precisely, then, the natural log of 10 is 2.302.

Logarithms, or *logs*, have a broad array of uses, but the characteristic that's important in this context is that they can have values that are well below zero—in theory, they can extend to negative infinity—but when you reverse the process and turn them back into the number they're based on, that number is always positive.

A natural logarithm is negative if it applies to a number smaller than 1. So the natural logarithm of 1 is 0. The natural logarithm of .5 is –0.69. The natural logarithm of .1 is –2.3. That means that we can use the prediction equation to return negative numbers and then turn those negative numbers, which we treat as logarithms, into the number that the logarithm represents.

Excel has two worksheet functions that are helpful in this process, LN() and EXP(). For example:

    =LN(10)

Returns 2.302, the natural log of 10. And

    =EXP(2.302)

returns 10, the number that we originally represented as the logarithm 2.302. (The EXP() function actually returns what's called an antilog.) The use of LN() and EXP() in the current context is as follows. Suppose that the prediction equation returned a logarithm of the odds that's negative—say, –15. That's entirely possible when the value of a predictor variable is very small compared to its mean. But we're not stuck with a negative value, because we know we're predicting logarithms. Once we have that predicted value of –15, we convert it from a logarithm to an odds:

    =EXP(–15)

Or 0.00000031. So, although those are small odds, they're not negative.

The result of all this is that we can use a prediction equation to return values considerably lower than 0, use logarithms (actually, antilogs) to convert negative numbers to odds, and use the P=O/(O+1) formula to convert odds to probabilities.

There's one more piece to the puzzle: Using Solver to maximize the accuracy of the values that come back from the prediction equation. Let's wait on that until we have something for Solver to work on. In the meantime, the next section shows how to assemble the original observations along with the odds and the logarithms that make logistic regression work.

From the Log Odds to the Probabilities

We start with data laid out something like that shown in Figure 5.4.

Figure 5.4
The range A1:D3 is reserved for use by the Solver.

	A	B	C	D
1			Coefficients	
2	Intercept	Sticker	Age	City
3	1.0000	0.0000	0.0000	0.0000
4				
5	Sell	Sticker	Age	City
6	No	34.261	12	Claremont
7	No	30.583	12	Claremont
8	No	31.522	9	Claremont
9	No	30.222	11	Claremont
10	No	26.516	4	Claremont
11	No	33.955	9	Claremont
12	No	25.347	11	Claremont
13	No	33.521	17	Claremont
14	No	25.600	13	Claremont
15	No	28.989	14	Walnut
16	No	33.754	14	Claremont
17	No	28.919	17	Claremont
18	Yes	29.164	11	Walnut
19	No	33.675	16	Claremont
20	Yes	34.124	17	Claremont
21	No	26.465	15	Claremont
22	No	29.180	6	Walnut
23	No	34.178	16	Walnut
24	No	25.327	15	Claremont

The data shown in Figure 5.4 represents sales data for two used car lots in different municipalities: Claremont and Walnut. The owner of the lots wanted to know how, if at all, the age and list price of a used car affected the probability that the car would sell. Additionally, he wanted to know if the city where the lot was located affected the probability of a sale. Not all the records are visible in Figure 5.4, but the data extends down through row 41.

The intercept and coefficient values in the range A2:D2 are set to initial values, just to give the analysis a place to start. The first step is to recast two text variables, Sell and City, as numeric variables. See Figure 5.5.

5

Figure 5.5
The numeric recoding
of the *Sell* and the *City*
variables is necessary in
Excel, but R takes care of
it for you.

H2			× ✓	*fx*	=SUM(I6:I41)			

	A	B	C	D	E	F	G	H	I
1			Coefficients						
2	Intercept	Sticker	Age	City			Sum log likelihood	-25.27742075	
3	1.0000	0.0000	0.0000	0.0000					
4									
5	Sell	Sticker	Age	City	Logit	Odds	Probability that Sell = 0	Prob of correct classification	Log Likelihood
6	0	34.261	12	1	1	2.718281828	0.731058579	0.731058579	-0.31326169
7	0	30.583	12	1	1	2.718281828	0.731058579	0.731058579	-0.31326169
8	0	31.522	9	1	1	2.718281828	0.731058579	0.731058579	-0.31326169
9	0	30.222	11	1	1	2.718281828	0.731058579	0.731058579	-0.31326169
10	0	26.516	4	1	1	2.718281828	0.731058579	0.731058579	-0.31326169
11	0	33.955	9	1	1	2.718281828	0.731058579	0.731058579	-0.31326169
12	0	25.347	11	1	1	2.718281828	0.731058579	0.731058579	-0.31326169
13	0	33.521	17	1	1	2.718281828	0.731058579	0.731058579	-0.31326169
14	0	25.6	13	1	1	2.718281828	0.731058579	0.731058579	-0.31326169
15	0	28.989	14	0	1	2.718281828	0.731058579	0.731058579	-0.31326169
16	0	33.754	14	1	1	2.718281828	0.731058579	0.731058579	-0.31326169
17	0	28.919	17	1	1	2.718281828	0.731058579	0.731058579	-0.31326169
18	1	29.164	11	0	1	2.718281828	0.731058579	0.268941421	-1.31326169
19	0	33.675	16	1	1	2.718281828	0.731058579	0.731058579	-0.31326169
20	1	34.124	17	1	1	2.718281828	0.731058579	0.268941421	-1.31326169
21	0	26.465	15	1	1	2.718281828	0.731058579	0.731058579	-0.31326169
22	0	29.18	6	0	1	2.718281828	0.731058579	0.731058579	-0.31326169
23	0	34.178	16	0	1	2.718281828	0.731058579	0.731058579	-0.31326169

A worksheet such as the one shown in Figure 5.5 is what takes up the lion's share of the effort in running a logistic regression in Excel. The following sections describe the tasks taken care of in Figure 5.5.

Recoding Text Variables

The Sell variable is recoded so that a Yes (that is, the car was sold) becomes a 1 and a No becomes a 0. These particular values, 1 and 0, are important because we want to predict the probability of a sale, given values on Age, Sticker Price, and City, as accurately as possible. When a car has been successfully sold, the probability of that event is 1; as long as it's not sold, the probability of that a sales event occurred is 0.

Matters are different when it comes to a predictor variable, instead of a predicted variable such as Sell. All we're trying to do with the City variable is distinguish the location of a car that's for sale (or where it was when it was sold). We do want the variable's values to be numeric, so that they can be multiplied by a coefficient. But granted that condition, the codes could just as easily be 3.1416 and 67 as 1 and 0.

Defining Names

This task is not truly necessary, but it makes matters more convenient later. Four names are defined, as follows:

- *Intercept.* The cell A2 is given the name Intercept.
- *StickerCoef.* The cell B2 is given the name StickerCoef, as in "sticker shock." The listed price of the car. The tag "Coef" is attached to the end of the defined name (as it is with

the remaining two names) to make it clear that the cell contents are coefficients in the prediction equation.

- *AgeCoef.* The number of years that have elapsed since the car was manufactured.
- *CityCoef.* The city where the car is offered for sale or where it was sold.

The names are defined solely to make it easier to understand the worksheet formulas and more self-documenting. We get to the first set of formulas in the next section.

Calculating the Logits

Here's the Excel formula, used in cell E6, for what logistic regression terms the *logit*:

=Intercept+StickerCoef*B6+AgeCoef*C6+CityCoef*D6

That formula looks a lot like one you'd use in standard multiple regression to predict an outcome after the optimum values for the regression coefficients have been calculated. In ordinary least squares regression, the result of the formula is often called the *predicted value*. In logistic regression it's called the *logit*.

In Figure 5.5, all the logits, the values in the range E6:E41, equal 1.0. That's because we haven't yet used Solver to find the coefficients that result in the best predictions. With the intercept set to 1.0 and all the coefficients set to 0.0, the logit formula just given can't help but return 1.0 for each record. That will change shortly.

Calculating the Odds

It's also true that the values in column F, in the range F6:F41, all equal 2.718. The formula in cell F6 is

=EXP(E6)

That formula returns the antilog of the value in cell E6, and it's copied and pasted down through F41. Recall that the base of the natural logarithms is 2.718. The natural logarithm of a number is the power you raise 2.718 to in order to obtain another value. If you want to obtain 2.718 itself, you raise the base of the natural logs, 2.718, to the first power, and the result would be 2.718.

The EXP() function returns the antilog. If you pass a natural logarithm such as 1 to the EXP() function, the result is the *base*: the number that you raise to the power of the logarithm. In column F of Figure 5.5, you get the antilog of 1, which is 2.718. That is, the base 2.718 raised to the first power is 2.718.

Earlier in this chapter, I pointed out that for several reasons (including the prevention of probabilities lower than 0% or higher than 100%) we want our prediction equation to calculate the logit or log odds: *odds*, to keep the associated probability less than 100%, and *log*, to keep the associated probability higher than 0%.

And that's what the logit is: the log of the odds of a result for a given combination of predictor variables. Then, when we take the antilog of the log odds, the *logit*, in column E, we get the odds themselves in column F.

Calculating the Probabilities

As soon as we have the odds in column F, it's a short step to the probabilities. The formula in cell G6 is

=F6/(1+F6)

That applies the more general formula given earlier in this chapter:

Probability = Odds / (1 + Odds)

or

P = O / (1 + O)

We're nearly there. Although we have probabilities in column G, they're not quite the right ones. The range G6:G41 contains the probabilities that, given the predictor values, the values in column A represent the probability that a car did not sell—that is, that a value in A6:A41 is 0.

What we want is the probability that, based on the three predictor variable values, the record has the value of Sell that was actually observed. That conversion is easy enough. Here's the formula in cell H6:

=IF(A6=0,G6,1-G6)

The effect of that formula is as follows: If the value of the Sell variable is 0, then the probability that's predicted by the equation is also the probability of a correct prediction. Therefore, copy the value in G6 into H6. But if the value in A6 is 1, then the probability in G6 is the probability of an incorrect prediction. Therefore, put 1 minus the probability found in G6 into H6. And copy H6 down through H41.

Getting the Log Likelihood

The final step before starting Solver is to get what's termed the *log likelihood* of the probability associated with each record. This process has *nothing* to do with the use of logarithms to convert the logits to probabilities. It has everything to do with assembling an estimate of the overall accuracy of the prediction equation.

Suppose that the nature of your observed data was so accurate that you were able to predict the outcome variable perfectly. In that case, the probability you would observe for each record would be 1.0: You would predict a sale that takes place with a probability of 100%, and you will predict, with equal accuracy, a sale that does not take place.

Granted that the sales, and the failures to sell, are independent events, the probability of predicting all the records correctly is the continued product of their individual probabilities. That is, multiply all the individual records' probabilities together to get the overall likelihood that the predictions are correct. Clearly, the closer the individual probabilities are to 1.0, the closer the overall probability is to 1.0. And the closer the individual probabilities are to 0.0, the closer their continued product will be to 0.0.

> **NOTE** In this example, the assumption that "the sales, and the failures to sell, are independent events" simply means that the sale (or failure to sell) of one car has no effect on the probability of selling a different car.

But the convention in logistic regression is to convert the probabilities (those shown in the range H6:H41 of Figure 5.5) to logarithms and to sum those logs. The outcome is the same, but summing the logs is less cumbersome than multiplying the probabilities— or it was so in the 1950s, when logistic regression was under development as an analytic technique. Bear in mind that the logarithm of the continued product of a set of numbers is the same as the sum of the logarithms of those numbers. For example, using Excel syntax

=LN(.9*.5*.1)

returns −3.101, and

=LN(.9) + LN(.5) + LN(.1)

also returns −3.101.

It's generally true of logarithms, regardless of the base they use, that the log of a number less than 1 is negative. For example, using natural logs as this chapter has done, this Excel formula:

=LN(0.9)

returns −0.105. And this formula:

=LN(0.7)

returns −0.357. The two general points to take from this are

- Probabilities range from 0.0 to 1.0. Therefore the logs of the probabilities are all negative numbers.

- As probabilities approach 1.0, the associated logarithms approach 0.0. Suppose the predictions are perfect and all the individual probabilities are 1.0. Then their continued product will be 1.0, and the sum of the associated logarithms will be 0.0.

Using the tools that were in common use 60 years ago, slide rules and engineering tables, calculating the continued product of all those probabilities was an exacting task. Much easier to get the logarithm of each probability and total the logs. And that's still the way it's done today. In Figure 5.5, cell H2 shows the total of the logarithms in the range I6:I41.

The closer that sum is to 0, the closer the continued product of the probabilities is to 1. And the closer the continued product is to 1, the more accurate the predictions returned by the equation.

> **NOTE** The continued product of perfect predictions is 1, and the sum of the logs of perfect predictions is 0. The relationship between the two may be easier to remember if you keep in mind that any real number raised to the power of 0 equals 1. Therefore if you raise the base of a set of logs, such as 2.718, to the power of 0 (the perfect log likelihood), the result is 1 (the perfect continued product).

With the worksheet set up properly, it's time to turn to Solver.

Deploying Solver

If you haven't encountered Solver before now, it's an add-in that comes with Excel. Its purpose, at least in this context, is to optimize the intercept and coefficients in A2:D2 of Figure 5.5 so that the sum of the log likelihood in cell H2 comes as close to 0.0 as possible.

Installing Solver

A long, long time ago, several versions of Excel in the past, you often had to specify that you wanted Solver on your computer when you were either installing a new version of Excel or updating your current version. That seems no longer to be the case, but you still have to bring Solver to Excel's attention so that it will appear on the Ribbon.

The process is almost identical to the steps you take to get the Data Analysis Add-in onto the Ribbon. Take these steps:

1. Click File on the Ribbon.
2. Choose Options on the nav bar.
3. On the Excel Options window, click Add-ins on the nav bar.
4. Make sure that Excel add-ins appears in the Manage drop-down at the bottom of the window.
5. Click Go. You'll get the Add-ins window. Fill the Solver Add-in check box.
6. Click OK.

If all has gone as it should, you'll now find a link to Solver on the Ribbon's Data tab. Click that tab and look for an Analyze group on the Data tab, usually at the right end. You should see the link to Solver in that group.

Using Solver for Logistic Regression

With Solver installed, switch to the worksheet that contains your data, including all the elements shown in Figure 5.5. Select cell H2, or wherever you've chosen to put the sum of the log likelihoods. Click the Solver's link on the Ribbon's Data tab. The Solver Parameters dialog box shown in Figure 5.6 appears.

Figure 5.6
The version of Solver's main dialog box may appear different in your version of Excel, but the important controls will nevertheless be available.

The dialog box in Figure 5.6 looks intimidating, but for present purposes only a few entries are needed. Here are the steps to take:

1. Solver might have picked up the address of the cell that was active when you click the Solver link. If not, just click in the Set Objective edit box and then click the cell in your worksheet where you have stored the formula that totals the records' log likelihoods. In Figure 5.5, that's cell H2.

2. Make sure the Max option button is selected.

3. Click in the By Changing Variable Cells edit box and drag through A3:D3 on your worksheet. If you have rearranged the worksheet, just be sure to include the intercept plus the coefficients for any predictor variables that you want to use.

4. Choose GRG Nonlinear in the Select a Solving Method drop-down.

5. Click the Options button. In the Solver Options dialog box, click the GRG Nonlinear tab. The Options dialog box now appears as shown in Figure 5.7.

6. Click the Central Derivatives option button and fill the Multistart check box. Click OK.

7. You are returned to the Solver Parameters dialog box. Click Solve.

Figure 5.7
Choosing Central Derivatives makes it more likely that the results will match R's results exactly.

After a few seconds of processing time, Solver informs you that it has reached a solution. Be sure that the Keep Solver Solution button is selected, and click OK. You should see the worksheet shown in Figure 5.8.

Figure 5.8
Optimized regression coefficients are in the range B3:D3.

	H2			×	✓	fx	=SUM(I6:I41)		

◢	A	B	C	D	E	F	G	H	I
1			Coefficients						
2	Intercept	Sticker	Age	City			Sum log likelihood	-20.21463676	
3	3.2517	-0.1079	-0.0332	1.9388					
4									
5	Sell	Sticker	Age	City	Logit	Odds	Probability that Sell = 0	Prob of correct classification	Log Likelihood
6	0	34.261	12	1	1.096304	2.993082982	0.749566937	0.749566937	-0.28825966
7	0	30.583	12	1	1.493017	4.450500638	0.816530615	0.816530615	-0.20269087
8	0	31.522	9	1	1.491438	4.443478498	0.816293938	0.816293938	-0.20298077
9	0	30.222	11	1	1.565189	4.783576678	0.827096612	0.827096612	-0.18983377
10	0	26.516	4	1	2.19756	9.00302055	0.900030196	0.900030196	-0.10532696
11	0	33.955	9	1	1.229012	3.417850283	0.773645566	0.773645566	-0.25664144
12	0	25.347	11	1	2.091011	8.093091065	0.890026396	0.890026396	-0.11650416
13	0	33.521	17	1	1.00995	2.745464977	0.733010452	0.733010452	-0.31059532
14	0	25.6	13	1	1.997254	7.368791156	0.880508429	0.880508429	-0.12725578
15	0	28.989	14	0	-0.34032	0.711539848	0.41573081	0.41573081	-0.87771732
16	0	33.754	14	1	1.084521	2.958023228	0.747348628	0.747348628	-0.2912235
17	0	28.919	17	1	1.506327	4.510132914	0.818516175	0.818516175	-0.20026212
18	1	29.164	11	0	-0.2595	0.771439402	0.435487322	0.564512678	-0.57179244
19	0	33.675	16	1	1.026574	2.791485764	0.736251153	0.736251153	-0.30618298
20	1	34.124	17	1	0.94491	2.572582576	0.720090445	0.279909555	-1.27328874
21	0	26.465	15	1	1.837486	6.280726673	0.862651072	0.862651072	-0.14774499
22	0	29.18	6	0	-0.09505	0.909325364	0.476254797	0.476254797	-0.74180228
23	0	34.178	16	0	-0.96648	0.380418748	0.275582136	0.275582136	-1.28886956

What you have in Figure 5.8 is similar to a least squares regression equation. Solver has tried different values for the predictor variables' coefficients and the equation's intercept, and it has followed some fairly sophisticated algorithms to arrive at the final values in the range A3:D3.

It probably wouldn't be wise to do so, but at this point it's at least possible to apply the equation to a car that hasn't yet been offered for sale. Just as with a standard least squares regression equation, you would plug a car's values on sticker price, age, and city into the equation so that they are multiplied by the coefficients and the results adjusted by the intercept.

> **NOTE** The reason that it might not be wise to apply these results to a different car or cars is that you don't yet have good reason to believe that the results will be stable with a different data set. It's best to first repeat the analysis with new data, a process called *cross validation*.

The equation returns a logit value, the log odds. In least squares regression, you would now have the predicted value that you're looking for: the result of the TREND() function, perhaps, or of using the coefficients and intercept returned by LINEST().

5

In logistic regression you still have a little work to do before you have the value you're after. The result of the prediction equation is the log odds or logit, and you want the probability of a sale. So finish up with a couple of easy steps:

1. Convert the logit to the odds by using the antilog function. If the logit for the car you're interested in is in cell J5, you might use this:

   =EXP(J5)

2. Convert the odds to the probability by applying the appropriate formula. If the odds are in cell K5, you might use this to get the probability:

   =K5/(K5+1)

You now have the best equation to predict the probability of selling a car that hasn't yet been put on sale, given the data set that you supplied in the range A6:D41 in Figure 5.8. Solver has ensured that it's the best prediction possible by finding the set of coefficients and the intercept that jointly maximize the sum of the log likelihoods in cell H2.

> **NOTE** Bear in mind that the logs of numbers between 0 and 1 are always negative, and therefore their sum is always negative. So, to maximize that quantity means to get it as close to 0 as possible. To maximize a log likelihood of −20 means to move it toward 0, not toward −30.

Of course you can test whether Solver has maximized the log likelihood in H2 by finding the optimum values for the coefficients. Try other values for the coefficients by entering them into A3:D3 and see if the log likelihood improves over the value returned by Solver's adjustments.

Statistical Tests in Logistic Regression

Theorists and practitioners have spent a considerable amount of time and ink in efforts to design analyses for logistic regression that behave in the same way as they do in ordinary least squares regression. It hasn't worked out as smoothly as we'd like.

R^2 and t in Logistic Regression

For example, we like to look at the R^2 statistic in a least squares regression, to get a descriptive (rather than purely inferential) sense of how well the regression equation predicts the outcomes that we actually observe. Efforts to derive an R^2 statistic for the maximum likelihood procedures used with binomial or multinomial outcomes have fallen short.

The results of these efforts are generally termed *pseudo R^2 statistics*. The term is a not-so-tacit acknowledgement that it does not behave as credibly as does R^2 in a least squares equation. Probably the best-known and best-behaved pseudo-R^2 is called *McFadden's R^2*.

> **NOTE**
> Many different methods to mimic the behavior of the least squares R^2 are labeled *Pseudo R^2* by statistical applications. If you are going to employ a pseudo R^2 in a logistic regression analysis, it's wise to nail down which one the application is handing you.

Another example of the difficulty involved in getting the statistics used in logistic regression to behave as they do in least squares regression is often termed the *Wald statistic*. Least squares regression offers two popular ways to determine whether a predictor variable contributes reliably to the accuracy of the equation:

- Divide the predictor's coefficient by its standard error. The result is a t-statistic. You can use that t-statistic along with the residual degrees of freedom to decide whether the coefficient *in the population* is likely to be 0.0. (Similarly, you can use the t-statistic to construct a confidence interval around the coefficient's value, which may or may not span 0.0.) If you decide that the population coefficient might be 0.0, there's a good argument for removing that predictor from the analysis. In that case, any information that the predictor adds to the equation is due to sampling error.

- Use the models comparison approach (more familiarly termed the *likelihood ratio test* or *LR test* in the context of logistic regression). Run the linear regression analysis on the full model, and then run it again with one (or more) of the predictors omitted. The full model will have a larger R^2 than the restricted model, unless something unusually bizarre has occurred. Use an F-test on the difference between the two R^2 values. If you judge the result insignificant in a statistical sense, then the only difference between the two models—the predictor's presence or absence—does not add reliably to the information that the regression equation provides. Again, you could remove the predictor from the equation.

The Wald statistic is analogous to the first of the latter two alternatives, which depends on a t-test and requires only one pass through the data. It is also possible to employ the Wald statistic as part of a least squares analysis. In that context, the Wald statistic and the models comparison approach return the same result.

But in the context of a logistic regression, the two approaches do not necessarily agree. Experience has shown that with relatively small samples, the models comparison approach returns more accurate distinctions than does the Wald statistic. With large samples, the two approaches are generally equivalent.

Because of the broader applicability of the models comparison approach, I'm going to cover it in this chapter in preference to the Wald statistic. (But you get the Wald statistic easily from R packages.)

5

The Likelihood Ratio Test

Most applications, including R, report the components of a likelihood ratio test applied to the full equation. You'll see what it looks like in R later in this chapter. Figure 5.9 has an example in the Excel context.

Figure 5.9
Multiply the log likelihood by −2 to get the Deviance.

	H3	▾	:	× ✓ *fx*	=-2*H2				
⊿	A	B	C	D	E	F	G	H	I
1			Coefficients						
2	Intercept	Sticker	Age	City			Log likelihood	-20.21463676	
3	3.2517	-0.1079	-0.0332	1.9388			Deviance or -2LL	40.42927353	
4									
5	Sell	Sticker	Age	City	Logit	Odds	Probability that Sell = 0	Prob of correct classification	Log Likelihood
6	0	34.261	12	1	1.096304	2.993082982	0.749566937	0.749566937	-0.288259656
7	0	30.583	12	1	1.493017	4.450500638	0.816530615	0.816530615	-0.202690872
8	0	31.522	9	1	1.491438	4.443478498	0.816293938	0.816293938	-0.202980771
9	0	30.222	11	1	1.565189	4.783576678	0.827096612	0.827096612	-0.189833768
10	0	26.516	4	1	2.19756	9.00302055	0.900030196	0.900030196	-0.105326965
11	0	33.955	9	1	1.229012	3.417850283	0.773645566	0.773645566	-0.256641435
12	0	25.347	11	1	2.091011	8.093091065	0.890026396	0.890026396	-0.116504159
13	0	33.521	17	1	1.00995	2.745464977	0.733010452	0.733010452	-0.310595318
14	0	25.6	13	1	1.997254	7.368791156	0.880508429	0.880508429	-0.127255778
15	0	28.989	14	0	-0.34032	0.711539848	0.41573081	0.41573081	-0.877717319
16	0	33.754	14	1	1.084521	2.958023228	0.747348628	0.747348628	-0.291223499
17	0	28.919	17	1	1.506327	4.510132914	0.818516175	0.818516175	-0.200262121
18	1	29.164	11	0	-0.2595	0.771439402	0.435487322	0.564512678	-0.571792438
19	0	33.675	16	1	1.026574	2.791485764	0.736251153	0.736251153	-0.306183978
20	1	34.124	17	1	0.94491	2.572582576	0.720090445	0.279909555	-1.273288745
21	0	26.465	15	1	1.837486	6.280726673	0.862651072	0.862651072	-0.147744989
22	0	29.18	6	0	-0.09505	0.909325364	0.476254797	0.476254797	-0.74180228
23	0	34.178	16	0	-0.96648	0.380418748	0.275582136	0.275582136	-1.288869559

Here's where the terminology starts to get really messy. We want a measure of how far the predictions go awry—the differences or deviations or residuals between the event's actual, observed probability and the probability predicted by the equation, given the optimized coefficients and a record's values on the predictor variables.

Furthermore, we'd like that measure to be one that we can compare to a reference distribution such as q, t, F, or chi-square. In that case we can objectively measure how rare, or how common, it is to observe a value of a given magnitude, absent a genuine relationship in the full population. Then we can infer that an F value of 3.0 or larger with 4 and 50 degrees of freedom occurs in a central F-distribution only 2.7% of the time.

The log likelihood that's calculated and shown in cell H2 of both Figures 5.8 and 5.9 is an aggregate measure of the difference between the actuals and the predictions. However, as it stands it's not comparable to any of the standard reference distributions:

- The F-distribution is based on the ratio of one variance to another. No variance can have a negative value, and so no F-ratio can be negative. But in logistic regression the log likelihood is always negative.

- Chi-square is always positive, and, again, you can't locate a negative log likelihood in a chi-square distribution.

- The t-and the q-distributions assume a difference in mean values, divided by a standard error. These are inappropriate comparisons for a likelihood ratio, which is simply a total of logarithms.

It turns out, though, that if you multiply the log likelihood by -2, you get a variable that follows a chi-square distribution with degrees of freedom equal to the number of constrained variables in the equation. So you can compare the result of that multiplication to a chi-square distribution, noting the number of constrained variables. (I'll discuss that notion shortly.)

In the meantime, we need a name for that new statistic. And things would be much more straightforward if we could give it a name. Unfortunately, we have to deal with a variety of names, each of which has been widely used in the literature on logistic regression for the product of the log likelihood and the quantity -2:

- Deviance, DEV and D

- $-2LL$; also, $2LL$

- D_0 for a model that includes the intercept only and D_M for a model with one or more variables in addition to the intercept

- G, presumably for *goodness of fit*; also, G^2

Recognizing and remembering that these are all different names for the same quantity is a headache. I'll use $-2LL$ in the remainder of this chapter because it's a reasonably popular designation and because it's reasonably precise: -2 times the log likelihood.

Figure 5.10 demonstrates how you can carry out a likelihood ratio test in Excel.

Figure 5.10
This worksheet is a rearrangement of the sheet shown in Figure 5.9.

	I	J	K	L	M	N	O	P
					Coefficients			
1								
2			Intercept		Sticker	Age	City	
3				-3.2518	0.1079	0.0332	-1.9388	
4								
5	Log Likelihood			Log Likelihood	-20.2146			
6	-0.288260463			-2LL	40.4293			
7	-0.202691007							
8	-0.20298099				LL	-2LL	Delta from intercept-only	df	P chi-square
9	-0.189833843		Intercept only	-24.0569	48.1139	#N/A		#N/A
10	-0.105326715							
11	-0.256642077		Intercept & Sticker	-23.7855	47.5710	0.5429	1	0.4612
12	-0.116503844							
13	-0.310596124		Intercept, Sticker & Age	-23.7269	47.4538	0.6601	2	0.7189
14	-0.12725547							
15	-0.877717539		Intercept, Sticker, Age & City	-20.2146	40.4293	7.6846	3	0.0530
16	-0.291224257							

The range L9:P15 in Figure 5.10 shows three separate likelihood ratio tests. Each of them tests the statistical significance of the addition of a variable to the prediction equation. To show all the pertinent operations in one figure, I have moved the intercept and coefficients into the range K3:N3.

The full set of tests requires running Solver four times. But only one change is made to Solver's parameters for each run, so the process can take place fairly quickly. Here are the steps:

1. Set the value of the intercept in cell K3 to 1.0, and the values of the three coefficients in L3:N3 to 0.0.
2. Select the log likelihood in cell L5.
3. Start Solver by clicking its link on the Ribbon's Data tab.
4. Make sure that the Set Objective edit box on the Solver Parameters dialog box contains the worksheet address of the log likelihood. In this example that's L5. Choose to maximize its value.
5. Enter the Intercept cell (here, K3) in the By Changing Variable Cells edit box.
6. Make sure that the Make Unconstrained Variables Non-Negative edit box is cleared.
7. Click Solve.

Solver maximizes the value of the log likelihood in L5 by changing the value of the intercept, and leaving the values of the predictor coefficients at 0.0. The result is sometimes termed the $-2LL_0$. With these data, the intercept is optimized to 0.4520.

> **NOTE** The value 0.4520 is the average of the logits in column E. With no other variable to use as a predictor, the analysis cannot do better than to use the average logit as the intercept.

Save the value of the log likelihood as a value, not as a formula. I have done so in Figure 5.10 in cell L9. It is needed as a comparative value later in the analysis, and the precedent cells will have changed by then—which is the reason to save it as a value.

That's one time through the process. You need to repeat it three more times because there are three predictor variables (Sticker, Age, and City) to evaluate. There are fewer steps:

1. Start Solver.
2. Leave the Set Objective cell at the address of the log likelihood.
3. Change the By Changing Variable Cells edit box to include K3 (the Intercept) and L3 (StickerCoef).
4. Click Solve.

Now Solver maximizes the log likelihood by changing both the Intercept and the Sticker coefficient, which is in cell L3 and which has been named StickerCoef. The remaining variables, Age and City, are omitted from the analysis by setting their coefficients to 0.0 and omitting them from the list of Changing Variable Cells.

Again, when Solver is finished, copy the log likelihood and paste it as a value for later use. In Figure 5.10, I have done so in cell L11.

Repeat the prior four steps twice, once by adding AgeCoef to Intercept and StickerCoef, and finally by adding CityCoef to Intercept, StickerCoef, and AgeCoef. Record the log likelihoods as values, as I have done in Figure 5.10, in cells L13 and L15.

With the log likelihoods established in the range L9:L15, you can multiply each by −2 and place the results in M9:M15. One more piece is needed, and for that we need to detour briefly into the issue of constraints.

Constraints and Degrees of Freedom

We're getting ready to compare three sets of models:

- Intercept only versus Intercept and Sticker
- Intercept only versus Intercept, Sticker, and Age
- Intercept only versus Intercept, Sticker, Age, and City

Consider the first comparison, Intercept-only versus Intercept and Sticker. There is one variable in the second model, Sticker, whose coefficient is free to vary.

Put another way, we run Solver twice for the first comparison. The first time it's run, we arrange things so that Solver changes only the cell that contains the intercept. The other three are constrained to have coefficients of 0.0—that is to keep them from having any effect on the equation's result.

The second time we run Solver, we allow it to vary both Intercept and StickerCoef. AgeCoef and CityCoef are still constrained to equal 0.0. The first model, Intercept only, has one more constraint than the second model. That difference in the number of constraints is taken to be the degrees of freedom for the chi-square test. That first comparison therefore has one degree of freedom. That degree of freedom applies to the difference in the values of −2LL between the two models. The difference in −2LL appears in cell N11 and is calculated by subtracting M11 from M9.

So, we can compare the difference in the values of −2LL in cell N11 of Figure 5.10 to Excel's CHISQ.DIST.RT() function. We use the number 1 from cell O11, the difference in the two models' constraints, as the degrees of freedom argument. Here's the formula in cell P11:

    =CHISQ.DIST.RT(N11,O11)

It returns 0.4612. That means that more than 46% of a chi-square distribution with 1 degree of freedom contains values as large as, or larger than, 0.5429. It's not at all an unusual value for chi-square in that distribution and can easily be chalked up to a touch of sampling error. Apparently the car's sticker price is not a useful predictor of the probability of sale in this data set.

The second comparison involves the Intercept-only model and the model that varies the Intercept, StickerCoef, and AgeCoef. Therefore, the second model constrains only the City variable to equal 0.0, and the first model still constrains all three variables to equal 0.0. The difference in the number of constraints is now 2. That value is passed along to the chi-square function in cell P13, along with the difference in the two models' values for –2LL:

=CHISQ.DIST.RT(N13,O13)

This time the CHISQ.DIST.RT() function returns 0.7189. With 2 degrees of freedom even a larger –2LL value is more likely than the first one of 0.5429 to occur in the chi-square distribution.

Similar reasoning and calculations are used for the third comparison, which tests the Intercept-only model against the full model in which Solver varies the three coefficients—StickerCoef, AgeCoef, and CityCoef. The difference in the values of –2LL, with three degrees of freedom, is large enough that the chi-square value is significant at the 0.053 level. A borderline result if you started out with an alpha of 0.05, but if you did so then you're obligated to decide that the prediction equation is not dependable—but it might be smart to run the experiment again, with a larger sample size.

Logistic Regression with R's mlogit Package

R offers several ways to perform logistic regression. One of them uses a contributed package named *mlogit*, and this section describes its use and how to interpret its results. Another, discussed in this chapter's final section, describes how to use the more general *glm* model to obtain similar results in a framework that accommodates more models than the logistic.

As you might expect, there's a lot less work involved with running the analysis in R than in Excel. The corollary is that you get a lot less intermediate information. If you have no particular need for that information, then R is surely the way to go. If you want to see what happens to particular cases in the process of carrying out the logistic regression, bear in mind that its usually a lot easier to get at in Excel (but at the cost of doing that additional work I mentioned).

Running the mlogit Package

To follow along with this description, you'll want to get the raw data out of Excel and into R via a data frame. Throughout this book I have suggested that the most straightforward way of doing so is via the DescTools package, specifically its *XLGetRange* function, and that's my suggestion here.

The worksheet shown in Figure 5.11 has numeric values for the Sell and the City variables, in order to show more clearly the options you have in structuring your raw data set. Begin by activating that worksheet.

Figure 5.11
The text values for the Sell and the City variables have been replaced by numeric values.

	A	B	C	D
1	**Sell**	**Sticker**	**Age**	**City**
2	0	34.261	12	1
3	0	30.583	12	1
4	0	31.522	9	1
5	0	30.222	11	1
6	0	26.516	4	1
7	0	33.955	9	1
8	0	25.347	11	1
9	0	33.521	17	1
10	0	25.6	13	1
11	0	28.989	14	0
12	0	33.754	14	1
13	0	28.919	17	1
14	1	29.164	11	0
15	0	33.675	16	1
16	1	34.124	17	1
17	0	26.465	15	1
18	0	29.18	6	0
19	0	34.178	16	0
20	0	25.327	15	1
21	0	31.487	18	1
22	1	27.337	19	0
23	0	29.083	13	0

Select cells A5:D41. Switch to R and enter these commands:

```
> library(DescTools)
> CarData <- XLGetRange(header = TRUE, stringsAsFactors = TRUE)
> head(CarData,3)
> LongFormat <- mlogit.data(CarData, choice = "Sell", shape = "wide")
> head(LongFormat)
```

Figure 5.12 shows the results.

Figure 5.12
Notice that the CarData data frame has one row for each record: One row, one car. LongFormat has two rows: One row, one alternative.

```
R R Console
> CarData <- XLGetRange(header = TRUE, stringsAsFactors = TRUE)
> head(CarData,3)
  Sell Sticker Age City
1    0  34.261  12    1
2    0  30.583  12    1
3    0  31.522   9    1
> LongFormat <- mlogit.data(CarData, choice = "Sell", shape = "wide")
> head(LongFormat)
     Sell Sticker Age City chid alt
1.0  TRUE  34.261  12    1    1   0
1.1 FALSE  34.261  12    1    1   1
2.0  TRUE  30.583  12    1    2   0
2.1 FALSE  30.583  12    1    2   1
3.0  TRUE  31.522   9    1    3   0
3.1 FALSE  31.522   9    1    3   1
```

Figure 5.12 illustrates a fundamental aspect of data sets in the mlogit package. The term "mlogit" is short for *multinomial logit*. There are profound differences between binomial logistic regression, in which the predicted variable has two values such as Buy/Don't Buy or Vote/Don't Vote, and multinomial logistic regression, where the predicted variable can take on more than two values such as Ford, Toyota, and GM. The differences are as major as those between simple single-predictor regression and multiple regression (but the differences are very, well, different).

One of the ways that the differences between binomial logistic regression and multinomial logistic regression is in the shape of the data set that you present to the mlogit function, which refers to the two shapes as "wide" and "long."

Consider the CarData data set. It has one row per record, and one record is sufficient to provide all the necessary values without repetition. A record—that is, a given car—is either sold or it's not, and that event shows up in the value of the Sell variable. Whether or not it's sold, there's only one Sticker price that applies, only one Age of the car, only one City where the car lot is located.

But what if you had a multinomial variable to deal with, one with, say, three alternatives instead just two as in the CarData set? Perhaps you're investigating how a consumer chooses to buy a Ford, or a Toyota, or a GM. Now a variable that could have only one value per record in CarData—say, the sticker price—can have three values: the price of the Ford alternative, that of the Toyota alternative, and that of the GM alternative.

This sort of thing is what relational databases handle so smoothly: You would probably regard a customer as a parent record, with values such as customer's income belonging to that parent record. Linked via IDs to the parent records would be child records, which would represent different cars that the customer is considering. The child records contain variables specific to the cars: sticker, age, GPS, and so forth. Each parent record can have as many child records as there are cars under consideration by that customer.

But R is not a relational database management system, and despite functions such as VLOOKUP() neither is Excel. With two dimensions, rows and columns, we have to make do with allowing for multiple alternatives by putting the alternative information in additional columns or additional rows.

If you're doing your data entry in Excel, you might decide to represent a multinomial situation by adding columns: for example, FordCost, ToyotaCost, and GMCost. This approach has advantages and disadvantages. It's advantageous that one record occupies one row. That makes various analyses ranging from simple correlations to pivot table reports perfectly straightforward.

The mlogit function refers to this arrangement as the "wide" shape. Using that arrangement, the data set becomes wider as more columns are added to accommodate additional alternatives for the predicted variable. As soon as someone wants to consider a Yugo besides a Ford, Toyota, or GM, you need another column for the price of that make.

Or you might decide to arrange things so that a record occupies several rows, one for each alternative. You could treat each record as having as many rows as there are alternatives to choose from. Each row would have a column that contains the sticker price of a particular make.

> **NOTE** This—a multi-row record—would be an unusual choice in Excel unless your sole purpose in entering the data is to move it into R for analysis there. Using that layout, the simplest way I can think of to get, for example, a correlation for something such as Sticker and Age would be to use Advanced Filter to copy the rows that represent a given choice to another location and run the correlation on the extracted data. Excel is generally much happier with data sets that mlogit would consider to have a wide shape.

This approach leads to the shape of data set that mlogit terms "long." Instead of adding columns that make the data set wider, you add rows that make it longer.

The mlogit function prefers to work with data that's oriented according to a long shape. If you have a wide data set, an mlogit command will convert it on your behalf to the long shape.

That's what this command:

```
> LongFormat <- mlogit.data(CarData, choice = "Sell", shape = "wide")
```

is doing in Figure 5.12. It takes the data frame that you pull into R via the XLGetRange function. It examines the values in the Sell variable, because the command specifies that Sell represents the choice. (Here, the choice is whether or not the car was sold; in another data set, it might indicate whether the purchase was of a Ford, Toyota or GM.) Finding that the data set contains just two alternatives in the Sell variable, the command results in two rows per record: one for TRUE, with data that applies if the car was sold, and one for FALSE, with data that applies if the car was not sold. Of course this may be redundant information with a binomial choice, but it's often unique to each choice when you have three or more alternatives.

The *shape = "wide"* specification in the command informs mlogit which shape you arranged for in the data frame. Arranging the shape is not the only task that's performed, so you'll want to run the mlogit.data command even if you have a long shape to begin with.

The next two commands establish and display the model, including the equation and summary statistics such as the log likelihood

```
> LogitModel <- mlogit(Sell ~ 1|Sticker + Age + City, data = LongFormat,
reflevel = "0")
> summary(LogitModel)
```

The first command assigns the results of running the mlogit function on the LongFormat data frame to a variable named LogitModel. The second command displays the contents of LogitModel, as shown in Figure 5.13.

Figure 5.13

Compare the intercept and coefficients in this figure with those shown in Figure 5.10.

```
R Console

> LogitModel <- mlogit(Sell ~ 1|Sticker + Age + City, data = LongFormat, reflevel = "0")
> summary(LogitModel)

Call:
mlogit(formula = Sell ~ 1 | Sticker + Age + City, data = LongFormat,
    reflevel = "0", method = "nr", print.level = 0)

Frequencies of alternatives:
      0       1
0.61111 0.38889

nr method
4 iterations, 0h:0m:0s
g'(-H)^-1g = 2.19E-07
gradient close to zero

Coefficients :
                 Estimate Std. Error t-value Pr(>|t|)
1:(intercept)   -3.251735   4.671437 -0.6961  0.48637
1:Sticker        0.107861   0.148653  0.7256  0.46809
1:Age            0.033234   0.085474  0.3888  0.69741
1:City          -1.938803   0.777846 -2.4925  0.01268 *
---
Signif. codes:  0 '***' 0.001 '**' 0.01 '*' 0.05 '.' 0.1 ' ' 1

Log-Likelihood: -20.215
McFadden R^2:  0.15972
Likelihood ratio test : chisq = 7.6846 (p.value = 0.053)
>
```

The intercept and coefficients, as well as the log likelihood, that are returned by mlogit are identical to those returned by the Excel analysis in Figure 5.10. Let's take a closer look at how the command calls the mlogit function:

```
> LogitModel <- mlogit(Sell ~ 1|Sticker + Age + City, data = LongFormat,
reflevel = "0")
```

The first argument shown in the mlogit function is a formula that can come with three segments that R's documentation refers to as *parts*. The parts are separated by vertical bars such as this one: |. So a schematic of the formula specification might look like this:

(Sell ~ Part 1 | Part 2 | Part 3)

followed by more arguments.

The parts, taken in reverse order, are as follows:

- Part 3 is optional and makes use only of alternative-specific predictor variables (such as the price of different makes of car, where the make of car is the predicted variable). We have no alternative-specific predictor variables in this example, so Part 3 is omitted from the formula.

- Part 2 of the formula in this case specifies that the model is to include Sticker, Age, and City, just as though these were predictor variables in an ordinary least squares analysis.

- Part 1, like Part 3, involves alternative-specific variables but we can't omit this one. I have inserted the 1 between the assignment operator (the tilde) and the vertical bar that indicates the start of Part 2. The presence of the 1 calls for mlogit to include the intercept.

The next argument to the mlogit function identifies the source of the data. Make sure that you're passing a long format data frame to mlogit; the surest and easiest way of doing so is to run it through mlogit.data first, as shown earlier in this section.

The third argument to the function as used here is *reflevel*. This requires some explanation, even though you could omit it entirely because it has a default. Nevertheless, I want to bring it to your attention: If you omit it, you might get results that are apparently in conflict with the results you get from an Excel solution. But at least with a binomial problem, it's easy to bring the two analyses into agreement.

When you have an outcome variable that can take on K values, K–1 vectors with values of 0 and 1 (termed *dummies* by mlogit) can be calculated for the predictor variables. These vectors are equivalent to those created in the analysis of covariance for the purpose of testing for the presence of interactions between factors and covariates.

One of the alternatives available for the choice variable (in this example, Sell) is not represented by 1s in its own vector. That alternative gets a 0 in all the dummies, whereas the other vectors get a 1 in one of the dummies. By default, the value that is not represented by its own dummy vector is the first one encountered by mlogit when it reads the formula.

However, you can use the *reflevel* argument to override that default and specify the value of the choice variable that does not get its own vector. You might want to do so if you periodically run mlogit on a data set that gets updated from time to time, so that you're not necessarily sure which choice value mlogit will encounter when it reads your formula.

It's worth noting that in a binomial situation such as the present example, the choice variable can take on only two values: e.g., 0/1, TRUE/FALSE, and yes/no. Then K equals 2 and only one dummy vector can be created. Therefore, only one instance of the product of the vector and a predictor's coefficient can be assessed.

In contrast, in a multinomial situation, if the choice variable included three makes of car, then there might be one vector representing Toyota (0 or 1) times the price coefficient, and one vector representing GM (again, 0 or 1) times the price coefficient. Ford might be omitted by default as the first value of the choice variable that mlogit encounters, but Ford would get a 0 on both the Toyota and the GM vectors.

To see what happens in the binomial situation when you specify a particular value, 0 or 1, as the reflevel, do so in the mlogit statement. Try running mlogit with reflevel equal to 0, and then again with reflevel equal to 1. Compare the results. You'll find that the outcomes that describe the full equation, such as the log likelihood, are unchanged. In the binary case only the signs of the intercept and coefficients differ.

For example, setting reflevel = 0, the equation's intercept is –3.2517. If you set reflevel = 1, the equation's intercept is returned as 3.2517. You can replicate this result in Excel, of course, where its effect is more readily apparent. In the worksheet shown in Figure 5.9, the formula in cell H6 is

=IF(A6=1,G6,1-G6)

Make a note of the values of the intercept and coefficients and then do the following:

1. Change the equation in H6 to this:

   =IF(A6=0,G6,1-G6)

2. Copy and paste the formula in H6 down through the bottom of the data set.

3. Run Solver again with precisely the same settings as before.

You'll note that just as with mlogit, the signs of the intercept and coefficients have changed but not their absolute values. This is due to swapping the role of 1 and 0 in the analyses, although Excel and mlogit go about implementing that swap in different ways.

Comparing Models with mlogit

Figure 5.10 shows the log likelihood and −2LL for four different models: Intercept only; Intercept and Sticker; Intercept, Sticker, and Age; and Intercept, Sticker, Age, and City. The purpose is to test the increment in −2LL as variables are added to the equation.

One straightforward way to perform a similar analysis in R is to run mlogit four times, just as in Figure 5.10 Excel runs Solver four times with different variable cells defining the model each time. There are functions in R that will complete the models comparisons for you automatically, but as this book is written mlogit does not have that capability. The following commands are an example of how you would go about picking up the log likelihood for each model:

```
> LogitModel <- mlogit(Sell ~ 1, data = LongFormat)
> summary(LogitModel)
> LogitModel <- mlogit(Sell ~ 1|Sticker, data = LongFormat)
> summary(LogitModel)
> LogitModel <- mlogit(Sell ~ 1|Sticker + Age, data = LongFormat)
> summary(LogitModel)
> LogitModel <- mlogit(Sell ~ 1|Sticker + Age + City, data = LongFormat)
> summary(LogitModel)
```

The likelihood ratio at the end of the mlogit summary provides the appropriate statistical chi-square test. You can also compare the actual chi-square values and associated p-values at the end of mlogit's summary with those shown in N11:P15 of Figure 5.10.

Using R's glm Function

The mlogit function in R's mlogit package is complex, both as to syntax and as to its requirement that the data frame conform to the "long" shape. But the complexity is understandable, given that the authors wanted to accommodate both binomial and multinomial choice variables. As I mentioned at the outset of this chapter's section on mlogit, the differences in analyzing binomial versus multinomial data are major and probably justify the use of a more complicated means of defining the model.

R also provides a general linear model function that is capable of performing a variety of analyses based on the model. The function is part of the base *stats* package and therefore you need not download a special contributed package to run it. You can point it at data that's arranged just as you would arrange data for use in Excel: that is, as a list that mlogit would refer to as "wide." Perhaps inevitably, the function is named *glm*.

It's easy to use *glm*, but it does not accommodate multinomial choice variables. If you will never need to analyze a multinomial variable (such as make of car including at least three makes), then you can probably get along just fine with *glm* and not have to struggle with long and wide data frame shapes and with trilobate formula specifications.

Figure 5.14 shows how to call *glm* and its results.

Figure 5.14

Notice that the *glm* function returns z-tests of the coefficients, whereas *mlogit* returns t-tests.

```
R R Console

> glmlogit <- glm(Sell ~ Sticker + Age + City, data = CarData, family = "binomial")
> summary (glmlogit)

Call:
glm(formula = Sell ~ Sticker + Age + City, family = "binomial",
    data = CarData)

Deviance Residuals:
    Min      1Q   Median      3Q     Max
-1.6055  -0.7603  -0.5285   0.9833  1.9267

Coefficients:
            Estimate Std. Error z value Pr(>|z|)
(Intercept) -3.25174    4.67144  -0.696   0.4864
Sticker      0.10786    0.14865   0.726   0.4681
Age          0.03323    0.08547   0.389   0.6974
City        -1.93880    0.77785  -2.493   0.0127 *
---
Signif. codes:  0 '***' 0.001 '**' 0.01 '*' 0.05 '.' 0.1 ' ' 1

(Dispersion parameter for binomial family taken to be 1)

    Null deviance: 48.114  on 35  degrees of freedom
Residual deviance: 40.429  on 32  degrees of freedom
AIC: 48.429

Number of Fisher Scoring iterations: 4

> |
```

The *glm* function as used in Figure 5.14 takes as its data frame the car data obtained directly from Excel via the XLGetRange function. That range appears in Figure 5.11.

Note that the *family* argument to the *glm* function specifies *binomial*. That's because here we're doing a binomial logistic regression. Other families available with *glm* include *gaussian*, *Gamma*, and *poisson*.

Apart from differences due to the use of the normal distribution rather than the t-distribution in the tests of the coefficients, the logistic equation is identical to that returned by mlogit and by Excel. The overall statistics do not include the log likelihood or $-2LL$, but you can pick up the log likelihood (and use it to calculate $-2LL$) with the *logLik* function:

> logLik(glmlogit)

where *glmlogit* is the result returned by the *glm* function. Be careful to enter the letters in logLik in the correct upper and lower cases.

Principal Components Analysis

With principal components analysis we move beyond the types of statistical analysis that you can design using Excel's built-in worksheet functions. When it's a matter of basic descriptive statistics, or inferential tests including t-tests and the analysis of variance and covariance, regression analysis, and logistic regression, you don't have to look further in Excel than worksheet functions such as AVERAGE(), DEVSQ(), LINEST(), F.DIST.RT(), and EXP() to assemble a complete analysis.

But when it comes to analysis that involves digging out underlying variables that are observed only indirectly, Excel needs an assist. That sort of analysis includes areas such as principal components analysis, the subject of this chapter, and its close cousin factor analysis.

> **NOTE**
> It can be difficult to differentiate factors from principal components. It often comes down to your point of view. Some regard a principal component as a composite of the available variables, and a variable as a composite of the derived factors. Others regard this as a distinction without a difference, like grand opera vis-à-vis hog-calling.

Those analyses seek to explain the relationships between observed variables by extracting from correlation matrixes—or, almost equivalently, covariance matrixes—unobserved variables that are related to the variables that we *can* observe and measure.

Our purpose in doing so might be something as pragmatic and practical as helping to make sense of a data set containing hundreds of variables. If there are four or five latent variables that together explain 100 overt variables, we'd much prefer to work with the smaller data set.

But we need a way to identify and extract those unobserved variables from the data, and Excel doesn't offer a worksheet function named EXTRACT() or EIGENVALUE() or even anything conceptually close to those.

> **NOTE**
> A function that would extract underlying components from a data set is perfectly feasible in Excel. With some experience using VBA you could write a user-defined function—a *UDF*—to extract components. A workbook that accompanies this chapter includes a VBA subroutine that does exactly that. It's coded as a subroutine rather than as a function, but you're welcome to make the few changes necessary to turn it into a UDF. The code is there for you to edit if you want.

After the analysis has extracted the principal components, in the form of eigenvalues and eigenvectors, you could turn matters over to Excel's worksheet functions if you wanted to do so. And if you're new to principal components analysis and factor analysis, then I suggest that you do so. I think it's a valuable learning device to walk through processes like these in order to understand what's going on inside the black box:

- How the square roots of the eigenvalues combine with the eigenvectors to result in the factor structure matrix

- How the inverses of the square roots of the eigenvalues combine with the eigenvectors to result in the factor coefficients matrix

- How the size of the eigenvalues can inform your decision of the number of components to retain

So this chapter walks you through the process of running a principal components analysis in Excel. Along the way it points out how to get the same analysis using R functions. My purpose, as in earlier chapters, is to ease the transition to R by showing how to arrange for the same set of results using both applications.

Principal Components Using Excel

The examples in this chapter are all based on the small data set shown in Figure 6.1. It includes three variables only, and only 20 records. Normally you'd want many more than 20 records to beef up the external validity of the analysis. Again normally, you'd expect more than just three variables. Because one of the primary functions of this sort of analysis is data reduction, you usually see, say, 10 observed variables, or more, to justify the effort of running a principal components analysis.

But the purpose here is not to carry out an analysis of all the variables captured by Google Analytics collected over a month's elapsed time. It's to show what goes into a principal components analysis done in the context of both Excel and R. Three variables and 20 cases are perfectly sufficient for that purpose, and restricting the number of both the records and the variables makes it possible to present much clearer figures—see Figure 6.1, for example—and, I hope, a clearer discussion.

Figure 6.1
You would normally expect to see substantial correlations between these individual observed variables.

| B24 | | ⌄ | : | ✕ | ✓ | *fx* | =STDEV.S(B2:B21) |

▲	A	B	C	D	E
1	**Visit**	**Visit Length**	**Page Views**	**Pages**	
2	1	7	4	3	
3	2	4	1	8	
4	3	6	3	5	
5	4	8	6	1	
6	5	8	5	7	
7	6	7	2	9	
8	7	5	3	3	
9	8	9	5	8	
10	9	7	4	5	
11	10	8	2	2	
12	11	9	5	2	
13	12	8	4	2	
14	13	9	2	3	
15	14	8	4	7	
16	15	3	1	4	
17	16	3	1	3	
18	17	8	2	6	
19	18	1	2	5	
20	19	3	1	7	
21	20	6	3	3	
22					
23	Means	6.35	3.00	4.65	
24	SDs	2.39	1.56	2.39	

One way to initiate a principal components analysis in Excel is to open the workbook named PCA.xlsm that you can find on the publisher's website for this book.

Open PCA.xlsm *before* opening the workbook that contains the data that you want to analyze. The reason is that if you open the data workbook first and then PCA.xlsm, you might not see the Add-ins tab on Excel's ribbon when the data workbook is active. That tab is where the link to the PCA code is found.

> **NOTE**
>
> Yes, the code in the PCA.xlsm workbook is accessible via the Add-ins tab even though it's not an add-in. (It would be an add-in if the file name's extension were .xlsa.) An .xlsm workbook winds up in the Ribbon's Add-ins tab if the workbook has a Workbook_Open() event associated with it. I left the workbook as an .xlsm file because I wanted to make it as easy as possible for you to be able to examine and edit the VBA code.

6

Navigating the Dialog Box

After opening PCA.xlsm first and then your data workbook, click the Ribbon's Add-ins tab and then click the Principal Components link. You'll see the dialog box shown in Figure 6.2.

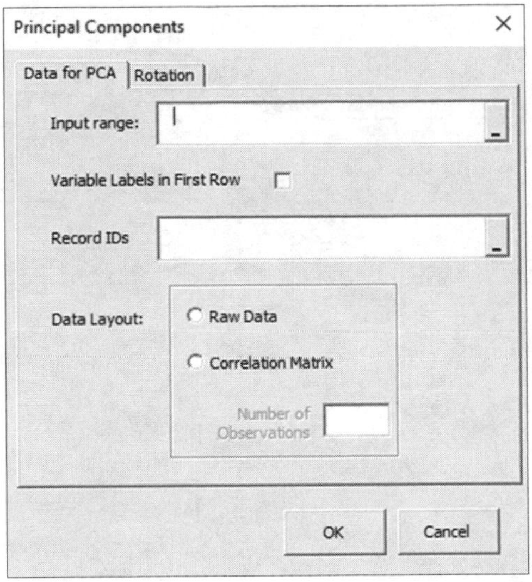

Figure 6.2
You can use either a correlation matrix or raw data as input to PCA.

To prepare the analysis, complete the options in the dialog box. Assuming that you want to analyze the data shown in Figure 6.1, take these steps:

1. Click in the Input Range box and drag through the range B1:D21. *Do not* include A2:A21 in this range.

2. Fill the Variable Labels in First Row check box.

3. Click in the Record IDs box and drag through A2:A21. Be careful not to include cell A1 in this range.

4. Choose the Raw Data option button.

5. Click the Rotation tab at the top of the dialog box. See Figure 6.3.

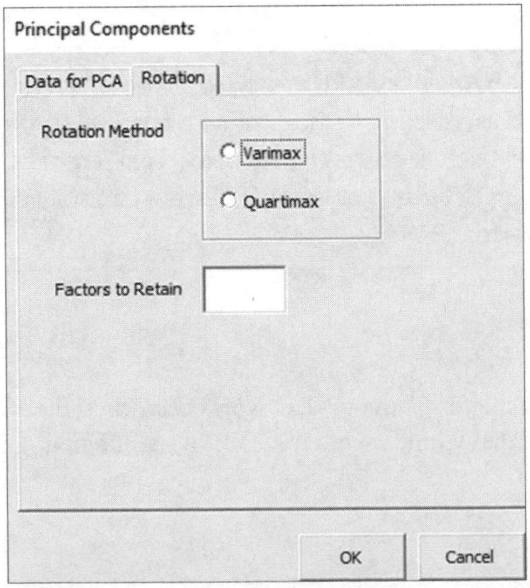

Figure 6.3
Normally you retain as many factors as you have variables on the first run through the data.

6. Choose the Varimax rotation.

7. Enter 3 in the Factors to Retain edit box.

A few item to bear in mind regarding the dialog box shown in Figures 6.2 and 6.3:

■ If you are using an Excel list (rather than a table) and you don't have column headers, leave the Variable Labels check box cleared. The code will supply variable names like Variable 1, Variable 2, and so on for you.

■ Record IDs are recommended so that you can more accurately associate both unrotated and rotated factor scores with the correct record. You can use names such as "Barry" instead of numbers as IDs if you want to.

■ You can use a square correlation matrix instead of raw data. That approach can make sense if you don't have access to the raw data but do have a correlation matrix, or if there's too much raw data to supply conveniently on an Excel worksheet. Note that the matrix must be square, not simply the values below the main diagonal of the sort produced by the Correlation tool in Excel's Data Analysis add-in. (Could I have allowed for that triangular input? Yes.)

■ If you do use a correlation matrix as input, you need to supply the number of records on which the correlations are based. It's needed to perform Bartlett's sphericity test. And if you supply correlations, you won't get individuals' factor scores. The raw data is needed to use in conjunction with the factor score coefficients to produce the factor scores.

■ Quartimax factor rotation is no longer used as frequently as it once was. I included it because it was easy to do so and I wanted to provide you a point of comparison with the results of Varimax rotation.

■ The first time you run a PCA on a given data set, it's normal to retain as many factors as you have variables. That puts you in position to judge how many factors to retain in subsequent runs. However, the number of retained factors applies to the rotated solution only. If you have five variables, you'll get a five-factor analysis in the basic unrotated results.

> **NOTE** The use of Bartlett's sphericity test requires some special care because it is sensitive not only to whether the population correlation matrix is the identity matrix, but also to departures from multivariate normality.

Click OK and you'll get the results, arranged on four different worksheets. The first worksheet, named *Principal Components*, appears in Figure 6.4.

Figure 6.4
This figure shows only the first few analyses on the worksheet.

	A	B	C	D	E	F	G	H
	F6	▼	:	×	✓	fx	{=MMULT(B3:D5,B9:D11)}	
1	**R Matrix**							
2		Visit Length	Page Views	Pages				
3	Visit Length	1	0.665126158	-0.115614924				
4	Page Views	0.665126158	1	-0.212274306				
5	Pages	-0.115614924	-0.212274306	1		=MMULT(B3:D5,B9:D11)		
6						1.0000	0.0000	0.0000
7	**R Inverse**					0.0000	1.0000	0.0000
8		Visit Length	Page Views	Pages		0.0000	0.0000	1.0000
9	Visit Length	1.795582653	-1.204496745	-0.048087558				
10	Page Views	-1.204496745	1.855176395	0.254548482				
11	Pages	-0.048087558	0.254548482	1.048474463				
12								
13	Determinant of R matrix = 0.531827							
14								
15	For sphericity test, Chi-square = 10.84, and df = 3							
16	P(Chi-square) = 0.013							

The Principal Components Worksheet: The R Matrix and Its Inverse

The worksheet named *Principal Components* contains most of the results of the PCA analysis. (The remaining three worksheets contain the rotated factor loadings, the rotated factor coefficients, and—if you supplied raw data instead of a correlation matrix—the rotated factor scores.)

The first portion of the Principal Components worksheet contains the correlation matrix for the original variables and its inverse. The correlation matrix is indispensable for the definition of principal components, and I'll get to that issue shortly. First, though, some information about the *inverse* of the correlation matrix.

The inverse of a matrix is analogous to the inverse of a single number. The inverse of the number 9 is 1/9, and if you multiply any number by its inverse you get the number 1. Matrix multiplication is a little more involved than multiplying one number by another, but not dauntingly so. If you multiply a matrix by its inverse, you get what's called an *identity matrix*. An identity matrix has 1s in its main diagonal and 0s everywhere else. Instead of a single 1, you get a matrix of 1s and 0s.

Figure 6.4 shows an identity matrix formed by multiplying the correlation matrix **R** by its inverse, **R**⁻¹. (It's conventional when writing about matrixes to show a letter symbol that represents a matrix in boldface.) The result of the matrix multiplication, the identity matrix, is in the range F6:H8 of Figure 6.4.

Note that Excel has a worksheet function, MMULT(), that performs the matrix multiplication for you. The basic rule (and there are some other rules) of matrix multiplication is that the first matrix must have the same number of columns as there are rows in the second matrix. At this point in a principal components analysis you seldom need to worry about this condition because you're almost always working with square matrixes of the same order (worry later, when you have dropped one or more components from the analysis).

To get the complete results from MMULT(), you need to start by selecting the appropriately sized range of cells, and to finish by array-entering the formula with Ctrl+Shift+Enter.

Excel has two other matrix functions that you should be aware of:

- MINVERSE() returns the inverse of a matrix. The code in the PCA workbook takes care of it for you, but if you want to do so you can array-enter this formula in a three-by-three range somewhere on the worksheet shown in Figure 6.4:

=MINVERSE(B3:D5)

You can calculate the inverse of square matrixes only.

- MDETERM() returns the *determinant* of a matrix. A matrix's determinant is a single number whose value depends entirely on the values found in the matrix. A matrix needs a non-zero determinant to be invertible. Some matrixes have determinants that equal zero, and as a practical matter this is because one column in the matrix of raw data is a perfect linear function of one or more other columns.

So, if you use the PCA.xlsm workbook (or any other that analyzes principal components) and get a set of error values instead of meaningful numbers, something to check on early is the determinant of the **R** matrix. If it's zero, you have a problem in your original data. You'll find the determinant in cell A13 of Figure 6.4. You can replicate that result with this formula:

=MDETERM(B3:D5)

Why is the inverse of the R matrix important? Largely because of its applicability to the notion of common, shared variance. A basic function of both principal components analysis and factor analysis is to derive variables that are not directly observed but that are closely related, in a quantitative sense, to variables that are observed. When an observed variable shares a substantial amount of its variance with an unobserved variable—a principal component or a factor—you can use that information to help develop an understanding about the unobserved variable.

Now, a variable such as Visit Length in the example shown in Figure 6.4 has some variance that it shares with other observed variables, as well as with a principal component. It also has some variance that it doesn't share with other variables. In many cases we'd like to restrict our analysis to the proportion of the variance of a variable such as Visit Length to the *shared* or *common* variance, and set aside the unshared, unique variance.

When you create a standard correlation matrix from a set of observed variables, you generally wind up with values of 1.0 in the matrix's main diagonal: A numeric variable has a correlation of 1.0 with itself. But that 1.0 includes variability that's unique to each variable. Some analyses use, instead of 1.0 in the main diagonal of the correlation matrix, the variable's common variance, the proportion of the variable's variance that's shared with other variables. One way to measure that shared variance is to treat a variable as

6

the predicted variable in a multiple regression. Then, the R^2 value from the multiple regression would express the proportion of variance shared with the best combination of the predictors. In terms of this chapter's example, you might find the R^2 associated with predicting the value of Visit Length from Page Views and Pages.

But you don't need to arrange a multiple regression for each variable in your analysis. The R^2 values are all available from the inverse of the **R** matrix, $\mathbf{R}^{-1}$. See Figure 6.5.

Figure 6.5
Compare the values in the diagonal of B13:D15 with the R^2 values from LINEST() in B19, F19, and J19.

B13		$\times$ $\checkmark$ f_x	=1-(1/B9)									
	A	B	C	D	E	F	G	H	I	J	K	L
1	R Matrix											
2		Visit Length	Page Views	Pages								
3	Visit Length	1.0000	0.6651	-0.1156								
4	Page Views	0.6651	1.0000	-0.2123								
5	Pages	-0.1156	-0.2123	1.0000								
6												
7	R Inverse											
8		Visit Length	Page Views	Pages								
9	Visit Length	1.7956	-1.2045	-0.0481								
10	Page Views	-1.2045	1.8552	0.2545								
11	Pages	-0.0481	0.2545	1.0485								
12												
13		0.4431										
14			0.4610									
15				0.0462								
16												
17		0.0268	1.0305	3.1341		-0.0893	0.4227	0.7315		-0.3729	0.0459	5.4776
18		0.1852	0.2845	1.4001		0.1167	0.1167	1.0048		0.4873	0.3172	1.6068
19		0.4431	1.8858	#N/A		0.4610	1.2077	#N/A		0.0462	2.4678	#N/A
20		6.7625	17	#N/A		7.2690	17	#N/A		0.4120	17	#N/A
21		48.0961	60.4539	#N/A		21.2045	24.7955	#N/A		5.0186	103.5314	#N/A

So the $\mathbf{R}^{-1}$ matrix makes it quick and easy to get the R^2 values—or, as principal component and factor analysis often term them, squared multiple correlations or SMCs. If you were to calculate the SMCs on the worksheet using LINEST(), not only would you have to run LINEST() once for every variable in your data set, you would have to replicate the data set K – 1 times, where K is the number of variables. (The reason is that LINEST() requires that all the predictor variables be adjacent. Therefore, you can't put a variable that's to be predicted in among the predictor variables.)

That's the main reason that I put $\mathbf{R}^{-1}$ on the Principal Components worksheet. Most of the time, you and I can proceed with our analysis quite nicely without it. But what if we get a result from, say, R that is a little bit off of what we expect? If you've provided all the arguments as shown in the R documentation? What if the results aren't just a little bit off but wildly discrepant from some benchmark? Both "a little bit off" and "wildly discrepant" are unacceptable, but the degree of apparent error is sometimes a clue as to where the problem lies. And if all you have to work with is a list of the eigenvalues, the pattern matrix, and the component weights, you might have a lot of trouble tracking down the source of the problem.

I'm sure that one of the many functions available in R's PCA packages routinely returns **R**$^{-1}$. It's just that for all my poking around in the R functions that perform PCA, I can't find it. If you want to use R to return the inverse of a matrix (which must be a square matrix, as noted earlier) R's contributed package *MASS* has a *solve* function that returns the inverse of a matrix. If *mymatrix* is a square, fully populated matrix, then after loading the MASS package, this command:

```
matinv <- solve(mymatrix)
```

stores the inverse of *mymatrix* in *matinv*.

Okay, let's move on to the eigenvalues and eigenvectors.

The Principal Components Worksheet: Eigenvalues and Eigenvectors

In a principal components analysis, each component is initially assumed to have variance of 1.0—very much like the unit normal distribution, which is taken to have a mean of zero and variance of 1.0. In the example this chapter has been using, there are three observed variables, therefore a maximum of three principal components, therefore a total variance of 3. This value is also termed the *trace*.

Our near-term goal is to derive three components that are orthogonal to one another (that is, that would be at right angles to one another if charted, and therefore uncorrelated and independent of one another).

The process of extracting the principal components from the correlation matrix results in two sets of values:

■ A set of *eigenvalues*, one for each principal component. Each eigenvalue expresses the amount of the total variance associated with each component. The total of the eigenvalues in a given principal components analysis equals the number of components—remember, each component has an initial variance of 1.0 when the source of the components is a correlation matrix rather than a covariance matrix. The process of more fully defining and orienting the components with respect to one another changes the amount of variance attributed to each component, and therefore its eigenvalue. In this example, the eigenvalues are approximately 1.7, 0.9, and 0.4. Note that they sum to the trace of 3.0.

■ A set of *eigenvectors*, which reorient the principal components in order to maximize the variance attributed to the first component, then to maximize the remaining variance to the second component, and so on—but always keeping the components orthogonal to one another.

> **NOTE**
> The sum of the eigenvalues is the matrix's trace. The *product*—actually, the *continued product*—of the eigenvalues is the matrix's determinant.

Both the eigenvalues and the eigenvectors are intimately related to the factor loadings (the correlation of each variable with each component) and to the factor coefficients (the value multiplied by each record's standardized value on each variable to get a record's factor score). Figure 6.6 contains some additional information from the Principal Components worksheet, and shows how to calculate the factor coefficients from the eigenstructure.

> **NOTE** The *eigenstructure* is the combination of the eigenvalues and the eigenvectors.

Figure 6.6
A little matrix algebra gets you from the eigenstructure to the factor coefficients.

F30   {=MMULT(B24:D26,J24:L26)}

	A	B	C	D	E	F	G	H	I	J	K	L
18	**Eigenvalues**											
19		Factor 1	Factor 2	Factor 3								
20		1.73827	0.93425	0.32749								
21											Inverses of square roots	
22	**Eigenvectors**						Eigenvalues				of Eigenvalues	
23		Factor 1	Factor 2	Factor 3		Factor 1	Factor 2	Factor 3		Factor 1	Factor 2	Factor 3
24	Visit Length	0.66392	0.28896	0.68972		1.73827	0.00	0.00		0.75848	0.00	0.00
25	Page Views	0.68463	0.13614	-0.71606		0.00	0.93425	0.00		0.00	1.03459	0.00
26	Pages	-0.30082	0.94761	-0.10744		0.00	0.00	0.32749		0.00	0.00	1.74745
27												
28	**Factor Score Coefficients**											
29		Factor 1	Factor 2	Factor 3		Factor 1	Factor 2	Factor 3				
30	Visit Length	0.50356	0.29896	1.20525		0.50356	0.29896	1.20525				
31	Page Views	0.51928	0.14085	-1.25127		0.51928	0.14085	-1.25127				
32	Pages	-0.22816	0.98039	-0.18775		-0.22816	0.98039	-0.18775				

In Figure 6.6, the ranges B20:D20, B24:D26, and B30:D32 are supplied by the code in PCA.xlsm. I have supplied the matrixes in columns F:L to show how the factor score coefficients are available from the eigenstructure.

The range F24:H26 takes the calculated eigenvalues from B20:D20 and rearranges them in a diagonal matrix, in F24:H26. This is simply to place the eigenvalues correctly for use in a matrix multiplication.

Then the range J24:L26 modifies the eigenvalues in the range F24:H26 by taking the square root of each eigenvalue, and then taking the inverse of the result. For example, here's the formula used in cell J24:

=1/SQRT(F24)

> **NOTE** Many of Excel's worksheet functions simply ignore empty cells. For example, SUM(A1:A5) returns the same result whether A3 is empty or contains 0.0. MMULT() is different: You need to put a 0.0 into any empty cells in MMULT()'s arguments.

The range F30:H32 contains this array formula:

=MMULT(B24:D26,J24:L26)

It postmultiplies the eigenvectors by the inverses of the square roots of the eigenvalues. Notice that the results are identical to the values, returned by PCA.xlsm, in the range B30:D32. Later in this chapter I show you that R's principal components functions return the same set of coefficients.

This set of factor score coefficients is useful if you want to calculate where each record in the underlying data falls on each factor. It's often enlightening to chart the factors against the original variables.

You can use similar calculations to go from the eigenstructure to the factor structure matrix. See Figure 6.7.

Figure 6.7
The difference with Figure 6.6 is due to *not* taking the inverses.

	F30			f_x	{=MMULT(B24:D26,J24:L26)}						
	A	B	C	D	E	F	G	H	I	J	K	L
18	**Eigenvalues**											
19		Factor 1	Factor 2	Factor 3								
20		1.73827	0.93425	0.32749								
21												
22	**Eigenvectors**										Square roots	
23		Factor 1	Factor 2	Factor 3			Eigenvalues				of Eigenvalues	
24	Visit Length	0.66392	0.28896	0.68972		1.73827	0.00	0.00		1.31843	0.00	0.00
25	Page Views	0.68463	0.13614	-0.71606		0.00	0.93425	0.00		0.00	0.96656	0.00
26	Pages	-0.30082	0.94761	-0.10744		0.00	0.00	0.32749		0.00	0.00	0.57226
27												
28	**Factor Structure**											
29		Factor 1	Factor 2	Factor 3		Factor 1	Factor 2	Factor 3				
30	Visit Length	0.87533	0.27930	0.39470		0.87533	0.27930	0.39470				
31	Page Views	0.90264	0.13159	-0.40977		0.90264	0.13159	-0.40977				
32	Pages	-0.39661	0.91593	-0.06149		-0.39661	0.91593	-0.06149				

The only substantive difference between Figures 6.6 and 6.7 is that the values in the diagonal matrix in J24:L26 are the square roots of the eigenvalues rather than the inverse of the square roots of the eigenvalues. The result of the matrix multiplication in F30:H32 is the factor loadings: The value of the R^2 between each factor and each variable.

You can verify this relationship for yourself by using Excel's RSQ() function, which calculates the R^2, the square of the correlation, between two variables. Supply as the arguments to RSQ() the original values of one of the variables and the unrotated scores for one of the factors. The result is the variable's loading on that factor as displayed in the factor structure matrix.

> **NOTE**
> You often see "factor pattern matrix" instead of "factor structure matrix." The two terms are synonymous.

Again, note in Figure 6.7 that the factor structure returned by PCA.xlsm in B30:D32 is identical to the factor structure returned by the matrix multiplication in F30:H32.

Variable Communalities

The notion of *communality* is an important one in principal components and factor analysis. Communality is generally expressed as a percent, and it is associated with one variable and with one or more principal components. Communality, which is often symbolized as h^2, expresses the percent of variance in a given variable that is accounted for by the factors.

Figure 6.8 shows the communalities for each variable. When a principal components analysis returns as many components as the underlying data has variables, then all the variance in those variables is accounted for and the communality of each variable is 100%. However, as you can see in Figure 6.8, if we kept two factors only the communality for Visit Length would be 77% + 8% = 85%.

The communalities are calculated as the sum of the squared loadings in the structure matrix. Referring back to Figure 6.7 and the range B30:D32—which contains the structure matrix—the squares of the loadings result in the communalities in the range B41:D43 of Figure 6.8.

Figure 6.8
The communalities do not change if the number of factors changes. Their totals decrease as factors are removed.

	A	B	C	D	E
39					
40	Variable	Communalities			SMCs
41	Visit Length	77%	8%	16%	0.443077712
42	Page Views	81%	2%	17%	0.460967699
43	Pages	16%	84%	0%	0.046233327

The SMCs appear in E41:E43 of Figure 6.8. These are the R^2 values that would result from treating each variable as the predicted variable in a multiple regression analysis with the remaining variables as the predictors (discussed earlier in the section titled The Principal Components Worksheet: The R Matrix and its Inverse).

The Factor Scores

Each of the 20 records shown in Figure 6.1 has a score on each of the three factors. The way to calculate these factor scores is a little involved mechanically, but it's straightforward conceptually.

Figure 6.9 shows the three factor scores for each of the original 20 records. The factor scores are produced by PCA.xlsm.

Figure 6.9
The factor scores are calculated as standardized scores with a mean of 0 and a variance of 1.

	A	B	C	D
45	**Factor Scores**			
46		Factor 1	Factor 2	Factor 3
47	1	0.628176578	-0.504953895	-0.346807632
48	2	-1.48233671	0.899087256	0.160233401
49	3	-0.107146868	0.099782322	-0.203977604
50	4	1.697232512	-1.019166481	-1.293811792
51	5	0.790757721	1.351314887	-0.960943353
52	6	-0.6120307	1.775003842	0.790234939
53	7	-0.126909625	-0.845627829	-0.551117913
54	8	0.905977529	1.886557539	-0.535252096
55	9	0.437262477	0.315381105	-0.50390953
56	10	0.266845513	-0.971093506	1.844333786
57	11	1.478719832	-0.574447461	-0.063946403
58	12	0.934310487	-0.790046243	0.235985523
59	13	0.38206532	-0.435850854	2.270025043
60	14	0.457025234	1.260791256	-0.156769221
61	15	-1.311185366	-0.866657895	0.02980501
62	16	-1.215728315	-1.276825395	0.048745939
63	17	-0.11498269	0.669576494	1.530129991
64	18	-1.494263645	-0.616117067	-1.921014503
65	19	-1.597556518	0.363844604	-0.265457857
66	20	0.083767233	-0.720552678	-0.046875707

Figure 6.10 shows how the factor scores are calculated. In that figure I have pulled together data and calculated values from different places, but you've seen them all in earlier figures.

Figure 6.10
Excel's MMULT() function is a handy way to calculate factor scores.

O2 ▾ : × ✓ fx =MMULT($F2:$H2,K$3:K$5)

	A	B	C	D	E	F	G	H	I	J	K	L	M	N	O	P	Q
1	Visit	Visit Length	Page Views	Pages		Standardized Scores				Factor Score Coefficients					Factor Scores		
2	1	7	4	3		0.2719	0.6427	-0.6903			Factor 1	Factor 2	Factor 3		0.6282	-0.5050	-0.3468
3	2	4	1	8		-0.9832	-1.2854	1.4015		Visit Length	0.5036	0.2990	1.2053		-1.4823	0.8991	0.1602
4	3	6	3	5		-0.1464	0.0000	0.1464		Page Views	0.5193	0.1409	-1.2513		-0.1071	0.0998	-0.2040
5	4	8	6	1		0.6903	1.9281	-1.5271		Pages	-0.2282	0.9804	-0.1878		1.6972	-1.0192	-1.2938
6	5	8	5	7		0.6903	1.2854	0.9832							0.7908	1.3513	-0.9609
7	6	7	2	9		0.2719	-0.6427	1.8199							-0.6120	1.7750	0.7902
8	7	5	3	3		-0.5648	0.0000	-0.6903							-0.1269	-0.8456	-0.5511
9	8	9	5	8		1.1087	1.2854	1.4015							0.9060	1.8866	-0.5353
10	9	7	4	5		0.2719	0.6427	0.1464							0.4373	0.3154	-0.5039
11	10	8	2	2		0.6903	-0.6427	-1.1087							0.2668	-0.9711	1.8443
12	11	9	5	2		1.1087	1.2854	-1.1087							1.4787	-0.5744	-0.0639
13	12	8	4	2		0.6903	0.6427	-1.1087							0.9343	-0.7900	0.2360
14	13	9	2	3		1.1087	-0.6427	-0.6903							0.3821	-0.4359	2.2700
15	14	8	4	7		0.6903	0.6427	0.9832							0.4570	1.2608	-0.1568
16	15	3	1	4		-1.4015	-1.2854	-0.2719							-1.3112	-0.8667	-0.0298
17	16	3	1	3		-1.4015	-1.2854	-0.6903							-1.2157	-1.2768	0.0487
18	17	8	2	6		0.6903	-0.6427	0.5648							-0.1150	0.6696	1.5301
19	18	1	2	5		-2.2383	-0.6427	0.1464							-1.4943	-0.6161	-1.9210
20	19	3	1	7		-1.4015	-1.2854	0.9832							-1.5976	0.3638	-0.2655
21	20	6	3	3		-0.1464	0.0000	-0.6903							0.0838	-0.7206	-0.0469
23	Means	6.35	3	4.65													
24	SDs	2.3902	1.556	2.3902													

6

Here's what's in Figure 6.10:

- A2:D21. This range contains the original data set. It first appears in Figure 6.1. The values in A2:A21 are just record IDs and play no part in the analysis itself.
- A23:D24. The means and standard deviations for each of the three original variables. The standard deviations are in the sample form, dividing the sum of squares by $(n-1)$ instead of by n.
- F2:H21. The standard score form of the original data. The difference between each value in B2:D21 and that variable's mean is calculated, and the difference is divided by the variable's standard deviation.
- K3:M5. The factor score coefficients. These are returned by PCA.xlsm and were shown earlier in Figure 6.6.
- O2:Q21. The calculated factor scores, which you might want to compare to those returned by PCA.xlsm shown in Figure 6.9.

Here's how the factor scores in O2:Q21 are calculated. Each factor has three coefficients—see K3:M5. You multiply the three *standardized* variable scores for each record by the associated coefficients and sum the results to get the factor score. So, the first record's score on the first factor could be calculated in this way:

    =F2*K3+G2*K4+H2*K5

There are plenty of ways to go wrong if you tried to calculate each factor score in that way. The MMULT() function can help out: This formula would also return the first record's score on the first factor:

    =MMULT($F2:$H2,K$3:K$5)

Notice the use of dollar signs to create mixed references. Once you have entered the first MMULT() formula, you can drag it to the right to get the scores on the second and third factors, and then drag the first three formulas down to get the three factor scores for the remaining 19 records. The mixed references keep the precedent cells in the correct columns of the standardized scores and the correct rows of the factor score coefficients.

Rotated Factors in Excel

The PCA.xlsm workbook will also perform a standard factor rotation for you. The rotation is the Varimax rotation, which is a rotation of the principal component axes to an alignment that simplifies the factor structure matrix. This sort of factor simplification aims at factor loadings that are either close to 0.0 or close to 1.0 for any given factor. That sort of pattern, often termed *simple structure*, seeks to make it easier to interpret the meaning of a factor by clarifying which variables load strongly on it.

> **NOTE**
>
> The PCA.xlsm workbook also does another type of rotation termed *quartimax*. The varimax rotation tends to simplify the structure of the components or factors. The quartimax rotation (which was developed before the varimax rotation) tends to simplify variables, so that they load strongly on one or two factors and weakly on others. Experience has shown that varimax rotation and simplified factor structures are more useful for research purposes than quartimax rotation and simplified variable structures.

In this book I am not going to dig into how factor rotation works and how the rotation method results in differently structured factors. I've already hinted that there's a lot of material to absorb, and I haven't even mentioned the oblique rotations that allow the axes to align at acute angles, not simply orthogonal rotations such as varimax that keep the axes at right angles to one another. I want to keep the focus here on how to perform these analyses first in the context of Excel and then in the context of R. There are plenty of good sources of information on factor analysis and rotation. I like to think that two of them are *Predictive Analytics: Microsoft Excel* and *Decision Analytics: Microsoft Excel*, both by Conrad Carlberg and published by Que.

When the rotation is complete, the loadings have changed. PCA.xlsm puts the factor structure matrix for the rotated solution on its own worksheet, named Rotated Loadings. See Figure 6.11.

Figure 6.11
The rotated loadings tend to show simple structure.

▲	A	B	C	D	E
1		Rotated Loadings			
2			Factor 1	Factor 2	Factor 3
3		Visit Length	0.93580	-0.04435	-0.34973
4		Page Views	0.35919	-0.11187	-0.92654
5		Pages	-0.04171	0.99481	0.09282
6					
7		Unrotated Loadings			
8			Factor 1	Factor 2	Factor 3
9		Visit Length	0.87533	0.27930	0.39470
10		Page Views	0.90264	0.13159	-0.40977
11		Pages	-0.39661	0.91593	-0.06149

Figure 6.11 shows the factor loadings as rotated by the varimax method. For convenience I have added the unrotated loadings, which appear in the Principal Components worksheet and which you've already seen in the range B30:D32 of Figure 6.7.

In Figure 6.11, notice that the unrotated loadings in the range C9:E11 don't clarify things much. Both Visit Length and Page Views have high loadings on Factor 1. Pages has a strong loading on Factor2, and no variable loads strongly on Factor 3.

6

By rotating the axes so that the data points have different projections on the axes, we can clean up the factor structure. The rotated loadings in the range C3:E5 of Figure 6.11 simplify the structure considerably. Visit Length is the only variable to load highly on Factor 1; Pages is the only variable to load strongly on Factor 2; Page Views is the only variable to load strongly on Variable 3.

Although the varimax rotation has simplified the factor structure, it hasn't told us much. We apparently have three factors, each of which represents one of our original three variables. We're back where we started out.

But at this point we're still dealing with three rotated factors. Bear with the analysis a little longer. Before this chapter is done we'll look at an analysis with the number of rotated factors limited to 2 instead of 3, and the outcome will be somewhat different.

Rotated Factor Coefficients and Scores

Rotation necessarily changes the factor structure, as shown in Figure 6.11, and it therefore also changes the factor score coefficients needed to calculate the score for each record on each factor.

PCA.xlsm reports these rotated coefficients on a separate worksheet named Rotated Coefficients. See Figure 6.12.

Figure 6.12
Rotated coefficients always differ from the unrotated coefficients.

	A	B	C	D
1	Rotated Factor Coefficients			
2				
3		Factor 1	Factor 2	Factor 3
4	Visit Length	1.249673	0.007277	0.483577
5	Page Views	-0.47143	0.099108	-1.27401
6	Pages	0.002697	1.016688	-0.12171

You can apply these coefficients to the standardized values of the original values, just as shown in Figure 6.10. The quickest way to make the calculations yourself is to copy the range that contains the coefficients in Figure 6.12 and paste them over the unrotated coefficients in Figure 6.10. You'll get the results in Figure 6.13.

Figure 6.13
The estimated factor
scores based on rotated
components.

	A	B	C	D
1	**Rotated Factor Scores**			
2				
3		Factor 1	Factor 2	Factor 3
4	1	0.034994	-0.63616	-0.60327
5	2	-0.6189	1.290389	0.991555
6	3	-0.18259	0.147808	-0.08863
7	4	-0.0504	-1.35643	-1.93669
8	5	0.259352	1.131994	-1.42342
9	6	0.647728	1.788571	0.728793
10	7	-0.70768	-0.70594	-0.18911
11	8	0.783308	1.560392	-1.27202
12	9	0.037251	0.214548	-0.7051
13	10	1.162657	-1.18586	1.287543
14	11	0.776538	-0.99173	-0.9665
15	12	0.556693	-1.05847	-0.35003
16	13	1.686613	-0.75746	1.438939
17	14	0.562335	1.068299	-0.60463
18	15	-1.14624	-0.41407	0.992918
19	16	-1.14737	-0.83942	1.043838
20	17	1.16717	0.515555	1.083866
21	18	-2.49375	0.06889	-0.28142
22	19	-1.14286	0.861991	0.84016
23	20	-0.18485	-0.7029	0.013207

Principal Components Analysis Using R

Let's turn now to how you can get a principal components analysis using R instead of Excel. By now you probably won't be surprised to learn that R offers a variety of packages and functions that return principal components analysis. Among them are *princomp* (in the stats package), *prcomp* (also in the stats package), *fa* (the psych package), and *principal* (again, the psych package), and there are several others.

I've had good results using the *principal* function in the psych package and I illustrate its use here. As I've done in earlier chapters, I start by using the XLGetRange function from the DescTools package to pull the selected range of cells in Excel's active worksheet into a data frame.

Preparing the Data

For this example, I have Figure 6.1 open as Excel's active worksheet, and the range B1:D21 selected. We want R to use the labels in the first row of columns B through D as variable names, so we set the *header* argument in *XLGetRange* to TRUE.

Notice that the selected range in Excel does not include column A with its record IDs. That's not a variable that we need for the analysis, and the *XLGetRange* function numbers the records anyway, so there's nothing to be gained by including column A in the data frame. We can name the data frame *PCAData*. See Figure 6.14.

6

Figure 6.14
Some of the warnings provided by R are worth your attention.

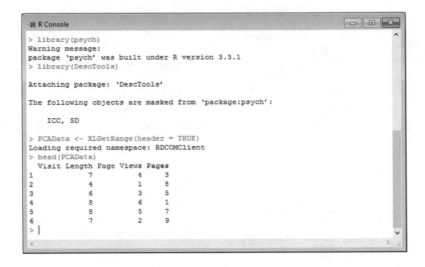

```
R R Console                                                    ☐  ☐  ☒
> library(psych)
Warning message:
package 'psych' was built under R version 3.3.1
> library(DescTools)

Attaching package: 'DescTools'

The following objects are masked from 'package:psych':

    ICC, SD

> PCAData <- XLGetRange(header = TRUE)
Loading required namespace: RDCOMClient
> head(PCAData)
  Visit Length Page Views Pages
1            7          4     3
2            4          1     8
3            6          3     5
4            8          6     1
5            8          5     7
6            7          2     9
> |
```

Before running the principal components analysis, we have to load the DescTools package and the psych package, in order to create the data frame with the *XLGetRange* function and to run the *principal* function.

When I started writing this book, the current version of R was 3.3.0. As I write this chapter, the current version is 3.3.1 and, for consistency, I am still using version 3.3.0. Therefore, R warns me that the current version of the psych package was built under R version 3.3.1, and I should be prepared for inconsistency.

In this case I'm not concerned about that, because I know what the functions in the psych package *should* return, so if need be I'll download and install the newest version of R as well as contributed packages I want to use. Furthermore, staying temporarily with version 3.3.0 gives me an opportunity to bring R's alert to your attention, as I've done here.

Another warning message, one that you should probably heed, appears in Figure 6.14 as follows:

```
The following objects are masked from 'package:psych':
    ICC, SD
```

Notice that the message appears immediately after the request to load DescTools is made. In this case, the message means that both DescTools and Psych give two objects—here, functions—the same names: ICC for intraclass correlations and SD for standard deviation. But even if the functions mean the same thing, they don't necessarily do the same thing in the same way, so R will recognize duplicated names from only one of the two packages and *masks* them from the other.

If you want to avoid this sort of conflict entirely, one way is to *detach* a package after you have used it and before you load a possibly conflicting package. In this example, you could do the following:

1. Load DescTools with *library*.
2. Use DescTools' *XLGetRange* function.

3. Unload DescTools with this command:

```
detach("package:DescTools", unload=TRUE)
```

4. Load *psych* and continue.

Another option, instead of detaching a package, is to qualify a duplicated name with the name of its package followed by two consecutive colons. For example:

```
DTICC <- DescTools::ICC(arguments)
```

and

```
PICC <- psych::ICC(arguments)
```

Calling the Function

The next step is to call the psych package's *principal* function and supply it with some arguments. Here's how it's called in Figure 6.15:

```
PCAModel <- principal(PCAData, nfactors=3, rotate="none", scores=TRUE)
```

The results are written to an object named PCAModel. The arguments are

- PCAData: The data frame containing the variables to be analyzed.
- nfactors: The number of factors to be extracted from the data frame's variables.
- rotate: The type of rotation to use. Specify "none" for no rotation, as here. As you'll see shortly, you can specify other methods such as varimax.
- Scores: Per the function's documentation, set the argument to TRUE if you want component scores to be output. But simply specifying TRUE does not cause the function to output the scores: You have to call for them specifically and in a separate command. Read more on this later in this section.

Figure 6.15
The factor loadings and eigenvalues are identical to those shown in Figure 6.7.

	A	B	C	D	E	F	G
1	> PCAModel <- principal(PCAData,nfactors=3,rotate="none",scores=TRUE)						
2	> print(PCAModel, digits=5)						
3	Principal Components Analysis						
4	Call: principal(r = PCAData, nfactors = 3, rotate = "none", scores = TRUE)						
5	Standardized loadings (pattern matrix) based upon correlation matrix						
6		PC1	PC2	PC3	h2	u2	com
7	Visit Length	0.87533	0.27931	-0.39470	1	-2.22E-16	1.6197
8	Page Views	0.90264	0.13160	0.40977	1	7.77E-16	1.4444
9	Pages	-0.39662	0.91592	0.06149	1	-1.11E-15	1.3726
10							
11		PC1	PC2	PC3			
12	SS loadings	1.73827	0.93424	0.32749			
13	Proportion Var	0.57942	0.31141	0.10916			
14	Cumulative Var	0.57942	0.89084	1			
15	Proportion Explained	0.57942	0.31141	0.10916			
16	Cumulative Proportion	0.57942	0.89084	1			
17							
18	Mean item complexity = 1.5						
19	Test of the hypothesis that 3 components are sufficient.						
20							
21	The root mean square of the residuals (RMSR) is 0						
22	with the empirical chi square 0 with prob < NA						
23							
24	Fit based upon off diagonal values = 1>						

6

The rotation methods you can choose from, using the *principal* function, include these (and there are others):

- none
- varimax
- quartimax
- promax
- oblimin
- simplimax
- cluster

The loadings shown in Figure 6.15, in the range B7:D9, are identical to those returned by Excel and given in B30:D32 of Figure 6.7. The *principal* function terms this the *pattern matrix*, another term for *structure matrix*. Notice that *principal* labels the principal components as PC1, PC2, PC3, and so on.

You also find the eigenvalues—the amount of the total variance attributable to each component—in B12:D12 of Figure 6.15. They are labeled "SS Loadings" because they are calculated as the sum of the squared factor loadings. For example, the eigenvalue for Factor 1 is 1.73827, and can be calculated as

=SUMSQ(B7:B9)

or

$$= 0.87533^2 + 0.90264^2 + (-0.39662)^2$$

The communalities, symbolized as *h2*, are given in the range E7:E9. When you have called for as many components as there are variables, the entire variability, equal to the number of variables, is accounted for and the communalities must equal 1. Uniqueness, the other side of the communality coin, is symbolized as *u2* and found in F7:F9. The column labeled *com* is Hoffman's index of complexity.

Three further items to note regarding the *principal* results:

- The *principal* function does not recognize an argument that specifies the number of decimals to display. If you want to exercise control over that aspect of the results, you need to first save the results to an R object—in Figure 6.15, that object is named *PCAModel*. Then, use the *print* function to display the results in the R console with the number of decimals you want. In Figure 6.15, the command is

```
print(PCAModel, digits=5)
```

- The *principal* code as of R version 3.3.0 apparently is missing a carriage return/line feed at the end of the results. R's command prompt immediately follows the last character of *principal*'s output.

Setting the *scores* argument to TRUE or FALSE or simply omitting the argument does not appear to have an effect on the results of the *principal* function. Neither the factor scores nor the factor coefficients appear in the results from *principal*. To get both the scores and the coefficients, set the *scores* argument as you prefer or omit it, and after directing the results of *principal* to an object such as *PCAModel*, enter the *factor.scores* command:

```
> factor.scores(PCAData,PCAModel)
```

You'll get the results shown in Figure 6.16.

Figure 6.16
The factor scores are shown along with the record IDs.

	A	B	C	D
27	> factor.scores(PCAData,PCAModel)			
28	$scores			
29		PC1	PC2	PC3
30	[1,]	0.628178	-0.50495	0.346807
31	[2,]	-1.48234	0.899068	-0.16023
32	[3,]	-0.10715	0.099781	0.203978
33	[4,]	1.697235	-1.01914	1.29381
34	[5,]	0.790752	1.351326	0.960946
35	[6,]	-0.61204	1.774997	-0.79023
36	[7,]	-0.12691	-0.84563	0.551117
37	[8,]	0.905969	1.886571	0.535255
38	[9,]	0.437261	0.315387	0.50391
39	[10,]	0.266849	-0.97109	-1.84434
40	[11,]	1.478721	-0.57443	0.063945
41	[12,]	0.934313	-0.79003	-0.23599
42	[13,]	0.382067	-0.43585	-2.27003
43	[14,]	0.45702	1.260798	0.156771
44	[15,]	-1.31118	-0.86668	0.029804
45	[16,]	-1.21572	-1.27684	-0.04875
46	[17,]	-0.11499	0.669576	-1.53013
47	[18,]	-1.49426	-0.61614	1.921014
48	[19,]	-1.59756	0.363823	0.265458
49	[20,]	0.08377	-0.72055	0.046875

Compare the scores shown in Figure 6.16 with those calculated by Excel in the range O2:Q21 of Figure 6.10.

You can use *factor.scores* to calculate the scores in different ways. See the documentation for terse descriptions of these methods.

TIP

You can get to documentation of most R functions and commands via a web browser. At the R command prompt, enter something such as this:

```
>??factor.scores
```

to get a web page with some information about, in this case, *factor.scores*.

The *factor.scores* command also displays the factor coefficients. See Figure 6.17.

6

Figure 6.17
The range B59:D61 shows a correlation matrix based on the factor scores.

	A	B	C	D
51	$weights			
52		PC1	PC2	PC3
53	Visit Length	0.503563	0.298965	-1.20525
54	Page Views	0.519278	0.140859	1.251274
55	Pages	-0.22817	0.980389	0.187756
56				
57	$r.scores			
58		PC1	PC2	PC3
59	PC1	1.00E+00	-3.39E-16	-1.38E-15
60	PC2	-3.37E-16	1.00E+00	-2.17E-15
61	PC3	-1.42E-15	-2.18E-15	1.00E+00
62				
63	$R2			
64	PC1 PC2 PC3			
65	1 1 1			

Compare the factor coefficients in B53:D55 with those in the range B30:D32 of Figure 6.6.

Although the method of extracting principal components from the correlation matrix causes the components to be orthogonal, and thus uncorrelated, it is not guaranteed that the factor scores calculated using the factor coefficients will themselves be perfectly uncorrelated. In Figure 6.17, the range B59:D61 shows the calculated correlations between the factor scores on the principal components. The different methods of calculating the factor scores I mentioned earlier can bring about slightly different results in the correlation matrix of the principal components.

The Varimax Rotation in R

You can easily arrange for different methods of rotation in R. Using the *principal* function in the *psych* package, the syntax is

```
> PCARotated<-principal(PCAData,nfactors=3,rotate="varimax")
```

Notice that the *rotate* argument has been changed from "none" to "varimax" and that the number of factors to retain has remained at 3. In Figure 6.18, I used the *print* command to display the results with the desired number of decimals.

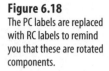

Figure 6.18
The PC labels are replaced with RC labels to remind you that these are rotated components.

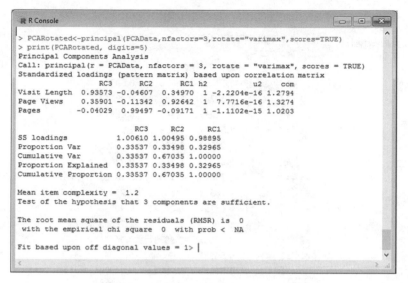

You can compare the rotated loadings in the range B7:D9 of Figure 6.18 with the rotated loadings shown in the range C3:E5 of Figure 6.11. Small differences tend to show up in the third or fourth digit following the decimal point, possibly due to the precision of the criterion used to judge whether a root is converging in the extraction process.

The *principal* function returns the eigenvalues of the rotated components, something that the PCA.xlsm Excel workbook does not do. They are labeled as *SS loadings* in Figure 6.18. Note that the variance attributable to each component is now almost equally distributed across the three components, although the total variance of 3 is of course unchanged. Also notice that the order of the labels given to the rotated components is reversed, although the documentation does not discuss the rationale for the change.

Figure 6.19 shows that you can pick up the rotated factor scores and their coefficients using the *factor.score* command in conjunction with the original data frame and the model created by *principal*.

6

Figure 6.19
Note that the order of the labels is still reversed as in Figure 6.18.

	A	B	C	D
26	> factor.scores(PCAData,PCARotated)			
27	$scores			
28		RC3	RC2	RC1
29	[1,]	0.03408	-0.63688	0.60256
30	[2,]	-0.61705	1.29238	-0.99012
31	[3,]	-0.18239	0.14797	0.08879
32	[4,]	-0.05237	-1.35852	1.93517
33	[5,]	0.26094	1.13003	1.42469
34	[6,]	0.65029	1.78846	-0.72678
35	[7,]	-0.70869	-0.70514	0.18831
36	[8,]	0.78551	1.55785	1.27378
37	[9,]	0.03754	0.21371	0.70535
38	[10,]	1.16099	-1.18607	-1.28885
39	[11,]	0.77511	-0.99391	0.96541
40	[12,]	0.55518	-1.05965	0.34886
41	[13,]	1.68556	-0.75825	-1.43976
42	[14,]	0.56384	1.06682	0.60583
43	[15,]	-1.14681	-0.41133	-0.99340
44	[16,]	-1.14854	-0.83662	-1.04480
45	[17,]	1.16792	0.51510	-1.08327
46	[18,]	-2.49365	0.07213	0.28145
47	[19,]	-1.14161	0.86456	-0.83922
48	[20,]	-0.18585	-0.70262	-0.01400

The labels of the components are still reversed, although the component scores themselves are not: Compare the rotated scores with those shown in Figure 6.13.

The rotated coefficients and the correlation matrix for the rotated components follow the scores themselves and appear in Figure 6.20.

Figure 6.20
The order of the labels remains reversed although the weights agree with the results of PCA.xlsm.

	A	B	C	D
1				
2	$weights			
3		RC3	RC2	RC1
4	Visit Length	1.249691418	0.006037826	-0.4835469
5	Page Views	-0.47131385	0.098354716	1.2741138
6	Pages	0.004141826	1.016546322	0.122845
7				
8	$r.scores			
9		RC3	RC2	RC1
10	RC3	1.00E+00	2.67E-16	-8.75E-16
11	RC2	2.68E-16	1.00E+00	-1.99E-15
12	RC1	-8.62E-16	-1.97E-15	1.00E+00

Compare the weights reported in Figure 6.20 with those shown in Figure 6.12. Both figures show weights for components rotated by the varimax criterion and are in agreement.

One purpose of both principal component analysis and factor analysis is *data reduction*: That is, explaining as much variance in a data set as possible with fewer components than the number of original variables. The example data set used in this chapter as has only three variables, and the point of keeping the data set small is to make the explanations clearer. So the notion of simplifying a three-variable data set probably seems pointless.

But when you're faced with a data set containing 25 variables, all of them apparently important and many of them strongly correlated, data reduction seems like a great idea. One problem is the question of the number of components to retain.

Henry Kaiser was largely, if not solely, responsible for the development of the varimax method of factor rotation. He argued that only components with an eigenvalue of at least 1.0 should be retained for subsequent analysis. Kaiser reasoned that components' eigenvalues are measures of common variance, not just specific variance: A component's variance ought to capture variance that is contributed by more than one variable. When, as in all examples in this chapter, the components are extracted from a correlation matrix rather than from a covariance matrix, each variable's contributed variance is exactly 1.0.

Therefore, because components are supposed to represent common variance, a component ought to have an eigenvalue of *at least* 1.0. It's an intuitive argument, but I've always found it appealing—more so than tools such as the scree test, which lay claim to numeric objectivity but which are every bit as subjective as Kaiser's criterion.

In the present case, we have two components with a respectable share of the total variance. See Figure 6.6: Components 1 and 2 have eigenvalues of 1.738 and 0.934; the third initial component has an eigenvalue of 0.327, rather low. Despite the fact that the second component's eigenvalue is less than 1.0, it's close, and in a real-world situation I'd be strongly tempted to leave it in the mix for further analysis.

So I'd run PCA.xlsm again, specifying varimax as the rotation method as before, but I'd opt to retain just two components. Figure 6.21 shows the resulting factor structure matrix, with the loadings on each component.

Figure 6.21
In a reduced model you generally find fewer components or factors and the original number of variables.

	A	B	C
1	Rotated Loadings		
2			
3		Factor 1	Factor 2
4	Visit Length	0.918748	-0.01047
5	Page Views	0.898174	-0.15927
6	Pages	-0.08809	0.994213
7			

And the factor coefficients for the reduced varimax solution are shown in Figure 6.22.

Figure 6.22
There are still three
coefficients for each
factor but only two for
each variable.

	A	B	C
1	**Rotated Factor Coefficients**		
2			
3		Factor 1	Factor 2
4	Visit Leng	0.572077	0.125228
5	Page View	0.537218	-0.02978
6	Pages	0.092085	1.002369

The factor coefficients matrix is no longer square, but the MMULT() formulas used in Figure 6.10 to get the factor scores for the unreduced solution will still work fine. The resulting factor scores appear in Figure 6.23.

Figure 6.23
The factor scores
change in the reduced
solution because the
axes rotate to a different
alignment with just two
components.

	A	B	C	D	E	F
1		Factor 1	Factor 2		Rotated Factor Scores	
2	1	0.437266	-0.67703			
3	2	-1.12391	1.320026			
4	3	-0.07029	0.12844			
5	4	1.290078	-1.50165			
6	5	1.175971	1.033666			
7	6	-0.0221	1.877423			
8	7	-0.38668	-0.76268			
9	8	1.453838	1.50542			
10	9	0.514317	0.16169			
11	10	-0.05244	-1.00572			
12	11	1.222683	-1.01075			
13	12	0.63808	-1.04401			
14	13	0.225423	-0.53397			
15	14	0.83071	1.052807			
16	15	-1.51736	-0.40982			
17	16	-1.55588	-0.82918			
18	17	0.10166	0.671728			
19	18	-1.61225	-0.11438			
20	19	-1.40178	0.848271			
21	20	-0.14734	-0.71029			

Let's test these results against those returned by R's *principal* function. These two commands display the summary results:

```
> PCARotated2 <- principal(PCAData,nfactors=2,rotate="varimax")
> print(PCARotated2,digits = 7)
```

The results appear in Figure 6.24.

Figure 6.24
With just two components instead of three, two variables load strongly on the first component and the third variable loads strongly on the second component.

	A	B	C	D	E	F
1	> PCARotated2 <- principal(PCAData,nfactors=2,rotate="varimax")					
2	> print(PCARotated2,digits = 7)					
3	Principal Components Analysis					
4	Call: principal(r = PCAData, nfactors = 2, rotate = "varimax")					
5	Standardized loadings (pattern matrix) based upon correlation matrix					
6		RC1	RC2	h2	u2	com
7	Visit Length	0.918801	-0.00385	0.84421	0.15579	1.000035
8	Page Views	0.899299	0.1528	0.832085	0.167915	1.057689
9	Pages	-0.09525	0.993553	0.996219	0.003781	1.01838
10						
11		RC1	RC2			
12	SS loadings	1.662006	1.010509			
13	Proportion Var	0.554002	0.336836			
14	Cumulative Var	0.554002	0.890838			
15	Proportion Explained	0.621888	0.378112			
16	Cumulative Proportion	0.621888	1			
17						
18	Mean item complexity = 1					
19	Test of the hypothesis that 2 components are sufficient.					
20						
21	The root mean square of the residuals (RMSR) is 0.0955395					
22	with the empirical chi square 1.095335 with prob < NA					
23						
24	Fit based upon off diagonal values = 0.9453229>					

Looking at the results of the reduced and rotated solution, I'd guess that the first component has to do with the time spent on the website: Both the Visit Length and the Page Views variables are likely to increase as time spent on the site increases. That the number of pages loads strongly on a different component suggests that the time spent is not divided equally across the site's pages, but that some pages cause more time to be spent there.

Let's finish by looking at the factor scores for the reduced, rotated solution and its factor coefficients. First the scores in Figure 6.25.

Figure 6.25
At this point you might want to see how the factor scores are related to variables that describe a user rather than a website.

⊿	A	B	C	D
1	> factor.scores(PCAData,PCARotated2)			
2	$scores			
3		RC1	RC2	
4	[1,]	0.44213	-0.67387	
5	[2,]	-1.13339	1.311899	
6	[3,]	-0.07121	0.12793	
7	[4,]	1.300859	-1.49232	
8	[5,]	1.168498	1.042105	
9	[6,]	-0.03562	1.877215	
10	[7,]	-0.38118	-0.76544	
11	[8,]	1.442961	1.515848	
12	[9,]	0.51314	0.165389	
13	[10,]	-0.0452	-1.00607	
14	[11,]	1.229931	-1.00192	
15	[12,]	0.645582	-1.03938	
16	[13,]	0.229263	-0.53233	
17	[14,]	0.823107	1.058761	
18	[15,]	-1.51437	-0.42073	
19	[16,]	-1.54987	-0.84036	
20	[17,]	0.096821	0.672443	
21	[18,]	-1.61139	-0.12599	
22	[19,]	-1.40785	0.838156	
23	[20,]	-0.14222	-0.71133	

The coefficients calculated by *principal* are in Figure 6.26.

Figure 6.26
Compare these coefficients with those returned by PCA.xlsm in Figure 6.22.

⊿	A	B	C
1	$weights		
2		RC1	RC2
3	Visit Length	0.571161	0.129345
4	Page Views	0.537419	-0.02592
5	Pages	0.084865	1.003006
6			

Index

Q

R

T